Qualifications Systems

BRIDGES TO LIFELONG LEARNING

OECD

ORGANISATION FOR ECONOMIC CO-OPERATION AND DEVELOPMENT

ORGANISATION FOR ECONOMIC CO-OPERATION AND DEVELOPMENT

The OECD is a unique forum where the governments of 30 democracies work together to address the economic, social and environmental challenges of globalisation. The OECD is also at the forefront of efforts to understand and to help governments respond to new developments and concerns, such as corporate governance, the information economy and the challenges of an ageing population. The Organisation provides a setting where governments can compare policy experiences, seek answers to common problems, identify good practice and work to co-ordinate domestic and international policies.

The OECD member countries are: Australia, Austria, Belgium, Canada, the Czech Republic, Denmark, Finland, France, Germany, Greece, Hungary, Iceland, Ireland, Italy, Japan, Korea, Luxembourg, Mexico, the Netherlands, New Zealand, Norway, Poland, Portugal, the Slovak Republic, Spain, Sweden, Switzerland, Turkey, the United Kingdom and the United States. The Commission of the European Communities takes part in the work of the OECD.

OECD Publishing disseminates widely the results of the Organisation's statistics gathering and research on economic, social and environmental issues, as well as the conventions, guidelines and standards agreed by its members.

This work is published on the responsibility of the Secretary-General of the OECD. The opinions expressed and arguments employed herein do not necessarily reflect the official views of the Organisation or of the governments of its member countries.

Also available in French under the title:
Systèmes de certification
DES PASSERELLES POUR APPRENDRE A TOUT ÂGE

Foreword

*I*n 2001, the OECD Education Committee launched a study whose ambition was to find a bridge *between national qualifications systems and lifelong learning. Its objective has been to identify processes and mechanisms through which the national qualifications system influences the motivation and opportunities to learn. The key question for the activity has been:* how can the qualifications system be shaped to provide the greatest incentive to learn? *The aim is to inform decision makers about possible policy actions based on the national qualifications systems that can promote lifelong learning for all.*

This OECD activity resulted from the necessity to address systemic issues when trying to meet the goal of lifelong learning for all. Its ambition was to review the existing policy responses to the lifelong learning agenda in the countries under study and to identify possible mechanisms within the qualifications system that could impact on the behaviour of the many stakeholders to trigger more and better lifelong learning. There are many other ways to impact on lifelong learning but they are not addressed in this book which solely focuses on the role of national qualifications systems.

Twenty-three countries took part in the activity. Fifteen of them fully participated in it by delivering a background report according to a set of agreed guidelines: Australia, Belgium (French Community), Denmark, France, Germany, Greece, Ireland, Japan, Korea, the Netherlands, New Zealand, Portugal, Slovenia, Switzerland and the United Kingdom. These reports were discussed with representatives from the country and authorised as valid descriptions of the respective qualifications systems and their effects on lifelong learning.

In addition to preparing their background report, countries were invited to identify the main issues for examination by international thematic groups. Three key themes were identified: the development and use of qualifications frameworks as a means of reforming and managing qualifications systems; standards and quality assurance in qualifications, with special reference to the recognition of non-formal and informal learning; and co-operation of different institutions and stakeholders of the qualifications systems. *Twenty countries contributed to one or more of the thematic groups: Australia, Belgium (Flemish Community), Czech Republic, Denmark, Finland, France, Germany, Greece, Ireland, Italy, Korea, Mexico, the Netherlands, New Zealand, Portugal, Slovenia, Spain, Sweden, Switzerland and the United Kingdom.*

The country background reports and the thematic groups' reports form part of the knowledge base of the study and have been used to prepare this book, in conjunction with a range of quantitative data and the published literature in the fields under study. All these unabridged reports, other relevant documents and useful links, can be found on the OECD dedicated website: www/ oecd.org/edu/lifelonglearning/nqs. *The thematic group's reports are also presented in summary form in Annex A. Even if a large amount of material and evidence has been gathered, this book should not be considered as the end of an activity but as a first step for countries to review their policies and practices. This book could indeed be used advantageously as a check list for policy makers aware of national qualifications system as a policy tool.*

National co-ordinators from each country, and members of international organisations, listed in Annexes C and D, were vital to the good functioning of the activity and the delivery of quality outputs. Equally essential to its success were the OECD Secretariat members who were successively in charge of this activity from 2001 on: Marianne Durand-Drouhin, Jack Keating, Friederike Behringer and Patrick Werquin. This book is authored by Mike Coles (Qualifications and Curriculum Authority, London) and Patrick Werquin (OECD, Education and Training Policy Division). Administrative assistance was provided by Sabrina Leonarduzzi and editorial assistance by Susan Copeland. The project was carried out under the supervision of Abrar Hasan, Head of the Education and Training Policy Division.

Barbara Ischinger
Director for Education

Table of contents

List of tables

List of figures

ISBN 978-92-64-01367-4
Qualifications Systems
Bridges to Lifelong Learning
© OECD 2007

Executive Summary

Background and rationale

Since the 1970s, the evolution of the OECD economies and societies, in particular the advent of information technologies, has made lifelong learning a key goal for education and training policy. Progress in technology and international economic integration is rapidly changing the economic landscape and putting an ever greater premium on the need to innovate, improve productivity and to adjust to structural changes painlessly. In this context, the 1994 International Adult Literacy Survey (IALS) of 12 OECD countries provided a sobering finding: at least one-quarter of the adult population fails to reach the third of the five literacy levels, which many experts regard as the minimum level of competence needed to cope adequately with the complex demands of everyday life and work. These results have been confirmed by follow-up surveys in 22 countries/regions. A population with this level of skills can hardly be expected to adapt rapidly and respond innovatively to the ongoing structural changes. "Lifelong learning for all" is a response to this challenge. This policy goal was identified by a meeting of OECD Education Ministers in 1996 (Lifelong Learning for All, OECD, 1996) and also echoed in publications by UNESCO and the European Commission.

The benefits of lifelong learning

A number of important socio-economic forces are pushing for the lifelong learning approach. The economic rationale for lifelong learning comes from two principal sources. First, with the increasing importance of knowledge-based economy and the progressive demise of Taylorism or Fordism (OECD 1988), the threshold of skills demanded by the employers is being constantly raised. There is a relative decline in demand for low-level skills. Second, as firms respond to a more volatile market and shorter product cycles, career jobs are fewer and individuals experience more frequent changes in jobs over the working life. The shelf-life of skills is shorter. There is a need for continuous renewal and updating of skills, which is essential for structural adjustment, productivity growth, innovation and effective reallocation of human resources.

On a broader, societal, level, the large structural changes threaten a new polarisation between the knowledge "haves" and "have-nots". The distribution of learning opportunities is quite uneven. Unemployed individuals have fewer learning opportunities than the employed; those in small and medium-size firms have poorer access than employees of larger firms; opportunities for those with secondary school education or less are significantly fewer than for those with post-secondary education; women are at a relative disadvantage compared to men. The large earnings gaps between those with and without post-secondary education, furthermore, widen over the lifetime. These discrepancies can damage the very basis of democracy.

Strategies for lifelong learning respond to the convergence between the economic imperative dictated by the needs of the knowledge society and the societal need to promote social cohesion by providing long-term benefits for the individual, the enterprise, the economy and the society more generally. For the individual, lifelong learning emphasises creativity, initiative and responsiveness – attributes which contribute to self-fulfilment, higher earnings and employment, and to innovation and productivity. The skills and competence of the workforce are a major factor in economic performance and success at the enterprise level. For the economy, there is a positive relationship between educational attainment and economic growth.

The OECD approach to lifelong learning

The OECD approach to lifelong learning, set out in a number of publications [OECD (1996, 1999, 2001, and 2004)], represents a major departure from the 1970s. It adopts a more comprehensive view that covers all purposeful learning activity, from the cradle to the grave, that aims to improve knowledge and competencies for all individuals *who wish to participate* in learning activities. The concept has four main features:

A *systemic view:* This is the most distinguishing feature of lifelong learning – all competing approaches to education policy are sector-specific. The lifelong learning framework views the demand for, and the supply of, learning opportunities, as part of a connected system covering the whole lifecycle and comprising *all forms of formal, non-formal, and informal learning.*

Centrality of the learner: This requires a shift of attention from a supply-side focus, for example on formal institutional arrangements for learning, to the demand side of meeting learner needs.

Motivation to learn is an essential foundation for learning that continues throughout life. It requires attention to developing the capacity for "learning to learn" through self-paced and self-directed learning.

Multiple objectives of education policy: The lifecycle view recognises the multiple goals of education – such as personal development, knowledge development, economic, social and cultural objectives – and that the priorities among these objectives may change over the course of an individual's lifetime.

Lifelong learning and qualifications systems

Lifelong learning is a vast agenda. Since 1996 the Education Committee's programme of work has systematically explored various aspects of lifelong learning strategies, especially on systemic features of lifelong learning. There are a range of policies in the economic and social domain that can be used to influence lifelong learning.

The link between lifelong learning and qualifications systems is evident from two features of lifelong learning: its systemic nature and its emphasis on all forms of learning, formal, non-formal and informal. A qualifications system, whether formally or implicitly, articulates which forms of learning form part of the qualifications systems and how they are standardised, recognised and valued by individuals, the economy and society. Individuals use the system to decide on their learning activities. A qualifications system can facilitate the individual in navigating along these pathways or can be a deterrent, depending on what incentives or disincentives it provides.

Country involvement and process

The Committee launched an activity in 2001 to explore the links between the qualifications system and lifelong learning. Given the labour market connections, the activity was also endorsed by the Employment, Labour and Social Affairs Committee. The purpose of the activity was to investigate how different national qualifications systems influence the overall volume of lifelong learning, its quality and distribution among different classes of learners. Based on this investigation, the activity aimed to identify what actions countries can take in designing and managing their qualifications system to promote lifelong learning.

In spring 2001, representatives from 22 OECD countries and representatives of five international organisations met to discuss the purpose and scope of the activity. On the basis of a concepts paper, an activity proposal and a guideline for preparation of country background reports, 15 countries (Belgium [French Community], Canada, Denmark, France, Germany, Greece, Ireland, Japan, Korea, the Netherlands, New Zealand, Portugal, Slovenia, Switzerland and the United Kingdom) agreed to participate in the work. A number of international organisations agreed to monitor the work: the European Centre for the Development of Vocational Training (CEDEFOP), the European Commission, the European Training Foundation, the International Labour Organization, and the World Bank. Several other countries agreed to participate at a later stage. The work was resumed in 2004 after an interruption of a year. Given the very complex and extensive nature of the work, it was agreed to create three country networks to prepare papers on specific topics. These reports and Secretariat drafts of a synthesis report were discussed at twice-yearly workshops during 2004-2005. A first complete draft was circulated to the Committee in March 2006.

There is a link between qualifications systems and lifelong learning

Under-researched but this link is possibly an under-researched area

Most educational policy makers believe that there is a link between qualifications systems and lifelong learning; however such a link has never been proven. This is because, whilst a lot is known about lifelong learning and about qualifications systems, until now the middle ground has been largely unexplored territory. Throughout this publication the focus is on this middle ground and the question is: how can national qualifications systems promote lifelong learning in terms of quantity, quality, efficiency and equitable distribution of learning opportunities?

The theoretical links between national qualifications systems and lifelong learning are termed *mechanisms* and each one should have the capacity to change the qualifications system to make it more conducive to lifelong learning. If such mechanisms can be identified, understood and then transformed into concrete robust relationships, policy makers will be provided with a rationale for reforming qualifications systems with lifelong learning benefits in mind.

Enabling policy learning

For some time countries have been trying to develop lifelong learning through reforming qualifications systems. Existing and planned policy from 15 countries has been analysed and classified into 9 generalised policy responses. They do not represent a model but an aggregation of all existing policies linking qualifications systems and lifelong learning. Because these nine policy responses are generic, they can be used for policy learning among countries.

The value of this list is that it represents a set of policy responses countries have considered and the list can be used for review of the existing and planned policies within a country:

1. Increase flexibility and responsiveness.

2. Motivate young people to learn.

3. Link education and work.

4. Facilitate open access to qualifications.

5. Diversify assessment processes.

6. Make qualifications progressive.

7. Make the qualifications system transparent.

8. Review funding and increase efficiency.

9. Better manage the qualifications system.

Changing behaviour of stakeholders

If lifelong learning is to develop further in countries, then the patterns of behaviour of individuals, employers as well as learning and qualification providers will need to change. Qualifications systems may play a role in the process of changing behaviour and the qualification-based factors that might influence behaviour are analysed by reviewing empirical evidence and theoretical literature that relates to national qualifications systems. An evaluation of the drivers of change influencing lifelong learning and the barriers to learning that confront individuals and employers, as well as learning and qualification providers, generates mechanisms that can be used to optimise the impact of lifelong learning policies.

The analysis so far shows that there is significant qualitative evidence that the learning behaviours of individuals, employers and providers of learning and qualifications are directly and indirectly influenced by the kind of qualifications system operating in the country. The analysis leads to the identification of specific changes in terms of structure or operating conditions, which will in turn change the likelihood of each of these groups participating in, using and providing qualifications. These change agents have been labelled mechanisms and now it is possible, using the evidence, to support the theoretical idea with concrete evidence and lay out 20 mechanisms for consideration as tools to strengthen policy responses for improving lifelong learning into positive outcomes. The 20 mechanisms are:

1. Communicating returns to learning for qualification.

2. Recognising skills for employability.

3. Establishing qualifications frameworks.

4. Increasing learner choice in qualifications.

5. Clarifying learning pathways.

6. Providing credit transfer.

7. Increasing flexibility in learning programmes leading to qualifications.

8. Creating new routes to qualifications.

9. Lowering cost of qualification.

10. Recognising non-formal and informal learning.

11. Monitoring the qualifications system.

12. Optimising stakeholder involvement in the qualifications system.

13. Improving needs analysis methods so that qualifications are up-to-date.

14. Improving qualification use in recruitment.

15. Ensuring qualifications are portable.

16. Investing in pedagogical innovation.

17. Expressing qualifications as learning outcomes.

18. Improving co-ordination in the qualifications system.

19. Optimising quality assurance.

20. Improving information and guidance about qualifications systems.

The two concepts of "**policy responses**" and "**mechanism**" are distinct. Policy responses are broad categories of policies which are currently being used by countries to address the pressures for change in the qualifications system. A mechanism is a conceptual link between the qualifications systems and lifelong learning that is based on the analysis of evidence of behavioural change of the main stakeholder groups. The evidence for these mechanisms comes from both the country background reports and the available research literature.

The 20 mechanisms can be classified using the different policy responses in an attempt to see how the evidence for mechanisms can provide useful tools for policy makers as they introduce and refine policies for lifelong learning.

Adding value to the evidence

The 20 mechanisms are a means by which qualifications systems can be more conducive to lifelong learning. National qualifications systems will not include all mechanisms. This is because every national qualifications system is unique and the functioning of mechanisms will be influenced by the conditions operating the qualifications system. Therefore it is not always possible to generalise about the strength of these mechanisms in bringing about more lifelong learning. However, by linking the mechanisms to the generic policy responses, we can get an idea about which mechanisms are likely to have a strong effect.

It has been possible to make a first approach on how strong the effect of a mechanism might be on a policy response. It is possible to separate *strong* mechanisms from mechanisms having a *supporting*, but not necessarily strong, role and those having no role at all. There is another way of considering the effect of a mechanism, this time on other mechanisms rather than directly on policy responses. Three are believed to have a catalytic role on some of the other mechanisms and are called *change mechanisms*.

Combining the different ways of analysing the effect of mechanisms leads to identify some particularly powerful mechanisms:

- Five highly ranked strong mechanisms: *Providing credit transfer; Optimising stakeholder involvement in the qualifications system; Recognising non-formal and informal learning; Establishing a qualifications framework;* and *Creating new routes to qualifications.*

- Three change mechanisms: *Establishing qualifications frameworks; Communicating returns to learning for qualifications;* and *Investing in pedagogical innovation.*

- Five highly ranked supporting mechanisms: *Monitoring the qualifications system; Establishing qualifications frameworks; Investing in pedagogical innovation; Expressing qualifications as learning outcomes;* and *Improving information and guidance about qualifications systems.*

Same words: same meaning?

Common understanding of the main elements of a qualifications system is an issue. Almost every element is understood in different ways and this is typified by the word *qualification*. The study has tried to develop consensus across countries about defining these elements. Significant progress has been achieved in developing common understanding of qualifications systems, qualifications frameworks and qualifications themselves.

For the benefit of the reader, and because these terms have been used extensively in this book, the following terms and concepts have been defined: competence, credit, lifelong learning, recognition of learning, formal learning, non-formal learning and informal learning.

Policy recommendations on how to best use the three main tools policymakers could use

---

Policy making for lifelong learning in the arena of qualifications systems is difficult, underdeveloped and possibly undervalued. This book suggests that it is useful to review the role of qualifications systems in promoting lifelong learning and discusses some of the practical issues for policy makers. From the wide ranging discussion of evidence generated by this study, it is clear that there are opportunities to use qualifications systems to develop lifelong learning. Three main tools can be identified that policy makers could use.

Review policy responses

The first tool is applied to existing policy responses to lifelong learning. The set of mechanisms can be used to discover whether the original logic underpinning the creation of each national policy response remains robust. For example, have the benefits they promised been delivered or are they still expected?

Systematic review of current policy responses to lifelong learning that involve qualifications systems is a good starting point. It is possible to use the mechanisms as ways to build new policy responses to lifelong learning that draw on the knowledge that each mechanism is defined as a means of influencing the behaviour of main stakeholders and therefore offers potential for optimisation of policy responses. Mechanisms are therefore valuable new tools for policy making.

Review powerful mechanisms

The second tool is more specific than the first and involves analysing policy responses to ensure they incorporate the powerful mechanisms identified in this book as incisive in making qualifications systems more responsive to the lifelong learning agenda. This tool involves the use of a specific set of mechanisms that appear to have a potentially greater influence on policy responses to lifelong learning than others, either in their wide applicability to policy responses or in their potential as "agents of change". Recently, the importance of mechanisms such as the ones reported above to support specific reforms has been evident and countries could benefit from reviewing them in their own context. Some of the practical applications of these powerful mechanisms in policy responses to lifelong learning are also examined in this book.

Contextualise and analyse a combination of mechanisms

A third tool for policy makers arising from the study is the opportunity mechanisms offer to appreciate the interaction between different reforms in the country context. The country context matters a great deal when considering the usefulness of mechanisms and will make the deployment (or otherwise) of mechanisms unique to each country.

An issue that arises immediately is the complexity of interactions between mechanisms and how they can be used to support one another (and therefore the policy response) and how counterproductive interactions can be avoided. This issue is also examined through examples in this book.

Setting a research agenda for the future

Linking quantitative indicators describing national qualifications systems and lifelong learning variables has proven a difficult exercise and there is little quantitative evidence, even if some is interesting and encouraging. Many conditions would need to be met in addition to having appropriate variables available for the appropriate period of time. Therefore, there are lessons to be learned and the following represent key elements of a research agenda for the future:

- There is a need for sound conceptual work about the best way to define systemic variables and to produce appropriate indicators describing national qualifications systems.
- There is a need for research on the best way to relate national qualifications systems to lifelong learning through quantitative variables.
- There is a need for international data to be collected as an empirical counterpart for the conceptual work proposed above.
- There is a need for a stronger focus on micro relationships, at the level of the components and sub-components of qualifications systems.

In addition to specific data, trend data will also be necessary. It will take time and effort but it would allow for more appropriate reflection on the way national qualifications and lifelong learning systems evolve over time. This may require some stability in the way variables are measured. If national qualifications systems are to become a more commonly used context for policy responses, policy makers will have to be more thoroughly informed of current data as well as trend data to avoid fragmentation of policy making.

References

OECD (1988), *New Technologies in the 1990s: A Socio-Economic Perspective*, OECD, Paris.

OECD (1996), *Lifelong Learning for All*, OECD, Paris.

OECD (1999), "Resources for Lifelong Learning: What Might be Needed and How Might it be Found?", *Education Policy Analysis*, Chapter 1, OECD, Paris.

OECD (2001), "Lifelong Learning for All: Policy Directions", *Education Policy Analysis*, Chapter 1, OECD, Paris.

OECD (2004), Lifelong Learning, *Policy Brief, February,* Paris.

ISBN 978-92-64-01367-4
Qualifications Systems
Bridges to Lifelong Learning
© OECD 2007

Chapter 1

Scope and Structure of the Study

In 2001, the OECD Education Committee launched a study on the role of national qualifications systems in promoting lifelong learning. The objective of the study, which directly involved 22 countries, has been to ascertain how national qualifications systems can be shaped to provide the greatest possible incentive to learn, in terms of both motivation and opportunities. What are the policy options open to decision makers that can promote lifelong learning for all?

The core ideas in this study are complex, and many different words and phrases are used to communicate them. This chapter, based on input from country experts and international organisations, attempts to arrive at a common understanding of what precisely is meant by key terms and ideas.

Section 1.1 describes the rationale for the study; Section 1.2 clarifies the basic assumptions underpinning it and examines some of the reasons for the paucity of literature on the topic. In Section 1.3 each of the key ideas is discussed and given a firm definition that represents the consensus of all study participants. Section 1.4 considers the different ways qualifications systems affect lifelong learning and classifies these effects. In Section 1.5 the key idea of a mechanism is amplified further and clearly defined in terms of meaning, structure and potential applications. The idea of a policy response to lifelong learning that is based on qualifications systems is also clarified. The description of this book's structure in Section 1.6 will help the reader find sections of particular interest.

1.1. The primacy of lifelong learning

Modern societies offer their people a broad range of benefits. These can be direct benefits reaped from participating in the labour market (wages, social status, other social benefit, etc.), or they can be broader benefits from living in the community and sharing public goods. Increasingly, attention is paid to the global benefits of living in a modern society – and also to the fact that not everyone enjoys them. Many policies respond by attempting to guarantee citizens these benefits. One way to do so is to establish better lifelong learning practices.

Many authors have stressed the value of lifelong learning as a tool for achieving society's benefits. Through that tool, skills are often acquired that can be used in a variety of contexts – at work, at home and in the community (EC, 2001; IJLE, 2004; NCVER, 2003a). Employers view these skills as drivers of productivity and competitiveness that are relevant across all systems and cultures (Béduwé and Planas, 2003; Brown, 2003; NCVER, 2003b; Ottersten, 2004). They are a response to the demands of globalisation and the dawning knowledge economy that requires their continual upgrading as production shifts from tangible goods to abstract goods. This need to maintain the volume of skills supply while raising its level is the core justification for raising the investment in human capital and lifelong learning. From the individual's point of view (but again with regard to the labour market), these skills bring employability and, among other things, better wages and more rewarding career opportunities. Employability is a key component for (re-)entering the labour market in some countries where unemployment rates remain uncomfortably high, especially for young people. There is also abundant literature on the many ways to acquire the skills necessary to cope with modern life including work (Evans, Hodkinson and Unwin, 2002; Feinstein, Galindo-Rueda and Vignoles, 2004; Guile and Griffiths, 2001).

Lifelong learning for all has become a widely shared policy objective among OECD countries and beyond (OECD, 2001). It is seen as a necessary condition for individual success in the labour market and social well-being as well as a basis for democracy and citizenship. It is also believed that the competitiveness of national economies depends heavily on the capacity of societies to encourage and facilitate lifelong learning. Since certain groups of the population are experiencing difficulties in undertaking learning activities – especially within the adult population (OECD, 2003, 2005) – policy responses have been adopted to help develop lifelong learning activities and/or improve the skills and competences of the population. Some governments and stakeholders have come to view national qualifications systems as a tool for promoting lifelong learning. In 2001, the OECD set up a study that sheds light on the usefulness of these systems, and the extent to which they influence the quantity, quality, equity and efficiency of lifelong learning. The results of that study are presented in this book. The reported outcomes are intended to be presented in practical terms and to inform decision makers about possible policy responses. The one overarching outcome of this study is that an agenda has been set for the future development of national qualifications systems that will enhance lifelong learning.

The OECD study is not just about national qualifications systems, nor indeed about lifelong learning: it deals with the ground between the two and specifically the impact of the former on the latter. It has proved necessary to review the huge amount of information about national qualifications systems and about lifelong learning, but the focus of the study remains on the link between the two. This link is comprised of "mechanisms", the principal concept in this book; mechanisms are fully explained in Chapter 1, and illustrations are offered in Chapter 4.

The national qualifications system is but one influence on lifelong learning, and it is stressed that other influences are not considered here. With regard to lifelong learning itself, this study does not restrict itself to improvement in quantity, such as increased participation of adults. It also addresses improvements to quality, such as optimising returns to learners; to distribution, such as involvement of groups traditionally excluded; and to efficiency. In terms of national qualifications systems, the study defines its scope to include all arrangements leading to the recognition of learning, including non-formal and informal learning. While current national qualifications system structures form the backbone of the study, the findings are likely to be relevant for future systems, since the basic architecture remains the same.

In summary, the prime objective of this book is to provide insight into a policy decision-making process that will facilitate improvements to lifelong learning through reform of national qualifications systems. The themes involved are broad: lifelong learning is a huge subject and national qualifications systems are invariably large and complex. However, the intersection of these two themes – and specifically the focus on changes to national qualifications systems – is a smaller, important and previously under-researched area of study.

The OECD study that led to this book is based on experiences in 23 countries. Fifteen of these countries produced a detailed background report describing their qualifications system, details of current and future policy development, and a case study of the impact of a change in the system. In addition, three thematic groups examined a different specific issue in depth.[1]

1.2. Assumptions and existing evidence

The first assumption underpinning this work is that there is indeed a link between national qualifications systems and lifelong learning, and that this link may be used to inform policy responses intended to improve lifelong learning. The assumption is based on experience of qualifications both as a motivator for people to learn and as an obstacle preventing some people from having their learning recognised. Success in gaining recognition can lead to financial rewards as well as enhanced self-esteem and improved life chances. In some countries, entry to the labour market is regulated by qualification requirements. Some people fear that their learning will not reach the required standard and resist participation for that reason. Others may lack basic skills or may be unable to express the skills they do have through a particular means of assessment. Some social groups support the qualifications system and encourage participation in learning for qualification; other groups are unwilling to engage in formal recognition processes. There are costs involved in qualification assessment; these may inhibit some people from participation and have little effect on others who are financially more secure. All these factors suggest that a qualifications system can both invite and discourage participation in learning. The full range of influential factors is discussed in detail in Chapter 4.

An important second assumption is that any qualifications system will have an optimum configuration that yields high levels of quality-assured recognition of learning. The system will then meet the needs of learners, employers and other stakeholders without erecting unnecessary barriers to learning as a result of its recognition procedure. This optimum configuration will inevitably differ across countries and regional contexts, because the systems will differ. It is therefore not possible to identify a universal best point of balance between all the competing factors within qualifications systems. Chapter 6 investigates how these competing factors can be better understood through the mechanisms referred to earlier.

A mechanism is a means of changing an aspect of a qualifications system so that lifelong learning is enhanced in some way. Immediately however, one should add that mechanisms need to be considered in a wider context than qualifications systems and lifelong learning. Social constructs are not usually independent of the social, economic and cultural conditions in which they exist. For example, the condition of the labour market, with its demands regarding the volume and structure of work, translates into job opportunities and the necessity to acquire higher skills and possibly qualifications. Innovation and technological development require workforce skill development. Institutional regulations also clearly have a bearing on demand for qualifications, for example the requirement in some countries to undertake training in order to be entitled to unemployment benefits. The degree of compression of the wage structure and the general rate of labour turnover can determine the returns of training for employers – and in turn, opportunities for individuals to train. Together with basic cultural values, these factors influence anticipated costs and benefits of training. They can moreover differ between various population groups in a country. Each country's qualifications system is bound up in these social, economic and cultural factors. A third assumption therefore becomes necessary: a mechanism will work in different ways in different countries, and there can be no universal message that a particular mechanism will work in all situations.

Literature on the *interaction* of qualifications systems and lifelong learning is rare. In the vast literature on the former, the notion of qualifications is implicit in discussions on learning and delivering learning programmes. Sometimes, in relation to accrediting prior learning, qualification is referred to through the use of words such as *educational attainment, outcomes* or *competences*. The lifelong learning literature that does make implicit or explicit reference to qualifications often points out that recognition of poor achievement in compulsory schooling has a negative influence on motivation to participate in learning later in life.

Care is needed in interpreting the scarce literature that links lifelong learning and qualifications, because often the latter are taken to refer to education and training (Keating, 2002). For example, literature on national targets for lifelong learning participation often refers to proportions of the population reaching certain levels of qualification. The use of the word qualification should refer only to the *outcome* of education and training. The report from Thematic Group 3 on co-operation of different institutions and stakeholders of the qualifications system (Annex A) underlines this and explains that qualifications are commonly understood to specify learning programmes.

A European Commission report on quality indicators for lifelong learning (EC, 2001) found that it was not possible to define a general indicator covering qualification (referred to in the report as *accreditation and certification*) because it would not incorporate significant aspects of learning outside the formal qualifications system. In evaluating lifelong learning internationally, qualifications levels are invariably and explicitly linked to phases of education and training and benchmarked to ISCED 97; once again this shows a strong link with participation in programmes rather than defining outcomes of learning programmes through qualifications.

1.3. A consensual view of terminology

Definitions are important: the spoken and written words need to carry the meaning for others that the speaker or writer intends. This chapter is designed to help develop common meanings for common words and phrases as well as to heighten awareness of different perspectives.

At the heart of this book are a number of central concepts. The following list refers to those linked to qualifications systems:

- Qualification.
- Qualifications system.
- Qualifications framework.
- Competence.
- Credit.
- The relationship between assessment, validation, accreditation and qualification.
- Standard.

On the lifelong learning side, the following concepts are central:

- Lifelong learning.
- Recognition of learning.
- Formal learning.
- Non-formal learning.
- Informal learning.

In the earliest phases of the OECD study these terms were defined, usually through the work of the three Thematic Groups that included members from many countries. However, as the study developed and more people worked with these terms, different interpretations came to the surface. Attempts to reconcile the views of participants have produced an evolution of definitions, as the different meanings have been accommodated. In this chapter an account is given of the evolution of each of the central concepts, followed by its final agreed definition. Existing OECD, European Union and CEDEFOP definitions have been used as a basis wherever possible.

Qualification

Discussions in the course of the OECD study produced the following definition:

A qualification is achieved when a competent body determines that an individual has learned knowledge, skills and/or wider competences to specified standards. The standard of learning is confirmed by means of an assessment process or the successful completion of a course of study. Learning and assessment for a qualification can take place during a programme of study and/

or workplace experience. A qualification confers official recognition of value in the labour market and in further education and training. A qualification can be a legal entitlement to practice a trade.

This definition is in line with those of international organisations, although there may be some reconciliation required with the more extensive definition of a qualification produced by the International Labour Office that has three parts:

● The requirements for an individual to enter, or progress within, an occupation.

● The education and training experience and attainments that an individual has.

● An official record of achievement, which recognises successful completion of education or training, or satisfactory performance in a test or examination.

A simplified version of the definition above will be useful in some circumstances: qualification is a formal outcome of an accreditation or validation process. A qualification confers official recognition of value in the labour market and in further education and training.

Qualifications system

The agreed definition is:

Qualifications systems include all aspects of a country's activity that result in the recognition of learning. These systems include the means of developing and operationalising national or regional policy on qualifications, institutional arrangements, quality assurance processes, assessment and awarding processes, skills recognition and other mechanisms that link education and training to the labour market and civil society. Qualifications systems may be more or less integrated and coherent. One feature of a qualifications system may be an explicit framework of qualifications.

Behringer and Coles (2003) propose a deconstruction of a qualifications system into components and sub-components; this is included in Annex 1.A2 and provides a perspective on how broad qualifications systems can be.

Qualifications framework

A qualifications framework is a component of a qualifications system.

A qualifications framework is an instrument for the development and classification of qualifications according to a set of criteria for levels of learning achieved. This set of criteria may be implicit in the qualifications descriptors themselves or made explicit in the form of a set of level descriptors. The scope of frameworks may be comprehensive of all learning achievement and pathways or may be confined to a particular sector – for example, initial education, adult education and training or an occupational area. Some frameworks may have more design elements and a tighter structure than others; some may have a legal basis whereas others represent a consensus of views of social partners. All qualifications frameworks, however, establish a basis for improving the quality, accessibility, linkages and public or labour market recognition of qualifications within a country and internationally.

Competence

Considerable work has been done to clarify the meaning of competence, especially when the word is used in connection with work. The OECD study DeSeCo (Rychen and Salganik, 2003) reviewed the meaning of the concept and categorised a range of competences.

Using the report of that project and examining published literature from France, the United Kingdom and the United States yielded the following composite definition.

> *Competence is an ability that extends beyond the possession of knowledge and skills. It includes: i) cognitive competence involving the use of theory and concepts, as well as informal tacit knowledge gained experientially; ii) functional competence (skills or know-how), those things that a person should be able to do when they work in a given area; iii) personal competence involving knowing how to conduct oneself in a specific situation; and iv) ethical competence involving the possession of certain personal and professional values.*

Credit

Credit is usually associated with determining the *value* of a specific amount of learning, usually a unit of assessed learning or a module in a learning programme. Sometimes credit is deemed portable and can be included in a setting different to the one in which it was gained or awarded. Credit *transfer* is used to describe this process, and it is worth noting that credit can move to another qualification and count for more or less than its original value depending on the relative size of the destination qualification. Sometimes credit is allowed to accumulate until it reaches or exceeds a value required for the award of a qualification. Credit *accumulation* is used in many flexible learning programmes. Finally, because credit systems can sometimes become complicated, the processes involved in valuing, transferring and accumulating credit may be governed by rules contained within a more general credit *framework*. Combining these ideas, we have:

> *Credit describes the value of an amount of learning. It can be transferred to a qualification other than the one in which it was gained. Credit can be allowed to accumulate to predetermined levels for the award of a qualification. The processes involved in valuing credit, transferring credit and accumulating credit are governed by rules in a credit framework.*

The relationship between assessment, validation, qualification and certification

The meaning of qualification as a way of conferring a status of being qualified and the ownership of a certificate of qualification is a source of confusion. In an attempt to root the meaning of qualification and certification in commonly understood terms, the following sequence of ideas is suggested:

> *Learning is **assessed** against standards or criteria by an expert, or a group of experts, who follow established procedures.*

> *Achievement in learning is **validated** when assessment of learning is approved or confirmed by relevant legislative and professional authorities by having met predetermined criteria, following a standard assessment procedure.*

> ***Qualification** is a formal outcome of an accreditation or validation process. A qualification confers official recognition of value in the labour market and in further education and training.*

> *A **certificate** is an official document that records qualification and validation of learning.*

Standard

A term that arises in many discussions of qualification and learning for qualification is *standard*. It is a key term for establishing confidence in qualifications systems and in learning provision. There are at least three ways in which it is used. First, in the widest interpretation it describes benchmarks or expectations of learning that have been established with stakeholders. In this sense the standards can be related to the content of learning programmes (learning outcomes) or to the process of verifying learning outcomes through quality assurance procedures. Thus the term might be used to refer to the standard of qualification. In this meaning standards convey a sense of consistency and relevance that is commonly understood by users. But this definition is sometimes too wide for some users of the word. A second meaning of standard can be associated with specific criteria governing the content of learning programmes. Standards here refer only to the level of learning outcomes involved; the word gives a sense of reaching a required (predetermined) standard, *e.g.* a person has a standard of chemistry knowledge to work as a technician. Clearly this meaning implies that many standards or levels exist depending on contextual factors such as local workplace expectations. A third meaning of standard is associated with a procedure commonly accepted as replicable every time it is carried out. Clearly there is no variation due to context here. In this book the broadest meaning is used unless otherwise stated.

> *Standards are benchmarks or expectations of learning that have been established with stakeholders and include all factors that influence the consistency and relevance of qualifications.*

Learning

In this book, the definition published by CEDEFOP (Tissot, 2004) is used:

> *Learning is a cumulative process whereby individuals gradually assimilate increasingly complex and abstract entities (concepts, categories, and patterns of behaviour or models) and/ or acquire skills and competences.*

Lifelong learning

The OECD has adopted a "cradle to grave" concept of lifelong learning. However, in analysing literature on lifelong learning most writers ignore the learning that takes place in the years of compulsory education. Presumably this is because in those early years the learner is left little choice about whether to engage in formal learning or not. In effect, these writers regard lifelong learning as that which occurs after compulsory secondary schooling or from the beginning of a vocational education and training programme, and are possibly better identified as adult learning. The OECD's cradle-to-grave approach is distinct from this post-compulsory approach, and allows for the fact that compulsory education can have a profound effect on participation in learning later in life.

An issue that often arises is the richness of the lifelong learning concept, and in particular that it covers institutionalised learning, work-related learning, and forms of learning for leisure. The notion that lifelong learning is essentially geared toward the individual carries great weight with participants. In the paper Behringer and Coles (2003) produced to support the OECD study the definition used is as follows.

> *Learning activity that is undertaken throughout life and improves knowledge, skills and competences within personal, civic, social and/or employment-related perspectives. Thus the whole spectrum of learning – formal, non-formal and informal – is included, as are active citizenship, personal fulfilment, social inclusion and professional, vocational and employment-related aspects.*

Recognition of learning

In European literature *recognition* seems to be a broad term often used interchangeably with *validation*. Both terms appear to include the recording of achievements in learning and the progress made by individuals. For some users *recognition* also includes the processes leading to the issue of a qualification. Recognition of learning aims to make known an individual's knowledge, skills and wider competences; they can then use the credit so gained to benefit financially or in terms of status or self-esteem. In some countries the term *validation* specifically refers to legal processes that permit an individual to obtain a certificate (for instance a vocational diploma) linked to their skills, knowledge and know-how. In other countries *validation* is referred to as a means of making known a person's skills and competences without requiring prior achievement of predetermined knowledge targets. Recognition is also a component of the pedagogical process in adult education and an important instrument in work on recruiting and motivating participants to study. In Scotland *recognition* is seen as a process of linking knowledge, skills and competences – however learned – to criteria in a national benchmark. This is firmly distinguished from *accreditation* by definition: the latter contains a formal assessment process that includes elements of quality assurance.

CEDEFOP (Tissot, 2004) categorises recognition (of competences) as either *a) formal recognition,* which is the process of granting official status to competences, either through the award of certificates or through the granting of equivalence, credit units, or the validation of gained competences; and/or *b) social recognition,* through acknowledgment of the value of competences by economic and social stakeholders. This leads to the accepted definition for the OECD study:

> *Recognition of learning is the process of recording of achievements of individuals arising from any kind of learning in any environment; the process aims to make visible an individual's knowledge, skills and wider competences so that they can combine and build on learning achieved and be rewarded for it.*

Formal learning

This is usually associated with an institution of learning, such as a school or an employer offering formal training. An agency that manages an assessment process may also be involved. The learning results from an organised programme of instruction. Formal learning is intentional from the learner's perspective. Thus we have a definition:

> *Formal learning can be achieved when a learner decides to follow a programme of instruction in an educational institution, adult training centre or in the workplace. Formal learning is generally recognised in a qualification or a certificate.*

Non-formal learning

Like formal learning, non-formal learning takes place when an individual follows an organised programme of learning in an educational institution or in the workplace. This kind of learning is sometimes embedded in planned activities that are not explicitly designated as learning, but that contain an important learning element. Non-formal learning can be structured and is intentional from the learner's point of view.

Many countries explicitly acknowledge a difference between non-formal learning and informal learning. Where this distinction is made, there is a general agreement that non-formal learning is intentional, and often arises in an educational or labour setting, but does not lead to formal qualifications. In Sweden formal learning is undertaken within the formal education system and non-formal learning is organised alongside formal learning by private providers. Thus non-formal learning can be very strongly connected to formal education systems and other organised education.

Non-formal learning arises when an individual follows a learning programme but it is not usually evaluated and does not lead to certification. However it can be structured by the learning institution and is intentional from the learner's point of view.

Informal learning

Informal learning is achieved outside organised education or training provision. It is often referred to as "experience" or "unintentional learning" that occurs throughout life without the learner necessarily being aware of the knowledge or skill that they have gained. This type of learning is seen as a "side-effect" of life. Informal learning is also referred to as experiential learning. It is suggested that the CEDEFOP (Tissot, 2004) definition is the most useful.

Informal learning results from daily work-related, family or leisure activities. It is not organised or structured (in terms of objectives, time or learning support). Informal learning is in most cases unintentional from the learner's perspective. It does not usually lead to certification.

1.4. Effects on lifelong learning

What are the possible effects of a qualifications system on lifelong learning? These can be classified as relating to the:

- Quantity of learning opportunities.
- Quality of learning opportunities.
- Equity of access to learning.
- Efficiency of the lifelong learning processes.

The ranges of effects are shown in Figure 1.1.

Having identified how lifelong learning might be enhanced by qualifications systems, it is useful to explore what components of qualifications systems are responsible for this effect on lifelong learning. Behringer and Coles (2003) identified a range of these components and suggested how they might interact with lifelong learning. For example, they considered the possible effects of accreditation processes for qualifications and concluded that the cost of accreditation would be a factor influencing individuals' take-up of learning – and therefore, that an efficient accreditation process would have a positive influence. Similarly, if an accreditation process raises the quality of assessment and evaluation, then this might encourage take-up of accredited learning programmes. Another component of qualifications systems is credit transfer. Here Behringer and Coles concluded that increased flexibility of learning periods and of programme content, opportunities for partial certification and a spreading of the time and therefore the cost of gaining a full qualification were all likely to have a positive effect on lifelong learning. By considering the effects it is possible to anticipate the kind of features of qualifications systems that might influence the behaviour of different stakeholders (Table 1.1).

Figure 1.1. **How lifelong learning could be enhanced through a qualifications system**

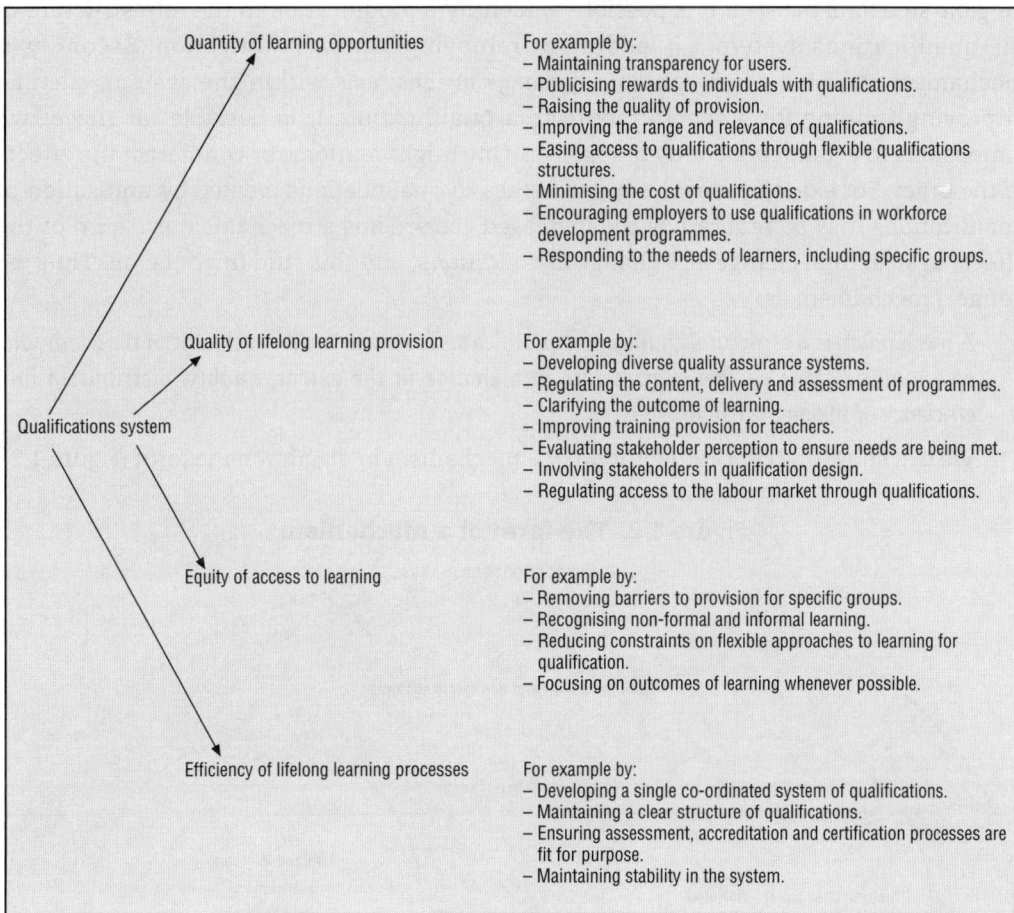

Quantity of learning opportunities

For example by:
– Maintaining transparency for users.
– Publicising rewards to individuals with qualifications.
– Raising the quality of provision.
– Improving the range and relevance of qualifications.
– Easing access to qualifications through flexible qualifications structures.
– Minimising the cost of qualifications.
– Encouraging employers to use qualifications in workforce development programmes.
– Responding to the needs of learners, including specific groups.

Quality of lifelong learning provision

For example by:
– Developing diverse quality assurance systems.
– Regulating the content, delivery and assessment of programmes.
– Clarifying the outcome of learning.
– Improving training provision for teachers.
– Evaluating stakeholder perception to ensure needs are being met.
– Involving stakeholders in qualification design.
– Regulating access to the labour market through qualifications.

Qualifications system

Equity of access to learning

For example by:
– Removing barriers to provision for specific groups.
– Recognising non-formal and informal learning.
– Reducing constraints on flexible approaches to learning for qualification.
– Focusing on outcomes of learning whenever possible.

Efficiency of lifelong learning processes

For example by:
– Developing a single co-ordinated system of qualifications.
– Maintaining a clear structure of qualifications.
– Ensuring assessment, accreditation and certification processes are fit for purpose.
– Maintaining stability in the system.

Table 1.1. **Example of how a qualifications system feature influences stakeholders**

Possible mechanism	Possible effects on individuals	Possible effects on employers	Possible effects on providers
Increase portability of qualifications.	Positive (qualifications could be used in another workplace/country).	Negative (risk of trained staff leaving the firm).	Positive (increased size of market, economies of scale).
		Positive (flexibility in recruitment and deploying labour).	Negative (complexity of entry requirements to programmes).

1.5. The meaning and structure of mechanisms and policy responses

Having explained the main concepts involved in the OECD study and explained the origin of definitions of key terms, it is useful to focus more sharply on the idea of a mechanism. So far a mechanism is defined here as a means of changing an aspect of a qualifications system so that lifelong learning is enhanced in some way. An example of a potential mechanism is the breaking up qualifications into units of assessment for learners with limited time or money to begin a programme of study for qualification by working on one or two units.

During the course of the OECD study, the nature of a mechanism evolved; currently it is conceived as comprising two parts that may interact. First, it can be considered as a tangible *structural change* if it is possible to identify a modification in the infrastructure of the qualifications system, *e.g.* adding or removing a new qualification. Secondly, a mechanism can be a more ephemeral *change in conditions* within the system, such as improving funding for a specific route to a qualification. It is possible for these two dimensions to act independently or together. One might reinforce or counteract the effects of the other. For example, any increased access to qualifications created by unitisation of qualifications may be reduced by the increased costs. Thus a mechanism is a sum of the effects of structural change and change in conditions, and this sum might be nil. Thus we define a mechanism as:

> *A mechanism is a structural change in a qualifications system and/or a change in the conditions of a qualifications system that results in a change in the extent, quality, distribution and efficiency of lifelong learning.*

We can show this conceptualisation of a mechanism in diagrammatic form (Figure 1.2).

Figure 1.2. **The form of a mechanism**

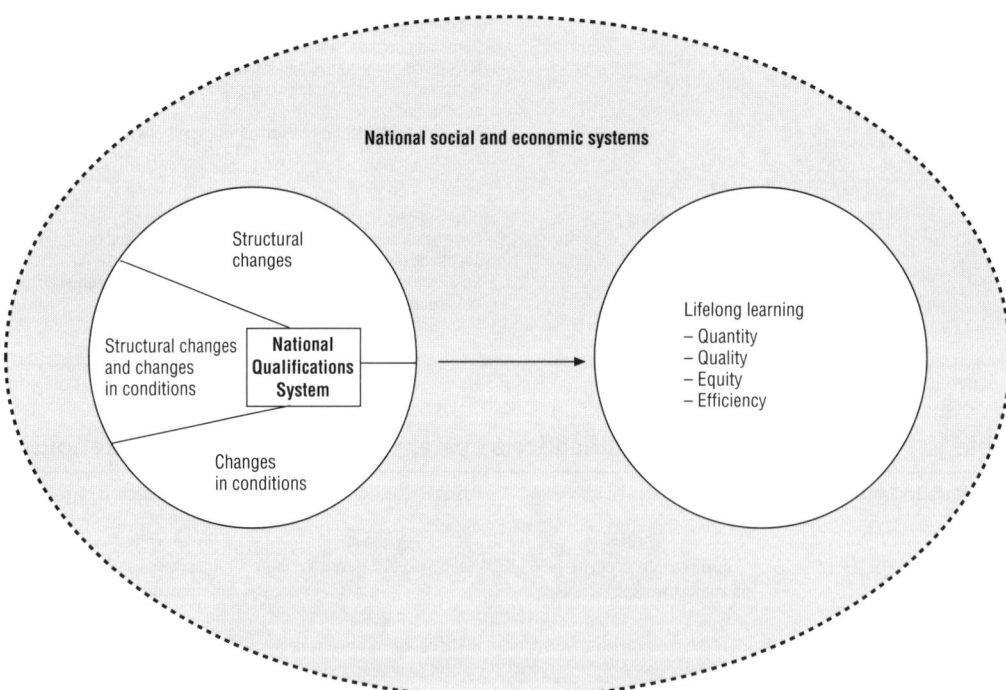

This understanding of a mechanism is used in Chapter 4. There, 20 mechanisms are identified through a comprehensive analysis of empirical and theoretical evidence related to the ways the behaviours of the main stakeholders could be changed. In Chapters 5 and 6 these 20 mechanisms are used to optimise the operation of the *policy responses* made by countries in order to enhance lifelong learning. Nine policy responses are identified in the next chapter. The term *policy response* is defined as:

> *A formal national policy statement covering the intention to develop major parts of the qualifications system in order to bring about improved lifelong learning.*

All of the above definitions have helped clarify the understanding of participants in the OECD study.

1.6. The book's structure

The above sections of Chapter 1 provide definitions and set the conceptual scene. They present all the definitions of the main concepts that emerged during the OECD study and where a common understanding of meaning was considered crucial to the success of the study. These definitions are now sufficiently robust to become the adopted definitions for further work in this field. It would useful to continue using these terms in a consistent manner over time but it is clear that the concepts behind these definitions are organic and that the definitions cannot be carved in stone once and for all. Chapter 1 also attempts to provide a conceptual basis for the ways of linking national qualifications systems and lifelong learning through potential mechanisms. It is important to establish a theoretical base before turning to evidence. The rest of the book is based on empirical work using the country background reports, the thematic groups' work and/or the data gathered during the study including published research and policy papers.

Chapter 2 summarises recent trends and developments in national qualifications systems. This chapter reveals a growing awareness on the part of decision makers in many OECD countries that national qualifications systems can be a policy tool. After a brief reference to pressure for change, empirical evidence is used to draw out a range of policy responses to the need to improve lifelong learning *through* qualifications systems.

Chapter 3 aims at providing quantified ways of mapping out the possible relationships between national qualifications systems and lifelong learning. It attempts to take account of groups at risk and the diversity of individual needs. Two types of data are used. First, aggregated or macro variables describe, at the country level, factors such as level of educational attainment of the population and the proportion of adults undertaking learning activities. A typology of qualifications systems that could be related to lifelong learning data is also presented. Second, micro data at the individual level are used to supplement the macro data and provide a better sense of the possible relationship between undertaking learning for a qualification and lifelong learning.

Chapter 4 extracts stakeholder evidence from country background reports and combines it with published information to identify incentives and barriers to learning. This evidence is synthesised into a series of mechanisms based on the conceptual framework outlined in Chapter 1. No attempt is made to consider operationalising the mechanisms, a topic treated in Chapters 5 and 6.

Chapter 5 shows how these mechanisms can be clustered under the policy responses identified in Chapter 2. It takes each of the policy responses and considers which mechanisms are likely help achieve its aim and which are likely to be counter-productive. Short case studies are provided to illustrate the practical application of mechanisms in actual country policy responses. The breadth of influence of mechanisms on policy responses is analysed and some indications are provided about how some mechanisms seem to strengthen the effects of others.

Chapter 6 targets policy makers and focuses on the practical issues of making mechanisms a useful part of policy making. Drawing on all the evidence and analysis presented in the previous chapters, it presents three tools that policy makers can use to develop qualifications systems into drivers that will deliver more and better lifelong learning.

Overall, the OECD study that has led to this book examined the impact of different qualification policies on lifelong learning. It has helped countries share know-how and policy experience gained from recent reforms and adjustments in qualifications systems. To do so, it has been organised to make research work as robust as possible. In addition to the fact-finding approach adopted for the country background reports, the work of the Thematic Groups focused on particular aspects of the relationship between qualifications systems and lifelong learning. It also included international meetings of national representatives and experts to monitor the progress of the study.[2] As a consequence, the study has been able to promote talk among country delegates, international organisation[3] representatives and experts, to moderate written material, and to initiate ideas. That input, together with the published literature and the OECD expert seminars, has been instrumental in shaping the structure and content of this book.

Notes

1. See Annex 1.A1 for a full description of the process.

2. Paris (France), St.-Gallen (Switzerland) and Cancún (Mexico).

3. The European Centre for the Development of Vocational Training (CEDEFOP), the European Training Foundation (ETF), the International Labour Organization (ILO), the World Bank and the Trade Union Advisory Committee (TUAC) have participated in this activity.

References

Béduwé, C. and J. Planas (2003), *Educational Expansion and Labour Market: A Comparative Study of Five European Countries – France, Germany, Italy, Spain and the United Kingdom – with Special Reference to the United States*, CEDEFOP Research Series, Office for Official Publication of the European Communities, Luxembourg.

Behringer, F. and M. Coles (2003), *The Role of National Qualifications Systems in Promoting Lifelong Learning: Towards an Understanding of the Mechanisms that Link Qualifications and Lifelong Learning*, OECD Education Working Papers, No. 3, Paris.

Brown, L.B. (2003), *International Models of Career-Technical Educations*, ERIC Clearinghouse on Adult Career and Vocational Education, *www.ericacve.org/pubs.asp*.

EC (European Commission) (2001), *Making a European Area of Lifelong Learning a Reality*, COM (2001), European Commission, Brussels.

Evans, K., P. Hodkinson and L. Unwin (2002), *Working to Learn: Transforming Learning in the Workplace*, Kogan Page, London.

Feinstein, L., F. Galindo-Rueda and A. Vignoles (2004), *The Labour Market Impact of Adult Education and Training: A Cohort Analysis*, Working Paper, Centre for the Economics of Education, forthcoming in the *Scottish Journal of Political Economy*.

Guile, D. and T. Griffiths (2001), "Learning through Work Experience", *Journal of Education and Work*, Vol. 15, No. 3, pp. 113-131.

IJLE (*International Journal of Leadership in Education*) (2004), "Lifelong Learning: A Simple Concept Oversimplifying a Complex Reality", Editorial, Vol. 23, No. 4, July-August, p. 315-317.

Keating, J. (2002), "Qualifications and Learning: Exploring the Relationship", Working Paper.

NCVER (National Centre for Vocational Education Research) (2003a), *Defining Generic Skills*, *www.ncver.edu.au/research/proj/nr2102b.pdf*.

NCVER (2003b), *Training and Competitiveness: An Asian Firm Perspective*, NCVER, *www.ncver.edu.au/research/commercial/op291.pdf*.

OECD (2001), *Education Policy Analysis*, OECD, Paris.

OECD (2002a), *Guidelines for Country Background Reports*, document prepared by the Secretariat for the activity on "The Role of National Qualifications Systems in Promoting Lifelong Learning", February, OECD, Paris, *www.oecd.org/edu/lifelonglearning/nqs*.

OECD (2002b), *The Role of National Qualifications Systems in Promoting Lifelong Learning – Thematic Issues Groups*, document prepared by the Secretariat for the activity on "The Role of National Qualifications Systems in Promoting Lifelong Learning", April, OECD, Paris, *www.oecd.org/edu/lifelonglearning/nqs*.

OECD (2003), *Beyond Rhetoric: Adult Learning Policies and Practices*, OECD, Paris.

OECD (2005), *Promoting Adult Learning*, OECD, Paris.

Ottersten, E.K. (2004), "Lifelong Learning and Challenges Posed to European Labour Markets", *European Journal of Education*, Vol. 39, No. 2.

Rychen, D.S. and L.H. Salganik, eds. (2003), *Key Competencies for a Successful Life and a Well-Functioning Society*, Report of the OECD DeSeCo (Definition and Selection of Competencies) Project, Hogrefe and Huber, Göttingen.

Tissot P. (2004), *Terminology of Vocational Training Policy: A Multilingual Glossary for an Enlarged Europe*, CEDEFOP, Office for Official Publications of the European Communities, Luxembourg.

ANNEX 1.A1

Process and Thematic Groups

At the national level, countries were invited to write a country background report according to a set of guidelines (OECD, 2002a); 15 countries did so.[1] The national reports were then discussed with representatives from the country and authorised as valid descriptions of the respective qualifications systems and their effects on lifelong learning. The reports were not primarily intended to form the basis for comparison, as they mainly describe and analyse issues from a domestic point of view and the study did not include independent review visits or external evaluation. Nevertheless they provided a solid primary source of data for analysis and the preparation of this book. They are the basis for the empirical work, and are used in conjunction with a range of quantitative data and the published literature in the fields under study. In preparing their national reports, countries were asked to consider four components.

First, they were asked to describe their qualifications system in broad terms, in particular the arrangements for recognition of formal, non-formal and informal learning. These include arrangements linking qualifications through credit systems and qualifications frameworks, and the governance arrangements for qualifications systems. Countries were then asked to provide summary information on the impact of qualifications systems as revealed through reviews or evaluations, or other information and data readily available. This included information on the benefits gained through the recognition of learning for qualifications. The third component was based on a review of the major changes in qualifications systems or key elements of systems introduced in countries over the past decade and the educational, economic and social pressures that led to these changes. They were also asked to describe the major initiatives or reforms in their qualifications system that were designed to enhance learning through such objectives as increased levels of participation in formal learning or improved outcomes. For the final component, countries were asked to examine and analyse providers' and learners' direct experiences of the impact of qualifications systems upon learning. It was proposed that this examination be at the level of practice and use – that is learning programmes in a variety of settings.[2]

In addition to preparing their background report, countries were invited to identify the main issues for examination by international Thematic Groups. Three key themes were identified and so three thematic groups were set up. The rationale for organising the groups was twofold. First, there was interest in having a comparative approach in addition to the descriptive country-centred approach of the country background reports. Second, it was an opportunity to focus on themes of particular interest to participating countries.

Qualitative data were gathered through consultations with the participants about their respective countries and by using a template (OECD, 2002b) to facilitate comparative analysis. Twenty countries contributed to one or more of the thematic groups.[3] The three corresponding thematic reports form part of the knowledge base of the study and have been used to prepare this book. They are presented in summary form in Annex A.

The first Thematic Group addressed *the development and use of qualifications frameworks as a means of reforming and managing qualifications systems*. Beyond the issue of definitions – key terms such as "qualifications system" and "qualifications framework" are clearly spelled out – the report of this group deals with the rationale for introducing a qualifications framework. Additionally it describes certain drivers for change, benefits, and the conditions for introducing a framework. The benefits are analysed according to whether they are general benefits or relate specifically to lifelong learning. General benefits have to do with qualifications systems and provision; career development, guidance and employment placement, and information and orientation including occupational mobility; the international and trans-national dimensions; and regulation, legislation and institutional arrangements. The benefits to lifelong learning are at the heart of the overall study. The first report summarises the possible impacts: to promote a culture of lifelong learning; to allow for the integration of lifelong learning provision into a coherent system; to enable non-standard forms of access; to enable further development of basic skills; to relate and compare qualifications; to focus learning on both individual and company needs; to minimise learning time and reduce costs; and to provide clarity and simplicity about competences held by individuals.

The report of the second Thematic Group addressed standards and quality assurance in qualifications, with special reference to the recognition of non-formal and informal learning. Here again, some terms are defined and the distinction between formal, non-formal and informal learning is clarified. The report also addresses the main reason why countries are interested in the deliberations of this second group: elaboration of the policy opportunity and challenges. In terms of opportunity, there is the possible contribution to the quality, quantity and distribution of lifelong learning. There are also issues in linking individual human capital – which can be improved through learning – with performance in the labour market, *e.g.* employability and mobility. The policy challenges, such as the difficulty of gaining acceptance in the labour market, are also spelled out. The report contains examples of current practices in several fields: legislation and policy; linkage with the formal education and training system; ways of decentralising the initiatives; the social partnerships; quality assurance; defining target groups; and demand for recognition systems. Barriers to the recognition of non-formal and informal learning are addressed from two points of view: individual motivation and the structures of the recognition systems. Looking to the future, proposals are made for removing these barriers and facilitating the recognition of non-formal and informal learning. They are provided along three lines: principles for recognition systems, addressing individual barriers, and developing recognition system. Finally, the report of this group provides some conclusions and opens up the debate by offering recommendations in seven domains: the purpose of a recognition system; the context; the establishment of national standards; quality assurance; the targeting of user groups; enhancing awareness and access; and the removal of existing disincentives.

The report of the third Thematic Group addressed the issue of *co-operation of different institutions and stakeholders of the qualifications systems*. In particular it examined the roles of partners in the development of occupational standards and vocational qualifications as well as their roles when the qualifications system is reformed. The report contains two chapters and some conclusions. The first chapter addresses the methodologies and development processes for improving or creating qualifications and standards. It then deals with an "essential but problematic" aspect of vocational qualifications: the description of the content of work. Potential biases in approaches to observation are then described as well as methodologies of observation. The focus then shifts to the development of qualifications, a complex process from a socio-political point of view. The first chapter finishes with a short analysis of the notion of "representation" in qualifications systems. The second chapter, on changes in qualification system regimes, focuses on the drivers, goals and initiatives for change and on structures of participation, including new forms of co-operation. The latter topic raises questions such as: who decides who should be involved? What is their relative power? What are their aims, aspirations and/or intentions in participating in the regulation and governance of qualifications systems? How well equipped are they to participate in the development process? What access do they have to the content of work in order to make judgements and assertions? What forms of support are available to specific groups in respect of participation? How tight are the structural arrangements and what are the rules within the discussions that take place? The report's conclusion discusses the potential significance of changes that have occurred in the past few years in countries' qualifications development processes.

Notes

1. Australia, Belgium (French Community), Denmark, France, Germany, Greece, Ireland, Japan, Korea, the Netherlands, New Zealand, Portugal, Slovenia, Switzerland and the United Kingdom.

2. Country Background Reports were coded with QSR NUD.IST software (Non-Numerical Unstructured Data * Indexing, Searching and Theorising), a flexible tool that is inclusive in nature. The framework used for the coding derives directly from the structure proposed in the guidelines (OECD, 2002a). It is therefore based on the four components, clearly spelled out by sub-themes to ease the coding process. The purpose of the coding is to allow thematic analysis of the country reports without having to read and code information in the 15 reports linearly.

3. Australia, Belgium (Flemish Community), Czech Republic, Denmark, Finland, France, Germany, Greece, Ireland, Italy, Korea, Mexico, the Netherlands, New Zealand, Portugal, Slovenia, Spain, Sweden, Switzerland and the United Kingdom.

ANNEX 1.A2

Components of a Qualifications System

The table below gives a list of components and sub-components that best describe a qualifications system. The way they are combined and used in the countries reveals to some extent how well the qualifications system is working. The performance of a qualifications system can be judged by such things as adaptation to learning pathways, accessibility, efficiency, flexibility, responsiveness and transparency.

Component	Potential sub-component
1. **Scope** of application of the qualifications system	Breadth (international, national, regional). Legal status. Sector/industry. Collective agreements or agreements by professional organisations.
2. **Control** of the qualifications system	Government. National agency or agencies. Social partners. Awarding body. No clear control. Extra-national. Stability of control.
3. **Accreditation** processes for qualifications	Status of institutions involved. Extent of public information about process. Establishing standards. Maintaining standards. Conditions for award. Process for recognising prior learning. Control of accreditation. Supply and demand considerations. Stability.
4. **Framework** within the qualifications system	Horizontal and vertical relationships. Equivalencies (general/vocational). Initial education/training only. Inclusiveness. Regulated or part of a regulatory function.
5. **Descriptors** present in qualifications	Requirement. Optional. Qualification types. Purpose (general, vocational). Content. Assessment. Levels.

Component	Potential sub-component
5. **Descriptors** present in qualifications *(cont.)*	Learning arrangements.
	Prior attainment.
	Types of assessment.
	Recognition of non-formal and informal learning.
	Links to qualifications frameworks.
6. **Access** to qualifications for individuals	Entry points.
	Entry requirements.
	Preparatory courses.
	Recognition of prior learning
7. **Progression** for individuals	Linkages between pathways, qualification types.
	Routes and pathways explicit.
	Transferability, equivalence of standards.
	No routes.
8. **Stability** of the qualifications system	Permanent, fixed term, mixed.
9. **Awarding** processes	Process of assessment (formal, informal).
	Recognition of prior learning.
	Extent of assessment in qualifications (flexible, minimum, maximum, modal size).
	Types of certificates.
	Level of regulation.
	Awarding institutions (type and number).
	Participation of social partners in awarding process.
10. Use of a **credit** system	Accreditation of learning elsewhere.
	Extent of unitisation/modularisation.
	Rules of combination of units/modules.
	Recognition of non-formal and informal learning/exemptions possible.
	Partial certification.
11. **International** reference points	ISCED.
	Trans-national (regional) frameworks, *e.g.* EU-level frameworks.
	Linkage to ISCO.
	Portability.

Source: Behringer and Coles (2003).

ISBN 978-92-64-01367-4
Qualifications Systems
Bridges to Lifelong Learning
© OECD 2007

Chapter 2

Policy Responses to Improve National Qualifications Systems

This chapter draws together recent policy responses to the lifelong learning agenda that involve national qualifications systems. Countries described the major pressures for changes and innovations over the past decade (inter alia from the various stakeholder groups), how policy has evolved to deal with these pressures, and any changes anticipated in the qualifications system. Country experts also identified the major constraints on reforms and innovations. This chapter is therefore a synopsis of evidence drawn mainly from background reports. It attempts to give an overview of the ways countries perceive policy development related to qualifications systems. This wide policy view sets the scene for more detailed work on mechanisms that link qualifications systems and lifelong learning.

Policy responses to lifelong learning that relate to qualifications systems are identified and elaborated in Section 2.2. This follows on from a brief exploration of the pressures countries feel to develop qualifications systems (Section 2.1). Some issues related to policy development in the area of qualifications systems are examined in Section 2.3. There is also a major annex to this book that is associated with this chapter (Annex B) – it provides a concise synopsis of the qualifications system and reform programme in each of the countries that provided background information.

2.1. Reasons for developing lifelong learning

There are major benefits to be gained for countries able to improve the quantity, quality, equitable distribution and efficiency of lifelong learning. Many of these benefits stem from improved economic performance based on better volumes and levels of skills supply to the labour market and the consequential gains in innovation, speed of product development and efficiency of work practices. There are also major social benefits related to an improved sense of citizenship and greater community involvement. Individuals can benefit from improved education services, lead healthier lives and gain a sense of creativity, responsiveness, self-worth and fulfilment. Together, the economic and social benefits can support cultural development and reduce the costs of maintaining services for the economically and socially excluded sections of communities.

A national qualifications system is a broad concept that includes all aspects of a country's activity resulting in the recognition of learning. These systems include the means of developing and implementing policy on qualifications, institutional arrangements, skills identification arrangements and processes for assessment, awarding and quality assurance. In some countries, the system is managed centrally and has the appearance of a well-structured arrangement of interacting elements; in others it is rather less integrated and coherent. A qualifications framework may or may not be in place. An understanding of all that is involved is important, since it clarifies the scope of the country reports with regard to pressures, reforms and constraints. Later in this volume, Annex B provides a concise synopsis of the qualifications system and reform programme in each of the countries that provided background information.

The key question here is, how can qualifications systems be used to deliver better lifelong learning? Countries value the potential benefits so highly that they have developed policy responses to meet the challenge. These responses are identified in this chapter and later (in Chapters 5 and 6) are examined in connection with mechanisms. Achieving a proper interface between the two can make greatly enhanced lifelong learning a reality. The lessons presented here can serve as grist for policy learning between countries (ETF, 2004).

2.2. Qualifications systems: drivers for change

Qualifications systems are evolving. There is a significant level of change in many countries and it is useful to identify the pressures driving this process. They are diverse; as one might expect, each country report provides a particular mix, and the mix differs from country to country. Rather than attempt to identify all the factors driving change, this section categorises these pressures on the basis of evidence furnished by countries in their background reports. There appear to be six different types of pressure.

Pressures to develop the economy

Many countries reported economic pressures to reform their national qualifications system, and that these are becoming more acute as the priority to strengthen the link between the education system and employment grows. Countries point to the gap between job training and qualifications as a reason for the development of qualifications frameworks and skill standards. Economic pressures have to do with global economic trends and national needs, *e.g.* to develop human capital and respond to skills shortages.

In many countries, raising the value of human capital is seen as crucial to development and progress. Qualifications are often taken as a proxy measure of the volume and quality of education and training. Qualifications systems are believed to have potential for improving the link between education and work; for establishing new pathways from education into employment; and for reducing barriers to learning, for example by using new forms of assessment.

Innovation in production has implications for training, and this in turn has implications for qualifications systems. Economic needs drive innovation, which often takes place via continuous learning in the workplace. The forms of this learning are changing; for example, learning is increasingly becoming self-directed. Consequently, learning structures in the workplace are becoming more complex. The focus is no longer solely on acquisition of knowledge but has widened to include new values, new codes of behaviour and the remodelling of past experience. This has resulted in the expansion of training provision and use of more diverse recognition systems through qualifications.

Some countries emphasise assessment of vocational ability, recognised in qualification, as important for employment stability, improved remuneration, and quick and efficient recruitment. Recognition of vocational ability is also expected to reduce risks related to employment, on both the employer's and the employee's side, by preventing mismatches arising from lack of information on workers' skills. Some countries report that rapid economic growth has produced skill shortages, and this has exerted pressure to have the qualifications system respond more quickly and efficiently to changes and emerging needs in the labour market.

Enterprises exert pressure as well. In many countries action is taken to overcome basic skill weaknesses (*e.g.* in communication, numeracy and problem solving) as these are believed to be found in the majority of jobs. Without this response it is feared that the low-skilled could be excluded from the labour market or forced into early retirement. On the other hand, some countries are interested in achieving higher-level competences through greater participation in higher education, and greater use of competence-based training and assessment as an alternative to traditional higher education. The system is under pressure to respond equally well to all levels of qualification development.

Promotion of greater mobility for workers and learners creates pressure on national qualifications systems. Firms' drive for greater flexibility at times can lead to shorter job tenures in the face of more volatile product markets and shorter product cycles. Career jobs are diminishing and individuals are now experiencing more frequent changes in jobs over their working lives. Then there is the expectation that systems deliver international recognition of skills, including recognition of formal, informal and non-formal learning that has taken place in other countries.

International pressures

Another type of pressure arises from international competition. Examples can range from the interpretation of performance data to making sure that qualifications achieved by different learning routes are genuinely comparable.

Several countries cited relative ranking in the OECD Programme for International Student Assessment (PISA) or Trends in International Mathematics and Science Study (TIMSS) as a key driver of current policy reform. Prior to this study, the International Adult Literacy Survey (IALS) had already shown major discrepancies in adult literacy performance among OECD countries (OECD and Statistics Canada, 2000). PISA is concerned with the 15-to-16-year-old population and pressure for change is targeted at managers in institutions, teachers and young learners. Such reforms can have effects on the wider system – including qualifications – by for example introducing new kinds of assessments and learning programmes.

Among the European Union countries, there is a commitment to increasing mobility of workers and learners across country boundaries. This requires transparency in qualifications systems and encourages countries to build education and qualification structures that are consistent with other countries in the EU. Recent proposals for a European Qualifications Framework are designed to facilitate compatibility among national systems. The Framework will also provide a further means of comparison through the referencing of national qualifications to a single set of levels.

Demographic pressures

In many countries, low population growth coupled with increased demand for high skills has drawn attention to potential skill shortages. Inevitably, older people need to be provided with learning opportunities reflecting change in work practices. However, the outflow of older skilled workers – which results in a waste of knowledge and expertise – can also lead to pressures on labour markets. Qualifications systems have to provide recognition for skills learned at any stage in life. This demographic shift has an impact on (re-)training needs, retirement schemes, pension funding and family life.

Several countries point to the challenges qualifications systems face as a result of immigration flows. These pressures include the need to relate qualifications gained in other countries to the national system and the need to recognise learning not previously recognised through qualifications.

Social and cultural pressures

Social and cultural issues are not divorced from the economic, demographic and immigration issues noted above. At the same time, it is generally known that people engage in learning for economic reasons – to improve employment prospects, for example – and for personal development and social reasons – social status, better citizenship, and so on. There is pressure to broaden the current provision of education to include such aspects as values, behaviour and citizenship, just as there is pressure to offer learners more choice and more flexible ways of gaining credit for their learning (including informal and non-formal learning). All of these aspects have implications for qualifications systems.

There is a call for more flexible vocational education and training systems for people in disadvantaged situations as a means of improving social inclusion through education and, subsequently, work.

Opportunities for training later in life depend heavily on the qualifications with which one enters the labour force and the learning opportunities open to the unemployed. Employees of small firms and in disadvantaged groups have far fewer opportunities for training than employees of larger firms. Disparities are also reflected in the large earnings gaps between those with and without post-secondary education, which furthermore widen over the lifetime. There is pressure on the qualifications system to give more individuals a chance to reach the minimum level of learning and qualification necessary for effective functioning in modern knowledge societies. Completion of upper secondary qualifications is a widely accepted benchmark.

Pressures from learners

Many countries identify strong pressures from learners to make qualifications systems transparent. They highlight the need for clarifying the possible progression routes in the qualifications systems. It is likely that this is especially important in countries where wage bargaining is linked to qualifications.

In the search for coherence and harmonisation, some countries describe pressure to rationalise their qualifications system, and in so doing create a more balanced view of all of the options available and reduce any differences in perceptions of academic and vocational qualifications. The countries sense a pressure to present a coherent system and in particular to forge stronger links between secondary education, higher education, and vocational education and training.

Pressure from technological change

Technological innovation and the global spread of communications technologies are creating pressure for countries to use the most up-to-date production methods. The move towards leaner production systems and the potential for rising unemployment rates bring a need for enhanced training and retraining in the use of new technologies. Qualifications systems must allow for the recognition of new knowledge, skills and wider competences. Skills shortages in the information and communications technology area are frequently reported. Qualifications systems must themselves optimise their own working practices through the use of new technologies.

Technological change has encouraged the growth of international qualifications, a development that raises important recognition, benchmarking, evaluation, quality assurance and jurisdiction issues. This generates a two-way set of pressures: "importing" qualifications from other countries and "exporting" a country's own qualifications. This is thought to be a major issue for the future, and it links strongly with the comparative pressures discussed above.

Demand-led pressures

The main pressures reported by the participating countries are all essentially demand-led. This theme runs through all six types of pressure outlined above. For example, countries expressed a clear need for their qualifications system to be more user-oriented in structure, presentation, management and functioning. Pressure to develop learning opportunities means that in some countries, providers have been required to differentiate course offerings in response to more selective demand. They have, for example, created qualifications delivered through general and vocational education, and provided programmes in new cross-disciplinary and more specialised fields.

2.3. Responses to pressures for changes in qualifications system

Given this diverse set of pressures, countries report that many reforms are under way, based on policies aiming to enhance lifelong learning. The term *policy response* is here used to describe an intention on behalf of countries to develop major parts of the qualifications system in order to improve lifelong learning. The nine areas of policy response elaborated later in this book have emerged from the country background reports. Where it is helpful and instructive to identify the country or countries of origin of these policy responses are given in the text. Where the policy response is more widespread this becomes cumbersome and is avoided. As stated previously, to make clear the origin of all policy responses, an annex has been prepared (Annex B) that describes each country's qualifications system and the major developments under way.

Before the policy responses are elaborated, it is important to review the notion of lifelong learning, since that rich and complex concept is the goal of all the policy responses identified here. What it involves is a reconfiguration of traditional views of learning, the recognition of learning, and management of the learning system. OECD (2004c) has identified four distinguishing characteristics of lifelong learning policy (Box 2.1).

Box 2.1. **Four distinguishing characteristics of lifelong learning policy**

A systemic view. This is the feature that most distinguishes lifelong learning – current approaches to education policy are sector-specific. The lifelong learning framework views the demand for and supply of learning opportunities as part of a connected system covering the whole life cycle and comprising all forms of learning.

Centrality of the learner. This requires a shift from a supply-side focus, for example on formal institutional arrangements for learning, to the demand side of meeting learner needs.

Motivation to learn. This is an essential foundation for learning that continues throughout life. It requires a capacity for "learning to learn", self-paced and self-directed.

Multiple objectives of education policy. The life cycle view recognises the multiple goals of education – such as personal development, knowledge development, and economic, social and cultural objectives – and that the priorities among these objectives may change over the course of an individual's lifetime.

Source: OECD, 2004c.

These four features of the lifelong learning concept have important implications for key parameters of education and training policy, such as its objectives; the structure of provision; the content of programmes; the quality and relevance of provision; resource provision and management; and the roles and responsibilities of different partners and stakeholders. Countries involved in this study accept that a more dynamic view of education and training is necessary if lifelong learning is to become a reality. They acknowledge the argument for giving lifelong learning goals scope to shape the way the education and training system operates. Stronger links are needed between learning at different stages of life and between the formal and the informal structures; more diverse settings are called for; different partnerships between funders, providers and qualification bodies will lead to more integrated provision. That suggests substantial departures from the existing infrastructure of education and training.

Qualifications systems have a significant role to play in this more dynamic view of education and training. Many countries commented on how this could happen. Both Australia and Ireland reported the need to bring together qualifications issued by the schools, vocational education and training, and higher education sectors into a single comprehensive system of titles and standards. Similarly, the report from the Netherlands described the route to increased institutional linkage. Denmark made a strong statement about the advantage to be gained through linking vocational qualifications to those offered by higher education. In Switzerland there is strong pressure for close interaction of educational tracks so that changing tracks is easier. This drawing together of qualification bodies could lead to an easier interchange among types of qualification, which might suit an individual's career ambitions.

Such a radically different view of structuring raises the issue of who controls the qualifications system in a country. Evidence in country reports suggests that governments see an increasingly important role for themselves. Diverse interests in the qualifications systems might be seen as running counter to pressures for openness and transparency and these probably call for some kind of central control.

Countries have made attempts to reform education and training systems in order to bring about more and better lifelong learning. Some of these *policy responses* bear directly on qualifications systems; nine examples are now considered in turn:

1. Increase flexibility and responsiveness.

2. Motivate young people to learn.

3. Link education and work.

4. Facilitate open access to qualifications.

5. Diversify assessment processes.

6. Make qualifications progressive.

7. Make the qualifications system transparent.

8. Review funding and increase efficiency.

9. Improve the way the system is managed.

Inevitably, some reforms will fit more than one category. For example, those that enable access to higher education from vocational education and training programmes could be classified under policy response 4 (facilitate open access to qualifications) or 6 (make qualifications progressive).

Policy response 1 – Increase flexibility and responsiveness

"Customisation" and "increasing choice" are the terms countries generally use when they speak of creating qualifications systems sufficiently flexible to be responsive to the changing needs of the economy, employment, and the personal ambitions of individuals. The Australian report highlights the importance of the learner-centred view and suggests that the individual should drive change if that will foster learning. The diversity and individuality in lifestyle, ambitions, learning patterns and choice of assessment method suggest that qualifications systems will need to be increasingly responsive and (therefore) flexible. It follows that mechanisms promoting this learner-centred flexibility are likely to be effective.

In Portugal the development of the recognition, validation and certification of competences involves elaborating individualised education and training pathways in accordance with each particular situation. Switzerland is opening up its education systems to the demands of its individuals. Denmark also has had reforms that individualise the learning and qualifications systems for adults. These now offer flexible learning pathways, advice and guidance; individual learning programmes are developed on the basis of counselling sessions and assessment of prior learning. In Ireland, the introduction of a national framework is the central concept in a comprehensive reform of the qualifications system, designed to make the system more responsive to learners' needs.

In contrast to this approach, many countries construct qualifications frameworks in terms of pathways or tracks. These tracks can imply rigidity rather than flexibility. They are not without their advantages, however; for example, they can define the accepted routes to skilled worker status or to membership of a professional body. To capitalise on these advantages and at the same time maintain flexibility, these countries are introducing easy ways to change track or keep options open that might otherwise be closed to those following certain tracks. The classic case is retaining access to higher education for people following a vocational track in upper secondary education. Another response to that tension is to introduce qualifications frameworks – these make explicit any linkage between different qualification types. By showing the linkages and where tracks intersect, the extent to which pathways are flexible becomes explicit. Some countries have already developed frameworks; others are considering the option (Annex A).

A closer look at country reforms reveals a steady trend over the last ten years towards modularisation of education and training programmes and the introduction of units of assessment that lead to qualifications. The intention is to develop programmes that are tailor-made to meet the needs of employment or of individuals. Modular programmes can also lead to more efficient use of time and other resources. The full range of secondary and tertiary programmes, including adult learning, has embraced the idea. The modularisation programme does not, however, always deliver sufficient transferable credit for individuals, and may provide inadequate or unreliable information for employers to make decisions about recruitment and training needs. Hence many countries are looking at ways of introducing credit transfer processes (and thus flexibility) into the qualifications systems.

Attempts have been made to increase the flexibility of national qualifications systems by managing the ways public funds are dispersed to support them. In some countries the funding has been increasingly associated with the demand side in order to induce providers to be more responsive to the market for training. In the United Kingdom, Denmark and New Zealand the drive for a learner-centred system involves changing the way learning and qualification are funded. Institutions receive public funding linked to the individual learner; the funds come when they register or enrol in a programme and when they reach qualification. There are also examples of achieving flexibility through the use of public subsidy to initiate a fresh institutional response to the qualification market. In some countries new infrastructures have been created to allow more diverse sources of evidence of competence to be accommodated within the formal qualifications system.

Local diversity in provision is usually associated with the aim of increasing the capacity of qualifications systems to respond to local needs. However, a high currency for qualifications will depend on how much employers are perceived to value them. These perceptions usually develop on a national scale and take time to develop and be disseminated

---

Box 2.2. **Spain's Vocational Education and Training Qualifications Framework**

Unitisation and modularisation have been, since the end of the 1980s, two of the principles applied in structuring qualification programmes in certain initial vocational training programmes (initial education, secondary+2 and higher, Bac+2 grades, amounting to diplomas) as well as in continuing training (occupational training leading to certificates for both the unemployed and employed).

These two principles inform the elaboration, now in progress, of the National Catalogue of Vocational Qualifications (NCVQ). The NCVQ and its associated Integrated Catalogue of Modular Training are basic components of the Spanish Vocational Education and Training Qualifications Framework. The Framework plays the role of institutional axis of the National Qualifications and Vocational Training System.

NCVQ constitutes the basic *referent* for public-private training offers; it has a *normative* role and an *integrative* aim, acting at the same time as national register of qualifications.

Regular updating is considered together with arrangements for the adaptation/adoption of the vocational training offers not linked to NCVQ.

Source: Spain's background report.

---

among potential learners. Equally, the interests of the learner are likely to be better served where it is possible to identify widely held national perceptions of quality and high returns in a qualification. Those too develop over time as quality assurance processes ensure consistency in application of approved procedures. Such extended timescales for developing high currency on a national scale may run counter to the need for change at local level. The report from the Netherlands points out the tensions between maintaining national standards for qualifications and allowing local diversity. The question arises about how far flexibility and diversity can be allowed to take hold before damage to other aspects of qualifications systems, such as transparency, reduces opportunities for lifelong learning. There is also a question of increased costs being associated with more diverse qualification provision.

One of the implications of a more learner-centred approach is that governments and managing agencies must know how the qualifications system is changing in *response* to need. Monitoring systems may be a good way for decision makers to secure the information they need (from learners, for example) to inform changes geared to greater flexibility. Ireland has embraced monitoring and set in place a system of data collection relating to the individual learner's view of qualification-based programmes. In Greek second chance schools there is systematic monitoring of student performance to identify gaps in learning at an individual level, so that programmes can be adjusted accordingly.

All of this evidence suggests that a greater emphasis on flexibility in the qualifications system – within the constraints of maintaining a cost-effective, quality-assured national system – is a policy response that many countries believe will lead to enhanced lifelong learning.

Policy response 2 – Motivate young people to learn

The lifelong learning approach entails a broader conception of foundation learning. It requires not just universal access to primary education but also a heightened motivation in young people to learn and a greater capacity to learn independently. There is substantial

---

Box 2.3. **Foundation Degrees in the United Kingdom**

Foundation Degrees were launched as an intermediate work-related higher education qualification in September 2001. They were set by the Higher Education Funding Council for England (HEFCE) with Department for Education and Skills (DfES). A multi-sector approach was taken. The Foundation Degrees address the skills gap at the associate professional and higher technician level. The business sector is involved in order to give people the intermediate technical and professional skills that are in demand from employers. Foundation Degrees are in fact designed, supported, and reviewed by businesses to ensure that the degrees meet their needs. Meanwhile the higher and further education sector is involved to ensure that this qualification meets the students' current and future needs.

Foundation Degrees contribute to widening participation in higher education by reducing the barriers to learning. They aim to offer flexible ways of learning, as well as to recognise relevant prior learning and experience. Foundation Degrees are set at the intermediate level between certificate and honours, and by definition take two years of full-time study. They include application of skills in the workplace and facilitate credit accumulation and transfer. To facilitate accessibility there are no set entry requirements; the university or college offering the course will decide on eligibility based not only on prior educational qualifications but also on appropriate working experience, considered more relevant for the degrees. Upon completion, the degrees aim at ensuring routes for embarking on a career change or progressing to a higher-level qualification.

Various attempts are being made to increase the visibility and value of the Foundation Degrees. The Universities and Colleges Admissions Service (UCAS) is hosting a comprehensive database of Foundation Degree courses to promote easy access to information and facilitate the application process. To raise the profile of or give value to the Foundation Degree, it is proposed that people with Foundation Degrees have the right to use the letters "FDA" (for arts-based subjects) or "FDS" (for science-based subjects) after their names.

The Government White Paper "The Future of Higher Education" places emphasis on expanding the Foundation Degrees as a way of expanding higher education to meet the needs of students as well as employers.

Source: United Kingdom background report; UK Department for Education and Skills, "The Future of Higher Education"; *www.foundationdegree.org.uk/; http://develop.ucas.com/FDCourseSearch/Gateway.html.*

---

research evidence that the early acquisition of qualifications leads to a higher level of participation in learning programmes later in life. Improving the motivation of young people to learn can involve the qualifications system. Country examples include: offering a wider range of vocational education programmes; opportunities to combine classroom learning with learning in work settings; encouraging co-operation with institutions outside the school; and introducing more learner-centred pedagogies. Often these approaches would involve reforming aspects of the qualifications system, including developing new qualifications.

Most countries report reforms in this area that are aimed to raise the level of qualification of school leavers and to retain more young people in upper secondary education. There are several themes to these reforms:

● The issue of relevance of initial education to work and building valuable work-related qualifications (Slovenia and the United Kingdom). In 2001 Australian ministers endorsed a new Framework for Vocational Education in Schools, and that signalled a broadening of the vocational education agenda. In Belgium (French speaking), through reinforced collaborations among the different partners such as the sectors of education and vocational training and its branches, the dual system is being reformed to create a better match between the objectives of the education sector as a whole and the more specific needs of the firm.

- A second theme is a reform of main school qualifications. This extends beyond the definition of knowledge, skills and wider competences to include the recognition of prior learning (Australia); the recognition of achievement across a whole programme rather than specific subject attainment (Ireland); the development of the National Certificate of Educational Achievement using "achievement standards" developed for the school curriculum and unit standards from the national qualifications framework (New Zealand).

- Better progression routes for young people within qualifications and between qualifications is a theme in many countries. Examples include enabling the easier vertical and horizontal transfer from one educational level to another (Slovenia) and flexible dual trajectories combining learning and work (the Netherlands).

- The introduction of credit transfer arrangements allows a range of learning outcomes to be recognised within certificates (Australia, Korea). Credits gained in initial education and training can count towards qualifications acquired in life.

Box 2.4. *Aimhigher* in the United Kingdom

Following the White Paper "The Future of Higher Education", the United Kingdom government launched a unified national programme. *Aimhigher,* built on the existing *Excellence Challenge* programme, has the goal of "Widening Participation". The focus of the programme is on raising the aspirations and attainment levels of young people entering higher education. Special attention is paid to young people traditionally underrepresented in higher education, *i.e.* students from non-traditional backgrounds, minority groups and disabled persons.

By building better links between schools, colleges and universities, *Aimhigher* attempts to transfer knowledge/experience about university life to students lacking role models who could give them a first-hand view of it and describe the benefits. A pilot project was funded to encourage students to undertake paid, part-time work in schools or colleges based on the existing programmes such as the Teacher Associate Scheme run by the Teacher Training Agency. With this scheme, students are able to share their experiences of university life with young people and get paid for valuable work experience. The programme is keen on further partnerships, especially innovative approaches such as mentoring, workshops, taster courses, the involvement of parents, etc.

An *Aimhigher* website has been created to offer all the relevant information about the road to higher education. The portal project was initiated by the Department for Education and Skills (DfES), concretised by the Higher Education Funding Council for England (HEFCE), and managed by Higher Education Research Opportunities (HERO). It is designed to encourage prospective students by showing how going into higher education will open up more opportunities in the future. It provides comprehensive information on career choices, higher education institutions and courses, financial support and advice, and student life.

Source: The United Kingdom Department for Education and Skills, "The Future of Higher Education"; *www.aimhigher.ac.uk/home/index.cfm.*

- Pedagogy has been examined in both the general and the vocationally oriented schools in Denmark to improve young people's study competence and thus strengthen the basis for more young people completing a higher education programme.

- Basic skills development in upper secondary schools has received attention in all countries.

- New school types have been developed in Greece with the establishment of Technical Vocational Schools (TEE) to provide technical and vocational knowledge, skills and wider competences as well as an occupational awareness to facilitate young people's entry into the labour market.

Many of these themes involve choice for individual learners and this supports the increased flexibility discussed above. The weight of evidence of reform of upper secondary education suggests countries feel that reform to upper secondary education is necessary if they are to create a springboard to lifelong learning for many citizens.

Policy response 3 – Link education and work

Vocational education and training dominate the programme of reform reported in many countries. There is a strong desire to see qualifications systems as a strong link between the education and training system and the labour market specifically and the economy more generally. Countries are attempting to strengthen this linkage through vocational qualifications and training. In some cases this has blurred the boundaries between what is considered general academic and vocational education, especially at high levels. Many countries are reforming their qualifications system in order to produce a seamless transition across the theory-practice continuum and aiming to blend work practices with academic study. In some fast-developing fields there is awareness that work-based expert knowledge is nearer the cutting edge of developments than the content of teaching and research programmes in higher education institutions.

New institutions have been set up in some countries to foster links between education and training provision and the labour market. These agencies have a range of activities that includes funding training; developing new training programmes; developing new qualifications; acting as a one-stop-shop for those needing guidance on education and training; broadening the range of educational institutions; and bringing together the diverse interests of other government agencies. One mode of action that seems to be attractive to many countries is to lead qualifications to a more outcome-based structure, where the method of programme delivery matters less than the knowledge, skills and competences that learners are expected to demonstrate. When qualifications become more outcome-related, there is an opportunity to engage employment interests in the qualification process; they can, for example, define key competences and become actors in the process of validating learning gained through experience.

As is evident already from the above, there is a strong move to introduce more choice into upper secondary education programmes. This additional choice is often offered through the introduction of vocational programmes leading to vocational qualifications, either as separate routes or as units that can be accommodated in a traditional general education route. The latter point should be emphasised because new, shorter and more flexible *alternance* schemes are appearing in addition to tried and tested apprenticeship or dual-system models. These work-oriented programmes are strengthened either by modernising programme content; extending the range of subjects or sectors involved;

Box 2.5. **Introduction of a Vocational Graduate Certificate and a Vocational Graduate Diploma in Australia**

In 1995, Australia introduced a system of competence-based vocational education and training. The system spanned four certificates and two diploma qualifications, and operated within a sector-comprehensive framework for all nationally recognised qualifications known as the Australian Qualifications Framework. Subsequently, the system was further streamlined into Training Packages that describe the skills and knowledge needed to perform effectively in the workplace. These training packages take the form of nationally endorsed standards and qualifications for recognising and assessing people's skills in a particular industry or enterprise.

In terms of lifelong learning, one distinctive advantage of the competence-based vocational education and training qualifications is that they can be assessed wholly or partly on the basis of previous work experience or through additional structured training in the workplace itself. This means that employment is acknowledged as a site of learning able to be recognised through the national qualifications system. These qualifications in turn allow access to promotion or further education and training, including university qualifications. As an integral part of the Australian Qualifications Framework, national quality assurance measures implemented by government authorities protect the standards of training and assessment to ensure that, irrespective of the particular learning pathway – workplace, institution, life experience – the qualifications carry the same status.

The original suite of competence-based qualifications did not extend to higher education, where standards for qualifications are set by the universities. However, as work-based learning and qualifications became well established over the past decade, there was increasing evidence of an unmet need for competence-based qualifications at graduate levels for a large category of "lifelong learners" – such as suitably experienced mature workers with or without existing qualifications, qualified and highly experienced trades people, or higher education graduates wishing to acquire new high-level skills originating in the workplace or tailored to a workplace environment.

Although the original range of qualifications in the Australian Qualifications Framework did not offer this choice of pathway, the market need was manifested through attempts to accredit higher education graduate certificates and diplomas to industry competence specifications. These attempts raised quality assurance issues for the higher education awards; at the same time, they failed to meet needs for streamlining the accreditation and delivery available through Training Packages. They also failed to establish the transparency of or confer appropriate status to expanded learner choice of vocational education and training pathways at graduate levels.

To address these issues and ensure that the new vocational education and training qualifications were able to support pathways to higher degrees on an equal if different basis from their higher education counterparts, extensive consultations involving all stakeholders and government authorities were conducted through the Australian Qualifications Framework Advisory Board. Following this, recommendations were made to the National Council of Education and Training Ministers for the addition of two new qualifications titles in the Australian Qualifications Framework: *Vocational Graduate Certificate* and *Vocational Graduate Diploma*.

Source: Australia background report.

improving pedagogy and assessment; or increasing funding for participants. Significantly, clarifying progression in learning and job opportunities and (in particular) easing entry to higher education will improve apprenticeship schemes and the introduction of new vocational routes and qualifications in general education. That improvement is high on the agenda of countries aiming to strengthen education-work links. Sometimes new forms of higher education programmes that are better linked to practice have been set up; some countries have created new higher education institutions that have a work practice orientation.

Policy response 4 – Facilitate open access to qualifications

One of the benefits from lifelong learning that countries recognise is that individuals wishing to gain qualifications can do so from a range of different starting points. For example, France has made progress in ensuring that national qualifications have specified routes of access that are essentially inclusive in nature. Taking account of different routes, particularly through recognition of prior, non-formal and informal learning – is a high-profile development in many countries and has been the focus of work by an OECD Thematic Group for this study (Annex A). These recognition processes involve offering a qualification after a positive assessment of an individual's knowledge, skills and wider competences gained through education, training, work and life experience.

Countries describe reforms aimed at producing qualifications that offer increased learning opportunities to excluded groups, such as the unemployed, women, indigenous populations and recent flows of immigrants. Lifelong learning is often mentioned in relation to the aim of better social inclusion. There are strong policy statements in country reports about the wider benefits of learning and qualification leading to stronger communities, and to the need to ensure that qualifications systems offer equitable access to all people. In several countries, the move towards more outcome-based models for qualifications is motivated by the belief that such systems allow fairer recruitment.

It is clear from country background reports that gaining access to qualification programmes is often a second step for some individuals and groups – the first step is to participate in an informal or unaccredited learning programme. Greece is typical of many countries in establishing schemes aimed at disengaged youth and the setting up of special provision. The latter could include – special work-related programmes (new technology schemes have worked well), work experience, and special programmes in basic language skills for immigrant workers. Subsequent access to qualification-based courses from this kind of special provision is a key step in developing better lifelong learning.

One of the areas where many countries are attempting to improve access is in higher education. Measures have been introduced in several countries to ensure that people with unorthodox qualifications or unrecognised achievement can join higher education programmes, often through special introductory programmes. More common are measures that ensure that learners in initial education with vocational qualifications do not close off their right to enter higher education at some later stage in their life, for example the Swiss *Maturité Professionnelle*.

Policy response 5 – Diversify assessment processes

One of the themes in country background reports is the need to examine how the assessment process – often referred to as evaluation – associated with qualifications affects the willingness of learners to participate in learning. There are two main aspects to this. Some people are driven to engage in learning in order to gain qualification(s) and the rewards associated with qualification. Others are fearful of failing to meet the requirements of qualification and are deterred from entering qualification-based learning programmes. These approaches are exemplified by Korea's wish to diversify assessment methods to broaden engagement in higher education. In Greece the use of written assessments is reported as a barrier to engagement in learning for some social groups. In Switzerland, the new Law for Professional Education states that qualification procedures guarantee equity of opportunity. Consequently, the related Ordinance foresees adequate procedures for specific groups (for instance for adults).

Assessment methods (and the administration and cost associated with them) are an important influence on the willingness of individuals to engage in learning for a qualification. If the procedures for assessment, quality assurance and certification are reviewed, the ensuing changes could lead to increased motivation to participate in qualification-based learning (OECD, 2005).

Evidence from across the range of country background reports suggests that qualification is growing in importance as a gateway to employment. However, there is a contrasting view in the research literature suggesting that employers are seeking to diversify the range of evidence used in recruitment, and that while initial qualification retains its importance for young people, for experienced workers some testimony of their experience is carrying more weight than previously.[1]

Learning comes in many forms and takes place in many different settings, from formal courses in schools or colleges to various types of experience in families, communities and workplaces. Many countries consider that a wider range of learning needs to be recognised according to content, quality and outcomes rather than location and form. Such recognition could act as a psychological and economic incentive for participation in learning activities.

Outcome-based assessment systems are believed to offer advantages to learners, according to the Australian, Danish, Dutch and Korean reports. These systems make clear to learners the required assessed outcomes of their learning from the outset of a programme, and so may allay some of their fear of failure. They also offer a chance to focus on developing specific areas of weakness that might prevent qualification. In these ways, they encourage lifelong learning. A point touched on in the Dutch report and other reports concerns the need to support these new recognition systems by developing more widespread use of quality standards and outcomes. Many countries have qualifications that are based on completion of a learning programme rather than on specified competence outcomes. The argument for outcomes acknowledges the inevitable access restrictions that apply when an individual has to be accepted for a learning programme, attend learning centres, complete a whole programme and undergo formal assessment. Outcome-based methods of assessment also facilitate the recognition of prior learning and raise potential learners' confidence in seeking qualification.

The United Kingdom offers the view that it might be possible to differentiate between "high stakes" and "low stakes" qualifications in terms of requirements for quality assurance. Their report argues that the administration and cost associated with assessment processes have weighed down those qualifications that rely on non-written assessment. The report concludes that rigorous quality assurance requirements are a proper feature of qualifications that open up scarce opportunities of work or education at higher levels for individuals. However, the report goes on to argue that much learning, particularly by adults, is not of this high-stakes variety and does not, by itself, unlock opportunities in the labour market and educational progression.

Policy response 6 – Make qualifications progressive

Accumulating learning experiences and developing competences throughout life is now a central concept across countries. There are many reforms that aim to shift the focus from a "once and for all" initial education and training that takes place early in an individual's life to one where the initial phase forms the foundation for further learning and inspires individuals to seek further learning experiences and qualifications. Hence the concept of encouraging progression – in learning programmes, skills acquisition and the job hierarchy – features strongly in the reform programmes of countries. Germany has adopted another method of achieving progressive learning, competence development and higher qualification. *Additional qualifications* build on the formal system and allow updating, recognition of specialisation and entry into specific work areas. Access is widened through recognition of non-formal and informal learning and the development of a credit system. Thus initial and continuing education and training are linked through qualification.

Some countries (including Portugal, Belgium, Germany and Denmark) mentioned the benefits of a sequence of qualification achievement throughout an individual's life and a move away from a system of once-and-for-all qualification early in one's career. The portability of qualification from one context to another is beneficial to many learners. Credit transfer systems were seen as playing a key role here, and many countries have in place development programmes to achieve this goal of portability, covering school qualifications, vocational education and training and higher education. For example, the Australian report described the development of credit transfer arrangements between Registered Training Organisations and schools, as well as between Registered Training Organisations and universities. These arrangements had proved efficient, whereas existing credit transfer was described as weak by many countries. Denmark is one of several countries that stress the potential power of credit systems to unify different types of qualification for parity of esteem.

Access to further learning is tightly bound to initial education achievements. People with poor records in school generally do not make use of later opportunities. Hence in reform efforts we see a strong focus on ways of creating a second chance to obtain school qualifications or basic educational knowledge, skills and wider competences. Systems for allowing recognition of non-formal and informal learning are in development to create a sense of "opening doors" instead of erecting barriers for those who have not achieved their full potential. Similarly, there is an expansion of adult learning in many countries.

A key factor in ensuring that qualifications systems perform optimally in supporting lifelong learning is the issue of making transitions from one part of the education system to another as straightforward as possible. Evidence advocated by countries suggests that this involves many devices such as:

- Encouraging transfer from non-accredited learning to learning recognised through qualification.
- Recognising informal and non-formal learning.

- Transferring credit for learning already recognised in an existing qualification or programme to a new qualification.
- Linking one qualification with a second one in a way that makes progression to the second one a natural step.
- Showing equivalences between qualifications through levels in frameworks.

In countries where there is a qualifications framework (e.g. Australia, Ireland, New Zealand, the United Kingdom), it is made explicit that the key purpose of the framework is to facilitate learning progression by clarifying relationships among different qualification types.

Policy response 7 – Make the qualifications system transparent

Country reports suggest that overlapping and competing qualifications, instability in the system and the involvement of diverse agencies lead to complex and confusing literature and communication about the benefits of qualifications. From the learner's perspective, a transparent system implies stability, a wide range of qualifications on offer, coherence, and above all quality assurance. Countries report a broad consensus about the need for more transparency in the structure of qualifications systems and the development of frameworks to achieve this (for example, Scotland and New Zealand). Some, such as Ireland and Portugal, report the establishment of a single institution to bring about this transparency.

Governments have invested in making qualifications systems clear to users; the rationale for this investment is indeed often directly associated with increasing lifelong learning. In other cases the link is more indirect; the goals are to increase the mobility of individuals (and thus the skills supply to the labour market), increase efficiency of the qualifications system, develop better quality assurance processes and encourage greater involvement from key stakeholders in the qualifications system.

Links between qualifications should be clear and classified in simple transparent ways; the clarity should be supported by guidance and counselling systems that are easy to access (OECD, 2004b). A unified system, where qualifications based in different sectors relate to one another with minimum (necessary) overlap, is the goal of many reforms.

Countries with a qualifications framework[2] sometimes have only partial coverage of qualifications because the whole system is complex and not easy to describe in a single framework. Many countries have implemented reforms to bring coherence to frameworks and others have policy discussions that signal intent to develop such a framework. Reform sometimes adopts a consensus-building approach to framework development, where inclusion of all qualifications is seen as necessary and all stakeholders are involved in shaping the framework. In other countries with a more top-down, reformist agenda, the qualifications framework is seen a tool to rationalise, modernise and simplify the qualifications system. Of course these are extreme positions and most countries are somewhere between the two. However, the positions give an indication of the ways qualifications frameworks are seen as effective tools for reform.

There are several references to reforms aimed at using information and communication technologies to create new, accessible and effective guidance processes for people wishing to learn for qualifications. These new systems depend to some extent on the success of other reforms such as the development of coherent qualifications systems and frameworks, and the recognition of non-formal and informal learning. It is therefore quite common to see reforms of guidance systems as part of a wider set of qualifications system reforms.

Transparent systems are also reported to require more systematic monitoring of the take-up, use and perceived value of qualifications. In Switzerland, a prospective study mandated by the Swiss Conference of Cantonal Ministers of Education (*Conférence suisse des directeurs cantonaux de l'instruction publique*) led to the construction of six possible scenarios for the future development of the entire education system in order to promote lifelong learning. A public debate on these scenarios is due to be launched (Rosenmund and Zulauf, 2004).

Policy response 8 – Review funding and increase efficiency

Almost all countries commented on how the cost of qualification(s) influences learners, governments and employers. In some circumstances costs were shown to be a strong deterrent to participation by individual learners. Evidence was also provided about limits to funding holding back training provision. Most adult and community education courses in Australia are non-accredited and few lead to the award of a qualification; providers have been reluctant to introduce award-based qualifications for cost reasons and because the formal assessment requirements (which are expensive) might act as deterrents to learners who lack confidence and have had poor experiences of formal learning. In Germany, the cost of continuing education and training is believed to have a considerable bearing on the decision to participate. New Zealand reports that an increasing portion of the cost of post-compulsory education has been borne by individuals. In the United Kingdom and the Netherlands steps are being taken to reduce the financial barriers to individuals through the introduction of entitlements for free or subsidised learning for a wide range of courses. In Denmark study support schemes have existed for many years; these include direct financial support for learners engaging in vocational education and training, and publicly funded continuing vocational training. The support also extends to employers providing training.

Costs are seen to discourage employer-provided training. In Japan and Korea the lack of investment in evaluation systems by private bodies is raising the question of whether public/private investment might be used to promote new methods and engage more learners. Inter-sector co-operation, which could render training and evaluation systems more practical and flexible, is being investigated.

There are also infrastructure costs. New Zealand has reported the costs to set up and maintain its national qualifications framework (a broad, inclusive, credit-based framework).

Recognition of non-formal and informal learning can cut costs for learners by reducing study duration, and increase net economic returns to learning. Such recognition incurs infrastructure costs which are sometimes initially subsidised by public finances. It requires standards and learning outcomes to be defined (against which the learning can be assessed) and agreement on assessment techniques, recognition methods and portability of credits. A balance needs to be struck between reducing what applicants pay and the cost of recognition systems. Cost savings arising from reducing the sensitivity of the system to the needs of individuals and other stakeholders and by limiting quality assurance procedures are likely to have a negative impact in the longer term. Recognition of non-formal and informal learning requires the active commitment and engagement of a number of stakeholders – within and between different education sectors, as well as those in education, and groups such as employers and trade unions.

Many countries are relying on expanded private capacity and increased competition in the provision of learning opportunities as a way to improve efficiency of the qualifications system and to increase its capacity to meet the needs of users. The costs of recognition of learning, validation, accreditation and certification are inextricably linked with this expansion. Over the 1990s the private share in total financing of education increased, and a clear trend in favour of greater private contributions is visible in many OECD countries. This is a result of strong incentives for investment in human capital for both individuals and firms. The limitations of capital markets and other institutional arrangements dilute these incentives, but countries are experimenting with financing mechanisms to overcome these limitations. At the tertiary education level there are a number of examples of innovative mechanisms to secure learner support, such as means-tested tuition fees and deferred income-contingent and differential contributions. For adults, countries are experimenting with new institutional arrangements to facilitate sharing of financial responsibilities and risks associated with investment in lifelong learning between individuals, employers and the state.

Policy response 9 – Improve the way the system is managed

In most countries, qualifications are supplied by several bodies. There are four main types of suppliers: government agencies, educational institutions, chambers of commerce and private charities. In addition, there is a small but growing supply of qualifications coming from vendors whose products are sold across the world. Government agencies regulate and manage the qualifications system. Several ministries operate within them, and a high level of co-ordination for developing and implementing policy is required – especially since lifelong learning and qualifications systems involve stakeholders beyond education ministries. OECD (2000, 2003) highlighted both the challenges of co-ordination and successful initiatives countries have taken in addressing them. The OECD study on adult learning in particular (2003) emphasised the close interaction required between education, training, labour market and social policies to meet the needs of adult learners. The other study, on the transition from initial education to working life (OECD, 2000), illustrated how countries are attempting to solve co-ordination challenges: through different ministries and agencies working together; through the involvement of employers, trade unions and other actors in policy development nationally and in programme delivery locally; through community involvement in local policy development and programme implementation. In Ireland, two ministries and several agencies are involved in the provision of opportunities for lifelong learning; however, recent reform of the qualifications system placed responsibility for the design and operation of the system with a single national authority, and relocated many award-making powers from a multiplicity of bodies to two newly formed awards councils.

One important issue is the ownership of qualifications systems. Typically these systems are closely linked to the formal sector of education and training provision. There is a sense of exclusion among those outside that sector – for example in the non-formal and informal sectors, which are becoming ever more important in the knowledge economy. An important challenge for management of the qualifications systems is to ensure inclusion by bringing more partners and stakeholders into the process of supplying and recognising qualifications.

Learners – at each stage of life – need to be provided with curricula, pedagogical practices, organised learning and co-ordinated qualification processes. Provision therefore needs to be structured in a way that creates appropriate linkages and pathways.

Improving the management of qualifications systems to enhance lifelong learning may be held back by the lack of performance data on the latter (OECD, 2004a).

2.4. Issues related to using qualifications systems as a tool for reform

Efforts to develop qualifications systems have encountered constraints, and countries explain these in some detail. Their descriptions are important and reported here because the mechanisms identified in this study are intended to be tools for overcoming such constraints. The latter can be grouped under the following headings: structures for governance, complexity of the national qualifications system, institutional structures, economic constraints, and finally social and cultural barriers to the development of the qualifications system.

Structures for governance

Federal systems of government and their constitutional division of responsibilities are reported to have a complicating effect on reform efforts. This is due to the complexity of processes involved in developing or implementing proposals for change and the divergent political views on the need for change or the directions it should take. Consultation processes in federal systems are reported to be more complex, as stakeholder groups can operate in different ways in different parts of the countries involved. Social and economic variations within regional jurisdictions can also have a direct influence on the weight of opinion supporting or opposing reform. National qualifications systems in countries with strong regional governance are often more diverse than those in countries with greater central governance of the system.

Complexity of qualifications systems

As national qualifications systems have evolved – usually under pressure to be more efficient and meet the needs of users more effectively – they have often become more complex. Consequently there are limits to which reforms can proceed without fundamentally altering the way the system operates. This can have the effect of making piecemeal change more desirable, as any substantial change is likely to destabilise the delicate balances (political, institutional and financial) within systems. Countries have reported that sometimes too little effort has been made to adapt infrastructures to support innovation. Insufficient investment in the capacity of experts and stakeholders in the qualifications system to make a new system operate well is often seen as a barrier to innovation.

Institutional structures

In many countries tertiary educational institutions, both universities and vocational education and training providers, enjoy considerable autonomy within broad frameworks of funding and accountability. This leads to divergent views regarding the merits of particular proposals.

One reason given for lower currency of vocational training compared to more academic provision – and the barrier to cross-sectoral reforms that creates – is that there is weak co-operation between education institutions or schools and work-based learning provision, and between the relevant government ministries.

Sometimes institutions are expected to cater for needs across large geographical areas. This can be because there are too few institutions, or because the specialisation of institutions means there are fewer with the capacity to deliver the level of general training required in an area. There is also a view that social expectations and inertia in the national qualifications system makes it easier for schools to deliver a core of trusted and well-known qualifications programmes and offer limited specialist provision. Falling birth rates also create barriers for providers to offer a range of specialist courses, as there is likely to be insufficient demand for some of them.

Economic constraints

Previous economic policy and labour market management have created a need for change and also act as a constraint on that change. For example, in some countries the focus on low-skilled and low-wage work and productive specialisation to reduce unemployment has produced a legacy of low regard for education and training within certain groups in society.

A shortage of resources is identified as a significant constraint on reforms. Their availability depends on economic performance and taxation revenues, and these have fluctuated in many countries. Reports of reforms being slowed by reductions in funding or changes in funding policies are common.

Social barriers to reforms of qualifications systems

The largest bank of evidence about barriers to national qualifications system reform is linked to social and cultural issues. Countries report the high status of academic education and that key stakeholders such as parents and schoolteachers have misgivings about the legitimacy of vocational programmes. In the eyes of many, schools are seen primarily as places for academic preparation leading to university entrance. Systems of selection reinforce this position. Within such a culture it is difficult to implement vocational programmes, and where these are accepted they may be used as a pathway for weaker learners, taught by teachers who feel less respected and valued. A limited understanding of vocational training and qualifications can slow the development of the qualifications system. This links to the often-mentioned barrier of tradition and traditional approaches.

Measures to broaden access to qualifications have encountered a series of constraints. For example, it is reported that people are suspicious of the quality of qualifications based on assessment of prior learning and work experience. There is concern in some countries that recognition of non-formal and informal learning might undermine the status and quality of formal education. Often a premium is placed on qualifications gained by standardised independent evaluation of learning that is external to the learning institution, and this has sometimes reduced the scope of what can be contained in a qualification. Yet some knowledge, skills and wider competences cannot be assessed through standardised tests – or only inadequately, artificially or at great expense. Thus they are not tested, and because of that they are sometimes not diligently learned or made the focus of teaching.

2.5. In short, many countries face the same kind of barriers

This chapter has drawn together information in accounts from countries of the pressures for innovation in qualifications systems, actual reforms, and the barriers that hold back development. The analysis has highlighted several kinds of pressure; economic ones in particular have increasing power to shape developments in national qualifications systems. Countries have embarked on a vast range of reforms for it is clear that qualifications systems are increasingly seen an effective vehicle for delivering important policy objectives: increased lifelong learning, social inclusion and (as a result) a greater skills supply to the labour market. Nine policy responses have been identified and discussed.

Many countries face the same kinds of barriers to reform mentioned in the chapter. Those related to institutional structures and social and cultural beliefs seem to be the most constraining.

The analysis reported here forms an important background to the proposed theory of mechanisms that link qualifications systems and lifelong learning. The evidence suggests that these mechanisms can become a tool with which to refine policy responses for improving lifelong learning through changes to qualifications systems.

Notes

1. See Keating *et al.* (2004) for a recent survey of employers' use of qualifications.

2. OECD (2004c) has explored the purposes, policies and likely benefits of frameworks in detail. See Annex A for a summary.

References

ETF (European Training Foundation) (2004), *Chapter 9: Policy Learning*, Annual Report, ETF, Turin.

Keating, J., T. Nicholas, J. Polesel and J. Watson (2004), *Qualifications Use in the Australian Labour Market*, National Centre for Vocational Education Research, Adelaide.

OECD (2000), *From Initial Education to Working Life: Making Transitions Work*, OECD, Paris.

OECD (2003), *Beyond Rhetoric – Adult Learning Policies and Practices*, OECD, Paris.

OECD (2004a), *Co-financing Lifelong Learning – Toward a Systemic Approach*, OECD, Paris.

OECD (2004b), *Career Guidance and Public Policy – Bridging the Gap*, OECD, Paris.

OECD (2004c), "Lifelong learning", *Policy Brief*, February, OECD, Paris.

OECD (2005), *Formative Assessment: Improving Learning in Secondary Classrooms*, OECD, Paris.

OECD and Statistics Canada (2000), *Literacy in the Information Age – Final Report of the International Adult Literacy Survey*, Paris (*www.nald.ca/nls/ials/introduc.htm*).

Rosenmund M. and M. Zulauf (2004), Trans Formation : quel système de formation pour un apprentissage a vie ? Études et Rapports 20B, CDIP, Berne (*www.edk.ch/PDF_Downloads/Dossiers/Stub20B.pdf*).

ISBN 978-92-64-01367-4
Qualifications Systems
Bridges to Lifelong Learning
© OECD 2007

Chapter 3

Do the Numbers Tell a Story? Quantitative Evidence about the Impact of Qualifications Systems on Learning

Quantitative analysis should contribute to a fuller understanding of the link between national qualifications and lifelong learning systems. Earlier chapters and those that follow provide qualitative evidence that comes largely from background reports. This chapter uses a statistical approach drawing upon both macro data (at country level) and micro data (at individual level).

Indicators of lifelong learning are available from several sources. Quantitative indicators of national qualifications systems, however, are not so common. This deficiency places serious limits on the quantitative analysis of their relationship. Two alternative "second best" approaches are used to derive aggregated information about country characteristics of national qualifications systems. The first is based on a typology developed for this study in co-operation with the experts from the participating countries. The second approach uses household surveys to derive aggregated indicators of both national qualifications systems and lifelong learning.

The chapter begins by addressing data availability and deficiency issues and presents some basic statistics (Section 3.1). It then seeks to establish correlations at the macro level between certain lifelong learning dimensions and national qualifications systems, using aggregated variables derived from the International Adult Literacy Survey, the European Union Labour Force Survey and some national surveys for non-European countries (Section 3.2). Finally the chapter examines the main issues and proposes to set an agenda for future data collection in the fields under study. The main conclusion (Section 3.3) is that qualifications systems do have a role in promoting lifelong learning in some circumstances, although much work needs to be done to measure that impact quantitatively.

3.1. The quantitative background for linking national qualifications systems and lifelong learning

This book is mainly concerned with national qualifications systems, not with individual qualifications as such. However, it is difficult to find existing quantitative data on that level, let alone the international level. Were that data to be available, they would be linked to specific features of lifelong learning at national level – in particular its volume, distribution, quality and efficiency. To conduct a meaningful analysis of the linkage, it would be ideal to have:

- Data on lifelong learning systems, including volume, distribution, quality and efficiency.

- Data on national qualifications systems such as those described in Chapter 1: accessibility, adapting to learning pathways, efficiency, flexibility, responsiveness and transparency.

- Trend information for both types of data.

- Data (mentioned above) that are comparable internationally.

Both national qualifications systems and lifelong learning have many dimensions. A consequence of that fact is that a given *policy response* to the lifelong learning agenda or a specific policy tool (*mechanism*) from the qualifications system may encourage a certain group of the population to learn while discouraging another group. This is so because not all potential learners share the same goal(s) when considering learning activities: some may learn for its own sake whereas others may seek a qualification or a job. Available data usually do not reflect this divergence of goal(s) among groups of learners. Therefore, before presenting some evidence, this section presents the available data, discusses methodologies, and identifies some of the difficulties in relating quantitative data in this field.

Available lifelong learning indicators

Figure 3.1 provides information on the proportion of the population with upper secondary education. A major deficiency is the limited availability of trend data. This stems from periodic changes (improvements) in the definition and measurements of key concepts, which make it difficult to develop a consistent series covering many years. An example is given by a reform of the International Standard Classification of Education (ISCED) that makes it difficult[1] to discern over time the proportion of individuals who have attained upper secondary education (Figure 3.2). In the absence of trend data, information on different age cohorts at a point in time (Figure 3.1) can be used as a proxy.

Upper secondary education attainment is a useful indicator of lifelong learning. Figure 3.1 shows that in most countries, a large fraction of the youth population is now reaching upper secondary education level. Improvement over the last two decades has been quite impressive, especially in Korea, Greece, Ireland and Spain (Figure 3.2). Therefore,

Figure 3.1. **Population that has attained at least upper secondary education (2002)**
(Comparisons of two age groups: 25-34 and 55-64)
Summary: More and more young people attain upper secondary education.

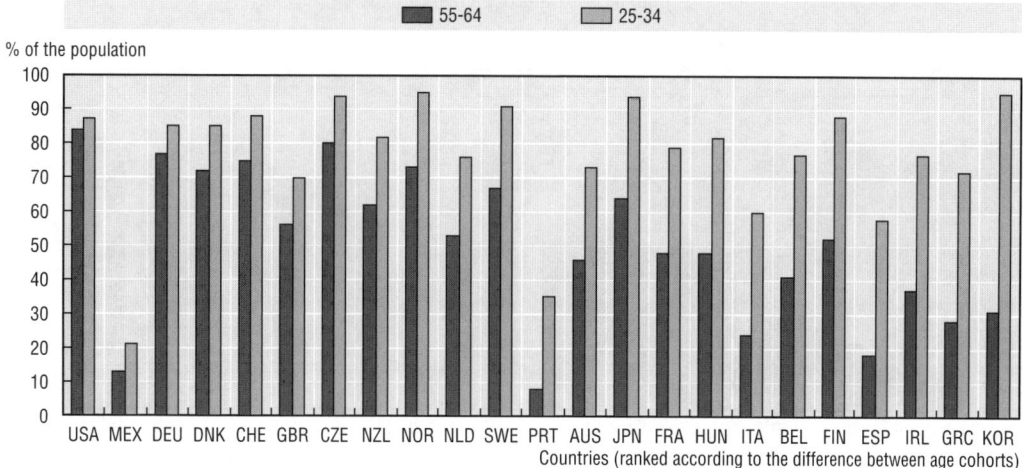

Source: OECD, 2004a, processed by the authors.

Figure 3.2. **Trends in upper secondary education attainment (1991-2002)**
*Summary: In most countries, there is a significant increase in the proportion
of the population with upper secondary education attainment.*

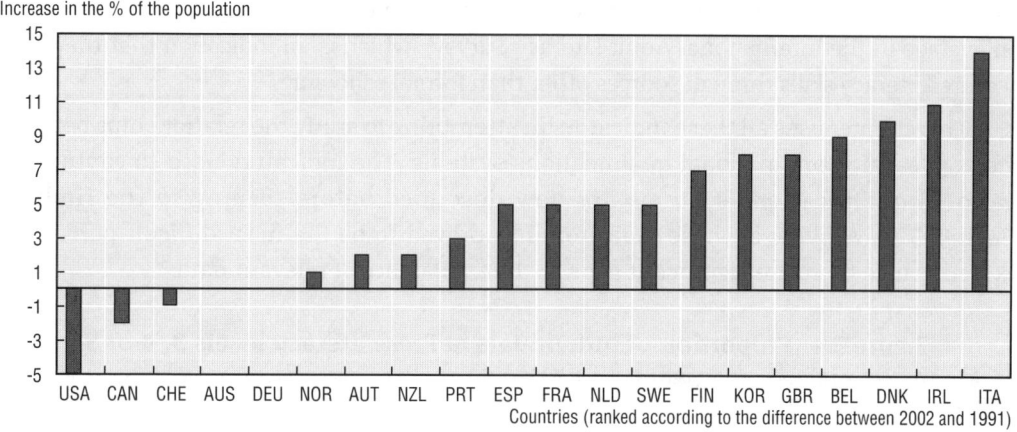

Source: OECD, 2004a, processed by the authors.

as far as volume is concerned, promoting lifelong learning through qualifications systems is more an issue for the adult population than for young people, since most of the latter now reach upper secondary education.

The percentage of people who have attained tertiary education is another interesting indicator of lifelong learning (Figure 3.3). Enrolment and/or success in tertiary education are likely to be good indicators of the reach of the qualifications systems and whether they promote higher levels of learning. It is unlikely that young people will engage in long studies if their qualifications systems do not lead to real reward in the labour market, or do not provide personal satisfaction or pathways to further learning.

Finally, literacy scores for the adult population are often used as a way of measuring non-formal and informal learning as well as lifelong learning. The benchmark is the minimum level

Figure 3.3. **Proportion of individuals that graduated from tertiary education institutions, 2002**

Summary: For most countries, between a quarter and a third of the population graduated from tertiary education institutions.

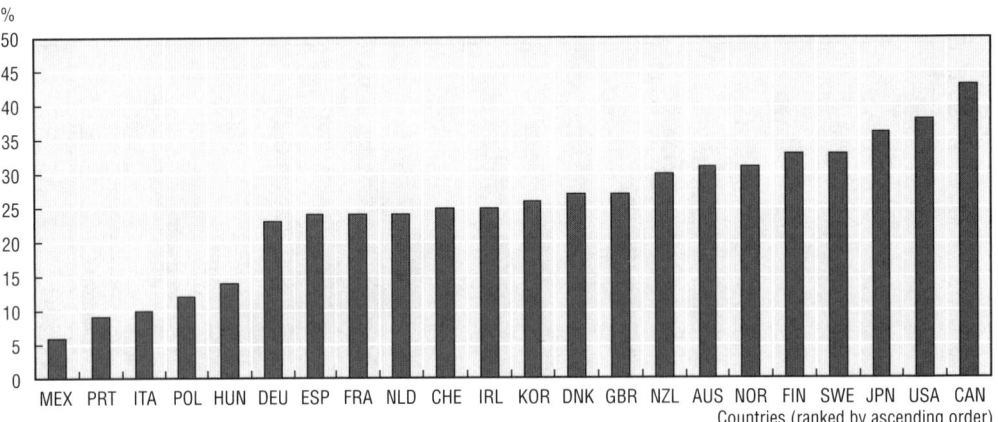

Source: OECD, 2004a, processed by the authors.

of literacy adequate for functioning in the knowledge society (Figure 3.4).[2] Measuring literacy offers a different perspective and additional information than educational attainments data because it sheds light on literacy skill loss and acquisition of that skill since formal schooling. For example, there is evidence that some poorly educated individuals are highly literate (10% on average in the International Adult Literacy Survey), which is an indication that they have acquired literacy skills through sources other than formal schooling.

This chapter uses all these indicators in attempting to study the relationships between lifelong learning and national qualifications systems. The indicators used to capture the national qualifications systems are now described before turning to the findings (Section 3.2.). Arriving at those indicators has proved to be the most difficult part of the exercise since there are significant gaps in the availability of relevant data.[3]

Figure 3.4. **Proportion of individuals at *Prose* literacy levels 3, 4 or 5**

Summary: For most countries, between 45% and 70 % of the population reached prose literacy levels 3, 4 and 5.

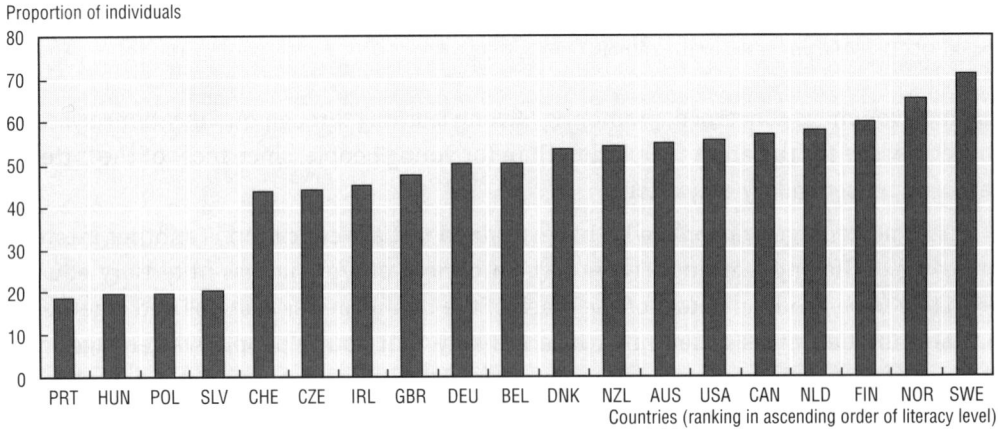

Source: International Adult Literacy Survey (2000), processed by the authors.

Constructing a typology of national qualifications systems

Chapter 1 provides a list of components that best describe a qualifications system. There are 11 (Annex 1.A2): the scope of application of the qualifications system; control of the qualifications system; accreditation processes for qualifications; a framework within the qualifications system; descriptors present in qualifications; access to qualifications for individuals; progression for individuals; stability of the system; awarding processes; credit system; and international reference points. The way these components are combined and used in countries explains the overall performance. A list of criteria for assessing this performance is also proposed in that chapter including, *e.g.*, accessibility, responsiveness and transparency. A quantitative analysis would ideally require measures of performance based on these criteria. However, such indicators do not exist.

It is therefore proposed to use some alternative proxy measures that can be described in quantitative terms. The approach adopted is to develop a typology of national qualifications systems based on some of their general structural elements on which agreement could be obtained among expert observers. The proposed typology uses the following eight general structural elements:

1. Whether the end of secondary education leads into an apprenticeship with responsibility for programmes shared between an educational institution and a firm.

2. Whether there is an explicit framework linking qualifications from different educational and occupational sectors.

3. Whether a large proportion of a cohort engages in studies linked to a specific occupational area.

4. Whether the qualifications system is unified throughout its regions and control lies with one main agency or with government.

5. Whether entry to the labour market is regulated through qualification and most occupational sectors use this regulation.

6. Whether there is a clear national programme or system for recognising non-formal or informal learning.

7. Whether unitised qualifications – with large uptake – exist, and units from different qualifications can be combined.

8. Whether credentials are essential for entry to the labour market or higher education and for further progress in work or study.

This list was developed in consultation with experts from countries participating in the OECD study. The experts were also asked to rank their country's qualifications systems along a four-point scale, from 1 (definitely true for my country) to 4 (not present in my country) (Table 3.1).

There are several ways of constructing the ordinal scale. For example, the scale could range between 1 and 4, as used here, or a scale from zero to ten could be used. The latter would have provided more variance, but this degree of differentiation would be difficult for the experts to use. In fact, consensus was difficult to achieve, even on a simple scale with four rankings. For example, when several institutions[4] were consulted in a country, the responses were not always the same, and what is reported in Table 3.1 is sometimes an average of the different rankings proposed. It was not always possible to consult with several experts in each country, but when it was possible, the relative homogeneity of the responses provided support in using this typology.

Table 3.1 could be further refined but it serves here as a first basis to organise the international comparison of qualifications systems and the linkage with variables describing lifelong learning. This typology is also useful as background information regarding national qualifications systems in the participating countries.

Table 3.1. **Typology of qualifications systems in selected countries**

	Dual system[1]	QF[2]	VET in school[3]	Centralisation[4]	LM[5]	RPL[6]	Credit system[7]	Credentialist[8]
Australia	2	1	1	1	2	1	2	2
Belgium (Flemish Community)	3	3	1	1	2	3	3	2
Belgium (French-speaking)	3	3	1	1	2	3	2	2
Czech Republic	4	3	3	1	2	4	3	2
Germany	1	3	2	2.5	2	3	3	2
Denmark	1	2	1	1	2	2	1	2
Spain	2	1	2	2	2	2	1	2
Finland	2	1	1	1	3	1	3	2
France	1	1	1	1	2	1	3	1
Greece	2	3	3	4	2	4	4	2
Hungary	3	2	2	1	1	3	3	1
Italy	2	3.5	4	3	2	4	3	1
Ireland	3	1	3	1	3	4	3	2
Northern Ireland	2	1	3	1	2	4	4	2
Japan	2.5	3	2.5	2.5	3	3	4	2
Korea	3	3	3	2	2	3	3	2
Mexico	3	3	1	1	4	2	3	1
Netherlands	2.5	2	1.5	2	3	2	2	2
Norway	1	2	2	1	2	1	2	2
New Zealand	2	1	2	1	2	2	1	2
Poland	2	2	1	2	3	3	4	2
Portugal	2	4	2	1	2	1	3	1
Scotland	1	1	3	2	2	2	1	1
Slovenia	4	3	2	1	1	2.5	3	2
Sweden	3.5	4	1	1	4	2	1	2
Switzerland	2	2	3	3	3	3	3	1
United Kingdom	2	1	2	1	3	1	3	2
United States of America	4	3	3	4	4	4	2	3

Legend: 1. This is definitely true for my country; 2. This is only partially true for my country; 3. There is only limited experience of this in my country; and 4. This is not present in my country.

General structural elements of national qualifications systems:

1. Countries where the end of secondary education leads into an apprenticeship with shared responsibility for programmes between an educational institution and a firm.
2. Countries with an explicit framework linking qualifications from different educational and occupational sectors.
3. Countries where a large proportion of a cohort engages in studies linked to a specific occupational area.
4. Countries where the qualifications system is unified throughout its regions and control lies with one main agency or with government.
5. Countries where entry to the labour market is regulated through qualification – most occupational sectors use this type of regulation.
6. Countries where there is a clear national programme or system for recognising non-formal or informal learning.
7. Unitised qualifications (large uptake) exist and units from different qualifications can be combined.
8. Credentials are essential for entry to the labour market or higher education and for further progress in work or study.

Source: OECD, consultation with the countries.

Constructing macro variables with micro data: another second-best approach

Another possible typology is to derive continuous quantitative indicators. Ideally one would like to measure whether the qualifications system promotes learning or not. An assumption made in the chapter is that the number of learners seeking a qualification, as

> Box 3.1. **What do old data mean? Comparing the 1994 International Adult Literacy Survey and the 2004 Adult Literacy and Life Skills Survey**
>
> The International Adult Literacy Survey took place between 1994 and 1998. New data, from the Adult Literacy and Life Skills (ALL) survey, were released in May 2005 (OECD and Statistics Canada, 2005). Since the two surveys are based on the same theoretical corpus and collect similar data ten years apart, they could offer observations on two points in time. Unfortunately, the way questions are phrased in the more recent background questionnaire is different from that in the earlier survey. In addition, only five countries have carried out both surveys: Canada, Italy, Norway, Switzerland and the United States. Nevertheless, subject to some caveats, the surveys can be used to produce information on the main reasons for undertaking learning activities. In regard to those learners who are primarily seeking a qualification, the changes between the International Adult Literacy Survey and the Adult Literacy and Life Skills Survey for different countries are: from 40% to 33% in Canada, from 43% to 59% in Italy, from 22% to 44% in Norway, from 19% to 42% in Switzerland and from 28% to 36% in the United States. Two conclusions can be made: 1) except in Canada, seeking a qualification seems more important in 2004 than ten years ago; and 2) the general pattern of the ranking of the countries is maintained, again with the exception of Canada. This stability over time suggests that International Adult Literacy Survey data may still be helpful for understanding individuals' behaviour in the context of this book, even though it was collected ten years ago. Therefore, mainly because of the small number of countries involved in the Adult Literacy and Life skills survey and its poor overlap with countries participating in the OECD study presented here, it was decided to concentrate on the International Adult Literacy Survey data; the Adult Literacy and Life Skills Survey was not explored further.

compared to those learners for whom obtaining a qualification is not the primary goal, could be used as a proxy variable for describing the overall "conduciveness" of a qualifications system in promoting lifelong learning. The second approach used in this chapter involves the International Adult Literacy Survey (Box 3.1 and Annex 3.A3), which provides information on the reasons why adults participate in learning.

Measuring conduciveness

The International Adult Literacy Survey, despite being rather old (Box 3.1), provides information on participation in adult learning and the motivations for it. Participation is therefore used as a way of measuring lifelong learning even if it is but one component. For some individuals, the primary reason for participation is to seek a qualification (Box 3.2), while for others the primary motivation could be, *e.g.*, career upgrading or learning for its own sake. Since the learners were asked to give only one reason, it would be reasonable to conclude that the three categories are mutually exclusive, at least as far as the primary motivation goes. It may well be that a person learning for her/his personal consumption ends up being recruited thanks to the competences acquired – but it would still be the case that the initial purpose of the learning was not job-related. The proportion of individuals undertaking learning activities primarily for a qualification (Table 3.2 and 3.A2.4 in this chapter's annex) is consistent with the figures reported in the country background reports on learner motivation. This similarity of findings suggests that the International Adult Literacy Survey data can be used with confidence.

Box 3.2. **Characteristics of learners whose primary goal is to seek a qualification**

To complement the evidence displayed on Figures 4.5-4.6 and 4.9-4.12, it is useful to describe the characteristics of the individuals primarily interested in achieving a qualification when they undertake learning activities. To some extent, informing decision making with the determinants of seeking a qualification also informs about the most effective ways to organise national qualifications systems. If the latter are to be used to promote lifelong learning, it is useful to know which subgroups of the population are more likely to be interested in using the qualifications system and which need extra attention, precisely because they are not interested in, and/or are deterred from, using it.

Throughout this chapter, the same question F5 from the IALS background questionnaire is used. It is phrased as follows: "Were you taking this training or education towards... (*read category/mark only one*).

1. A university degree/diploma/certificate?

2. A college diploma/certificate?

3. A trade-vocational diploma/certificate?

4. An apprenticeship certificate?

5. An elementary or secondary school diploma?

6. Professional or career upgrading?

7. Other."

For the purposes of this study, the seven categories are collapsed into two: seeking a qualification (items 1 to 5) or not (items 6 and 7). The variables obtained are used in a statistical model using many explanatory variables to describe those individuals primarily interested in a qualification when undertaking learning activities (Tables 3.A2.7 and 3.A2.8 in Annex 3.A2). In interpreting the following results, all other factors must be considered equal:

- Highly literate people are more interested in a qualification than people with low literacy. The variable measuring literacy level is more significant than the one describing initial educational attainment; the latter does not indicate the influence of initial education attainment on the primary objective of learning.

- Individuals in high-level occupations are less interested by a qualification when they undertake learning activities; blue collar workers and unemployed people are more interested in a qualification. Again, this finding must not be confused with the Matthew effect, which says that individuals already qualified are more interested in learning than others. Here, it is likely that individuals with poor labour market performance have realised that achieving a qualification is a necessity, evidence supported by the fact that the higher their income, the less individuals are interested in a qualification.

- Men want a qualification more often than women, and individuals who are not socially active want a qualification more often than those who are socially active.

- In countries such as Denmark, the Czech Republic and Australia, individuals are very interested in gaining a qualification. In countries such as Finland, Switzerland and Portugal, individuals undertaking learning activities do not seem very interested in a qualification. Finally, countries such as United States, Slovenia and Canada are in between these two extreme groups. This high level of discrepancy in the way individuals view gaining a qualification must have to do with the components and sub-components of their qualifications system as well as with its performance.

This evidence confirms the idea stated above that individuals engage in learning for a qualification for economic reasons and/or personal development.

Table 3.2. **Aggregated reasons for undertaking learning activities (first mention), 16-65 years old, 1994-98 (%)**

	Reasons for undertaking learning activities			Number of learning spells reported in the sample (%)
	Qualification	Career upgrading	Other	
Australia	47[1]	42	11	23[2]
Belgium (Flanders)	23	30	36	11
Canada	40	43	17	21
Chile	60	33	7	21
Czech Republic	53	17	28	14
Denmark	23	54	23	33
Finland	23	63	14	31
Germany	9	66	25	11
Hungary	21	46	28	14
Ireland	48	27	25	19
Italy	43	47	11	–
Netherlands	25	23	51	28
New Zealand	35	47	18	23
Norway	22	68	10	26
Poland	21	63	16	11
Slovenia	39	55	5	28
Sweden	6	–	93	31
Switzerland	19	41	28	24
United Kingdom	27	19	54	23
United States	28	48	17	19
Average	*29*	*44*	*24*	*22*

1. For example, in Australia, 47% of the adults reported undertaking learning activities to obtain a qualification for the first reported learning activity.
2. 23% of the individuals described a first education and training period.
The countries are listed in alphabetical order. The countries in bold are the ones involved in the OECD study.
Source: International Adult Literacy Survey, processed by the authors.

The proportion of learners seeking a qualification is relatively high in the Czech Republic, Ireland, Australia and Italy, in that order (Table 3.2 and 3.A2.4 in this chapter's annex).[5] At the lower end (by some distance) are Sweden and Germany, followed by Switzerland, Hungary, Poland, Finland and Denmark. These data can be interpreted in different ways. As noted above, they give one indication of whether the qualifications system is more or less conducive to learning in a country. In fact, countries where the culture of learning is strong do not rank very high in these tables. The argument here could be that if learning is part of the culture, more people are likely to participate in learning for its own sake – seeking a qualification may not be the dominant motivation.

Before using the numbers from the International Adult Literacy Survey, it would be useful to provide further evidence on the robustness of the data on qualification seekers. It is well known that learning activities leading to a qualification are longer, or more intensive, than other learning activities. As can be seen from Figure 3.5, there is indeed a high degree of correlation between the average number of hours spent on learning, (whether job related or general interest), and the proportion of learners seeking a qualification. The fit displayed on Figure 3.6 when using job-related training instead of any kind of learning activities confirms that the proportion of learners seeking a qualification seems to be a reliable indicator.

Figure 3.5. **Intensity of learning (any type) and qualifications**[1]

Summary: The higher the proportion of learners interested in a qualification the higher the duration of the individual learning period (any type of learning).

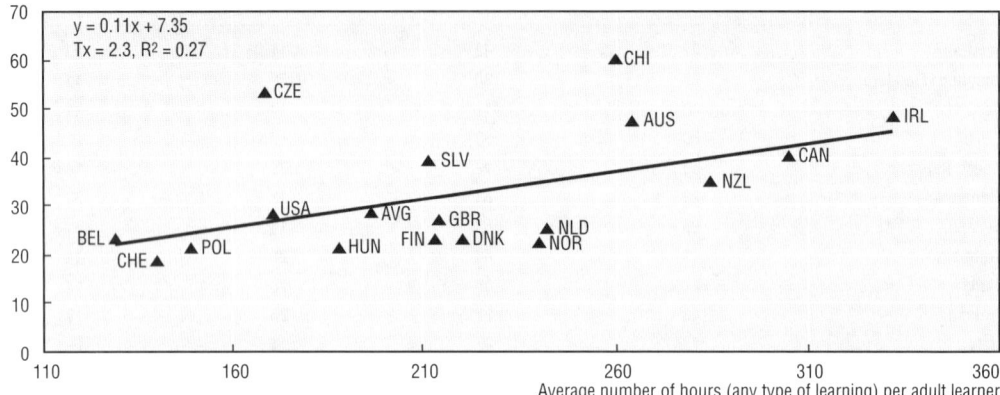

1. The quality of the model is acceptable but can be improved. Removing the potential outliers – Czech Republic and Chile (in italics) – ultimately results in a particularly good model: Tx = 4.2 and R^2 = 0.57 (where Tx is the student statistic – a value above 2 usually indicates a statistically significant parameter – and R^2 the goodness of fit indicator – R^2 varies between 0 [no correlation] and 1 [perfect correlation])

Source: International Adult Literacy Survey (2000), processed by the authors.

Figure 3.6. **Intensity of learning (on-the-job training) and qualifications systems**[1]

Summary: The higher the proportion of learners interested in a qualification the higher the duration of the individual learning period (on-the-job training).

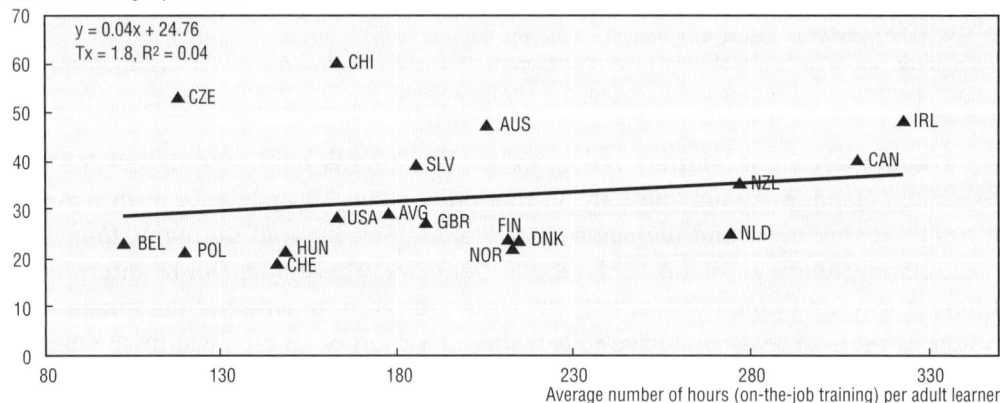

1. The quality of the model becomes reasonable when removing the potential outliers (Czech Republic and Chile): Tx = 2.8 and R^2 = 0.38.

Source: International Adult Literacy Survey (2000), processed by the authors.

Measuring adult learning using the European Union Labour Force Survey (EULFS) and some national surveys

Along the same lines, the EULFS is used to derive aggregated indicators of lifelong learning. This survey is more recent than the IALS but it covers only European countries; some national surveys are used to complement it (Annex 3.A1). The surveys provide information on participation in adult learning in a given reference period, which is usually over the last four weeks or during the last twelve months. For the purposes of this analysis, an additional indicator is used that provides information on the duration of the learning activity, which gives an indication of its intensity. Both indicators are used in

Section 3.2 but, before turning to these findings, the next subsection attempts to illustrate the expected relationships when trying to link national qualifications systems and lifelong learning in quantitative terms.

Expected relationships

Upper secondary education, tertiary attainment and national qualifications systems

If national qualifications systems have a significant impact on lifelong learning, it should be possible to see that impact at several stages in education and training. The end of upper secondary education is typically the point where general qualifications are awarded in all the countries, and those qualifications usually open up access to tertiary education. Therefore, if national qualifications systems have an impact on lifelong learning, some characteristics of the system should be reasonably correlated with the proportion of individuals having successfully reached upper secondary education. The rationale assumes that a conducive system would most likely lead to many young people gaining a qualification at upper secondary education level.

However, the variable describing the proportion of the population that has attained upper secondary education level does not correlate well with the eight general structural elements used for the typology of a qualifications system (Table 3.1). A somewhat strong link was anticipated – but not found – between a country being rather "credentialist" and the proportion of people reaching upper secondary education level; the latter being necessary for success in the transition from initial education and training to working life (OECD, 2000).

The same kind of argument applies to the tertiary education system. If the qualifications system in a country provides clear benefits to young people leaving upper secondary education, then clear correlation must be visible between it and enrolments in tertiary education or completion rates. If on the other hand it does not provide enough benefits to users, then even if participation in tertiary education depends on others factors, there may be limited interest in enrolment on the part of upper secondary graduates. Here too a somewhat strong link was anticipated but not found between the country being rather "credentialist" and the proportion of people enrolling in tertiary education. In fact, among all the indicators used for lifelong learning, none correlates well with any of the eight general elements of the typology.

Participation in adult learning and national qualifications systems

A qualifications system providing clear information about the outcomes of learning as well as guidance about the way to benefit from them can be expected to trigger interest in learning among the adult population. Lack of information and guidance may deter individuals. The data show that the proportion of 25-to-64-year-old individuals engaged in adult learning activities does not correlate well with any of the eight general elements of the national qualifications system typology. This is surprising because indicators such as the existence of a system that recognises prior learning or a credit system are supposed to be conducive to engaging in adult learning activities, because both provide transparency and information about outcomes and this motivates adults (OECD, 2003 and 2005a). Frameworks that provide the information about possible routes throughout the qualifications system similarly serve as incentives.

As noted above, deriving aggregated indicators that describe national qualifications systems using household surveys such as the IALS is a possible alternative and has been attempted as a second-best approach. Ideally, this requires having lifelong learning indicators for the same period, which are not available. However, existing data were used in many attempts to correlate the two sets of variables. One explanation for not finding a link between the proportion of adult learners seeking qualification and the eight general typology elements is the time lag between the IALS and the description of the country qualifications system according to the typology. In order to avoid the problem of time lags in data, the International Adult Literacy Survey could be used to derive indicators describing national qualifications systems, and lifelong learning indicators could be computed for the earlier period of the International Adult Literacy Survey. In doing so, both sets of derived indicators would be contemporaneous and the expected correlation better.

The above experiments represent only selected examples of how the available data could be used to explore the relationship between the qualifications system and lifelong learning. A comprehensive approach would require that all the components and sub-components of a system, as described in Chapter 1, be taken into account such as: flexibility, responsiveness and transparency, for example. For now, the next sections will show that national qualifications system characteristics and lifelong learning variables correlate to some extent.

3.2. An attempt at correlation

This section uses very broad descriptors of the national qualifications and lifelong learning systems to provide the reader with a first indication of possible links between the two. In view of the lack of data on the quality and the efficiency of lifelong learning, the section relies on data on two aspects: volume (participation) and equity (distribution).

Evidence on participation in adult learning and the national qualifications systems

The volume of lifelong learning can be measured, for instance, by counting the number of participants over a given reference period, such as over the last four weeks or the last twelve months. Two alternative measures were used, the standard participation rate and the weighted participation rate. The information in Figure 3.7 attempts to bring together a measure of lifelong learning volume and one measure of national qualifications systems: the degree to which a country has a dual system, which is one of the eight structural elements of the national qualifications system typology shown in Table 3.1. The participation rate variable refers to the number of adults involved in learning between the ages of 16 and 65, weighted by the duration of the learning period. The figure shows a relationship between the two variables.

However, the standard participation rate does not correlate with the existence of a dual system in a country. This shows that different measures of participation in lifelong learning are related in different ways to different measures of national qualifications systems and it is difficult to find a straightforward relationship between the two.

Overall, the participation rate data drawn from the European Union Labour Force Survey and one measure of the national qualifications system typology (dual system) seem to show linkages between national qualifications systems and lifelong learning. Aside from the measure of dual systems, significant correlations between other measures of national qualifications systems and the measures of lifelong learning were not found.

Figure 3.7. **Participation in adult learning and the existence of a dual system in the country**

(Both the number of adult participants in learning and the duration of learning are taken into account.)
Summary: If a qualifications system has a dual system, the level of adult learning is higher.

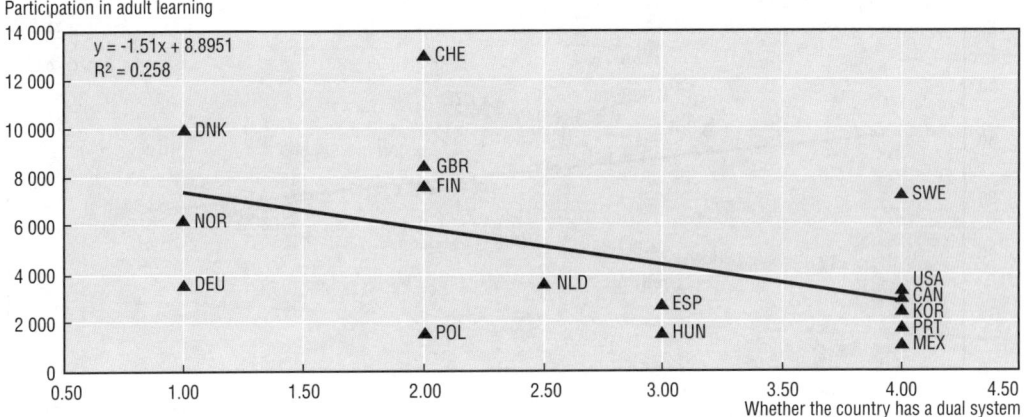

Source: Data from Miyamoto and Werquin (2006), processed by the authors.

Participation in adult learning and the conduciveness of qualifications system to learning

As mentioned earlier, the IALS provides information on the motives for participating in learning activities. Figure 3.8 shows the relationship between the aggregate participation rate (the vertical axis) and the percentage of adults participating in learning primarily to obtain a qualification. The figure shows a negative correlation: the higher the proportion of individuals in a country that are primarily interested in a qualification, the lower the participation rate in adult learning activities. When the figure is reproduced using job-related adult learning, instead of any kind of adult learning, the findings are similar and confirm a strong relationship (Figure 3.9). Attention was drawn earlier to the costs and constraints involved in gaining qualifications, as well as their benefits. One interpretation of the data could be that in those countries where adult learning is closely associated with the gaining of qualifications, its costs outweigh its benefits and this depresses its levels of participation. However, this may not be the principal reason. It is noteworthy that the Nordic countries, where generally higher levels of adult learning are long established, feature towards the top left of Figures 3.8 and 3.9; this indicates that these countries have high levels of adult learning, but relatively few individuals involved are learning for a qualification. It therefore seems likely that in certain countries where adult learning has become part of the general culture, the learning takes place over and above individuals' requirement for qualifications. In other countries though, adult learning is more confined to some kind of "baseline" requirement for qualifications. This point is reinforced in the case of those who do not hold a qualification. The data also illustrate the point, made earlier, that there is a wider range of motivations, and that obtaining a qualification is simply one among several (*e.g.* personal interest, job upgrading, etc.). The findings in Figures 3.8 and 3.9 both show that learning and seeking a qualification are two separate concepts. (See also Box 3.2 for additional developments on the motivations of individuals.)

Figure 3.8. **Extent of lifelong learning: participation in adult learning (16-65), 1994-98**[1]

(Standard participation rate, over the last 12 months, as defined in the International Adult Literacy Survey.)
Summary: The higher the proportion of learners seeking a qualification, the lower the proportion of adult learners in a country.

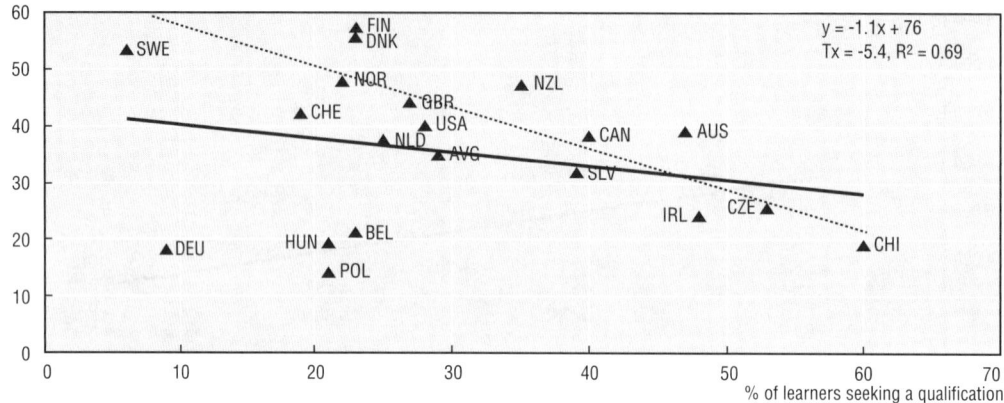

1. The quality of the model here also becomes reasonable when a few outliers such as Germany, Belgium (Flanders), Hungary and Poland are removed. It is not surprising that Germany, for instance, appears as an outlier because the German background questionnaire did not ask the question about adult learning in a comparable way to serve domestic purposes (OECD and Statistics Canada, 2000).

Source: International Adult Literacy Survey (2000), processed by the authors.

Figure 3.9. **Extent of lifelong learning: participation in job-related adult learning (16-65), 1994-98**

(Standard participation rate over the past 12 months, as defined in the International Adult Literacy Survey.)
Summary: The higher the proportion of learners seeking a qualification, the lower the proportion of learners involved in job-related learning.

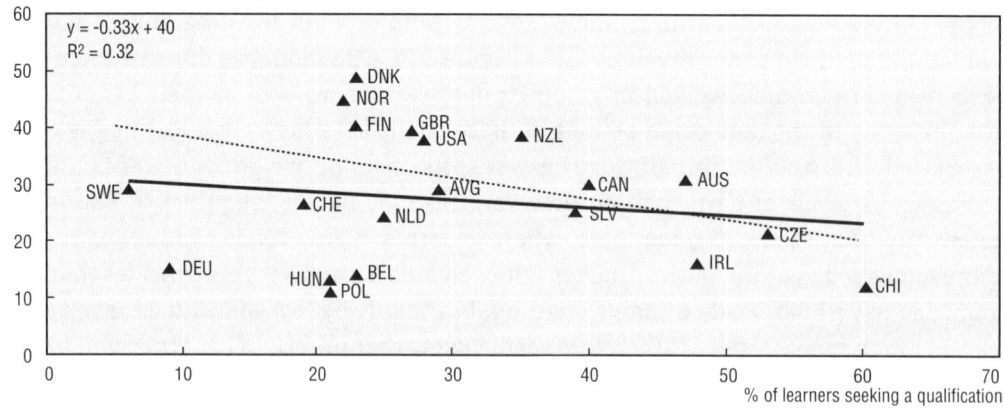

Source: International Adult Literacy Survey (2000), processed by the authors.

National qualifications systems and the distribution of lifelong learning

The second dimension relates to how equitably learning opportunities are distributed in the population. The question posed here is whether measures of lifelong learning distribution in some way relate to the features of national qualifications systems. Two distribution variables are used here: educational attainment (measured by the ISCED level of individuals[6]) and the current literacy level of the individuals (captured by their ability to read prose text), both from the International Adult Literacy Survey. As previously, the measure of national qualifications systems used is the proportion of adult learners who seek a qualification. Figure 3.10 brings these two variables together and shows that the higher the proportion of a country's population with low qualifications, the more likely learners are to be seeking qualifications. A simple conclusion might be that overall, learners with qualifications would not be as interested in seeking qualifications because they have some. However turning to individualised IALS data and then looking at those learners seeking qualifications by their current level of qualifications, we find that this simple conclusion is not true (Table 3.3). Whilst learners with qualifications still seek qualifications, those with low levels of qualifications are more likely to be seeking qualification than the highly qualified. Further statistical modelling confirms that those without significant initial qualifications are more likely to be motivated by qualifications when they undertake learning later in life (Box 3.2).

Figure 3.10. **Distribution of lifelong learning: low initial education and search for a qualification by learners**

Summary: The higher the proportion of a country's population with low qualifications, the more likely learners are to be seeking qualifications.

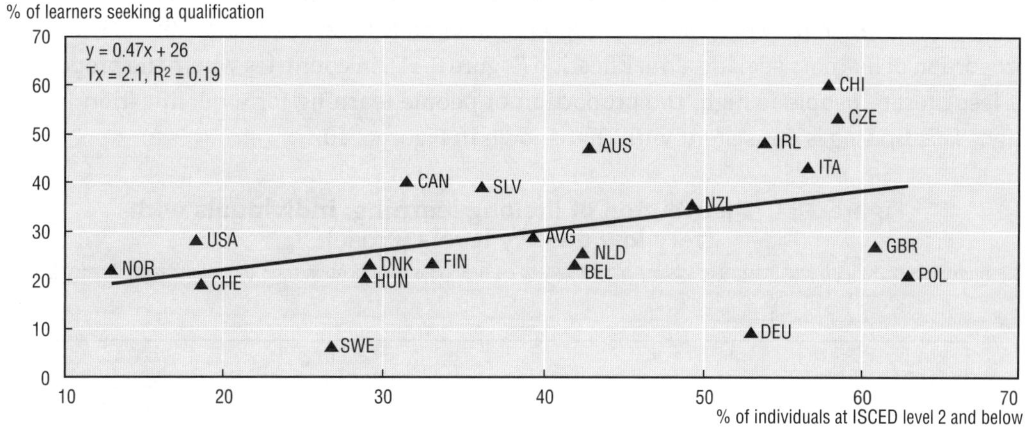

% of learners seeking a qualification

$y = 0.47x + 26$
$Tx = 2.1, R^2 = 0.19$

% of individuals at ISCED level 2 and below

Source: International Adult Literacy Survey (2000), processed by the authors.

Table 3.3. **Educational attainment and aggregated reasons for undertaking learning activities (first mention) 16-65 years old, 1994-98 (%)**

	Reasons for undertaking learning activities			
	Qualification	Career upgrading	Other	Unknown
Educational attainment				
ISCED 0-2 (Below upper secondary)	39	27	30	4
ISCED 3 (Upper secondary)	30	44	22	4
ISCED 5-7 (Tertiary)	22	53	22	3

Source: International Adult Literacy Survey (2000), processed by the authors.

This finding may be interpreted as an illustration of the "second chance" motivation, which is not just another chance for additional learning but also another chance for obtaining a qualification. On the face of it, the finding may be seen as contradictory to the Matthew effect (OECD, 2003): less qualified people participate less in learning activities than others. The Matthew effect is well documented and many reasons have been offered for the phenomenon: cost of learning, lack of time, dislike of assessment, fear of failure, and perception of stigma *vis-à-vis* the family, friends and the community. The finding here does not contradict the Matthew effect: issues of problematic access to learning are not relevant since only learners have been selected. This leaves motivation to learn as the key variable and it is perhaps not surprising that low-qualified learners wish to become more highly qualified. A clear conclusion is that the effect is more associated with barriers to learning; when only motivation to learn is considered, the effect is reversed. The Matthew effect is commonly accepted to be powerful. This conclusion suggests that barriers to learning are more influential than the evidence would indicate because the motivation factor of seeking a qualification may be hiding the effect's magnitude.

Literacy levels as a proxy for current competences

Adult learning is an important component of lifelong learning, whether undertaken in formal settings or not. ISCED is a good indicator of the level attained in initial education and training, but not a comprehensive indicator of real competences later in life at the time of the measurement. The International Adult Literacy Survey data are useful for this purpose. The distribution of lifelong learning can be captured by analysing the size of the proportion of those at the lower end of the literacy scale. Using this variable, we find a positive correlation between the proportion of individuals at level 1 of *prose* literacy and the proportion of learners seeking a qualification (Figure 3.11). In countries where the proportion of less literate people is high, the proportion of people learning for a qualification is also high. This finding is consistent with that shown in Figure 3.10.

Figure 3.11. Distribution of lifelong learning: individuals with very low literacy levels (Prose)

Summary: Learners with low literacy levels are more likely to be seeking a qualification than those with high literacy levels.

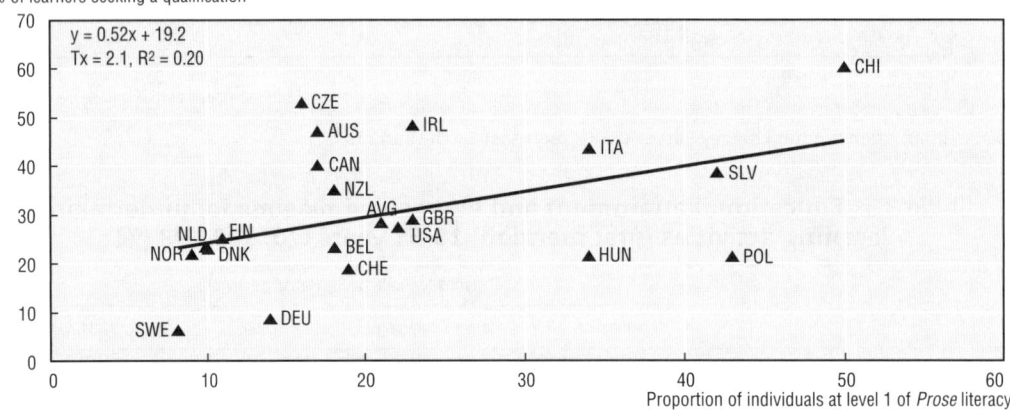

% of learners seeking a qualification

$y = 0.52x + 19.2$
$Tx = 2.1, R^2 = 0.20$

Proportion of individuals at level 1 of *Prose* literacy

Source: International Adult Literacy Survey (2000), processed by the authors.

Overall, the two previous sets of findings – about initial education attainment and current literacy level – offer interesting results. It seems that despite their weak participation rates in learning, poorly educated and less literate individuals are more interested in gaining a qualification. This finding is also supported by the information cited in Box 3.2. The explanation may be that individuals are aware of the potential benefits of holding a qualification, presumably in the labour market. One implication of the finding is the greater importance both of foundation qualifications for the poorly educated and of finding ways to address this need.

It is interesting to note that there is some clustering of countries in most of the figures. The data suggest that these countries have something in common, which may be systemic features of the qualifications system. However, it is difficult to test potential correlation within these groups because sub-sampling will necessarily involve small samples and the results may be unreliable.

3.3. Building a quantitative evidence base

It is now clear that quantitative evidence is limited and conclusions about relationships between national qualifications systems and lifelong learning have to be tentative. These limitations can come from three different sources: 1) it is possible that the national qualifications and/or lifelong learning systems have not been measured properly; 2) the relationship between national qualifications systems and lifelong learning is too complex to be measured at an aggregate level; and 3) there is, in reality, no relationship at all. These three limitations are now discussed.

National qualifications systems are not measured properly

The primary reason for finding only limited quantitative evidence in linking national qualifications systems and lifelong learning seems to be the failure to measure useful conceptual descriptions representing the former that can have implications for the latter. There exist quantitative data describing lifelong learning but, as pointed out above, the main problem is that indicators for describing a qualifications system do not exist or do not describe the system in an adequate way for sound quantitative analysis. Its features have been identified (Chapter 1) – accessibility, efficiency, flexibility, responsiveness, transparency, etc. – but they could not be measured. Therefore, a broader concept of conduciveness to learning has been derived from observing individuals' behaviour toward learning for a qualification. The chapter has presented a description of national qualifications systems through general structural elements in the form of a typology (Table 3.1) as a second-best approach.

The 20 mechanisms provided in Chapter 4 also describe the process through which the links between national qualifications systems and lifelong learning can be examined. However, they could only be established at a qualitative level and no attempt has been made here to find quantitative empirical counterparts. New conceptual work is therefore needed to identify the features of national qualifications systems that can be measured, or – if the ones proposed are satisfactory – to suggest a methodology to measure them.

Even with regard to lifelong learning indicators, where relevant data exist, some effort could be devoted to produce fresher data also in line with recent reforms likely to impact on lifelong learning activities. Trend data would also be necessary to appreciate changes over time and the impact of recent reforms.

A relationship too complex to measure at an aggregate level

In addition to the conceptual and empirical problems of measuring systemic features, it is possible that the quantitative findings reported above are limited, simply because the relationship between national qualifications systems and lifelong learning is too complex and has not been properly captured in the above experiment. In particular, it may be difficult to measure the processes through data at an aggregate level. The complexity of this relationship is underscored by the sheer number of *mechanisms* that can link national qualifications systems and lifelong learning (Chapter 4). Rather than map out broad quantitative variables measured at the macro level, it would probably be better to examine micro-level relationships between sub-components – *e.g.* the *scope of application* or *control* (Annex 1.A2) of qualifications systems and lifelong learning.

In addition to (and probably because of) this complexity, it is likely that there are cancelling effects too: different mechanisms may have impacts that run counter to each other. In this case, they would blur the clarity of the overall findings, or reduce the net effect. For example, a given policy targeted at qualifications systems may motivate a subgroup of the population to undertake learning activities but may discourage another sub-group from doing so. The overall effect would be difficult to observe. Attempting to identify a net effect between national qualifications systems and lifelong learning with aggregated variables is also not entirely appropriate, because aggregated variables are often correlated with other, hidden variables that must be controlled for.

A relationship that may not be displayable at a quantitative empirical level

Finally, there remains a possibility that there is no relationship at all that can be displayed at a quantitative empirical level. However, it is difficult to infer further and clearly deny such a relationship until the two sets of issues above are dealt with in an appropriate manner. The indications from Chapter 4, based on qualitative evidence, suggest that there is such a relationship.

A key positive finding of the quantitative analysis

In general, high levels of motivation to seek qualifications are not a necessary condition for achieving high levels of lifelong learning. However, there is a very important exception. Those who have not achieved a qualification at ISCED 3 or above and/or who have low levels of literacy are more likely than others to be seeking a qualification when they undertake learning. It may be that the offer of a credible "second chance" qualification can play an important part in motivating such people to learn.

Possible ways forward

Having considered the limitations, and having suggested that there are relationships between national qualifications systems and lifelong learning that can be described at the theoretical level, the discussion must now turn to proposals for overcoming those limitations.

First, it is necessary to gather evidence on the opinion of individual users and potential users about the conduciveness (transparency, responsiveness, etc.) of the qualifications system for promoting learning. Individual or household surveys should be used more systematically to collect information about the perception individuals have of their qualifications system. These additional short modules would have the merit of providing affordable key quantitative elements in a relatively short period. Such an approach would also, via an existing survey, allow for some enrichment of the analysis by using relevant variables usually collected in these surveys: for example gender, educational attainment, labour market status, social background and occupation.

Second, information should be gathered on the features that best describe qualifications systems for a sound quantitative analysis. One possible approach is to organise a group of international experts to ascertain these characteristics and the best way to conceptualise and define them at an international level. The proposed typology is a first step toward a quantitative knowledge of complex systems. It requires additional discussion with country experts and further refinement, but is a first step toward an agreed typology.

Setting an agenda for research

Linking indicators describing national qualifications systems and lifelong learning variables has proved a difficult exercise, because it requires many conditions to be met, and appropriate variables to be available, for the appropriate period of time. There are lessons to be learned; the following represent key elements of a research agenda for the future:

- There is a need for sound conceptual work about the best way to define systemic variables and to produce appropriate indicators describing national qualifications systems.

- There is a need for research on the best way to relate national qualifications systems to lifelong learning through quantitative variables.

- There is a need for international data to be collected as an empirical counterpart for the conceptual work proposed above.

- There is a need for a stronger focus on micro relationships, at the level of the components and sub-components of qualifications systems.

In addition to specific data, trend data will also be necessary. This will take time and effort but it would allow for more appropriate reflection on the way national qualifications and lifelong learning systems evolve. Stability in the way variables are measured may be needed as well. If national qualifications systems are to become a policy tool, policy makers will have to be more thoroughly informed about current data as well as trend data to avoid fragmentation of policy making.

Finally, the data collection process may have to leave the circle of direct benefits to lifelong learning, and gather information on broader social effects such as those related to crime or health factors.

Notes

1. The 1997 reform, for instance, created level 4. This had a direct effect on the number of people that used to be classified in the level 3 but it also produced inconsistent classification across countries. Along the same lines, the creation of sub categories A, B and C generated even more inconsistencies across countries as well as breaks in the time series.

2. The level considered by experts as a suitable minimum level for coping with the increasing demands of the emerging knowledge society and information economy is level 3 (OECD and Statistics Canada, 1995).

3. See for instance QCA (Qualification and Curriculum Authority) (2004) and Chapter 4 in particular for similar conclusions.

4. It was not possible to request a consensus decision from a range of stakeholders in each country. Nor was it possible to define in detail the parts of the education and training system that were to be covered, such as school education or tertiary education. Instead, country experts with an overview of education and training provision were asked to make a decision based on a general view of the country's provision.

5. Chile is the top-ranked country but did not participate in the activity.

6. Other variables, such as the average number of years of schooling or the proportion of individuals having ISCED level 3 and above, provide also good correlation.

ANNEX 3.A1

Assumption, Caveats and Technical Notes

The analysis of quantitative data is always based on certain assumptions about those data. This annex groups together assumptions, caveats and notes to the reader concerning the national qualifications system typology and adult learning data so as to avoid cluttering the main text with technicalities.

- Assumption – Chapter 3 assumes that individual motivation for learning for a qualification or for some other purpose carries useful information about the qualifications system. When more individuals are observed undertaking learning for a qualification, that is interpreted to mean that the qualifications system facilitates or leads to learning. Counting the number of individuals primarily seeking a qualification is thus an indicator of the qualifications system.

- Note 1 – For the sake of comparison, and to provide additional benchmarking points, all the countries where data are available are included in the figures and tables whether they have participated in the study or not. This is particularly useful for the countries involved in the study in some way other than through a country background report – thematic groups, for instance. From a technical point of view, this also allows for a larger sample size, which makes any reported correlations more robust.

- Note 2 – Not all the countries are systematically displayed in the tables and figures because there are missing values for some countries and/or particular year(s).

- Note 3 – In some cases the available data may refer at times to the country as a whole (Belgium, Canada, Switzerland or the United Kingdom) but in other instances the data may only cover a region of the country (Belgium's Flemish Community, Québec, the German-speaking Swiss cantons or England).

- Note 4 – The European Union Labour Force Survey (EULFS) does contain interesting questions related to education and training. However, it does not include questions related to individuals' main goal(s) when undertaking learning activities. This survey is therefore used only to derive an indicator of participation in adult learning – except for the Netherlands (2001) and Switzerland (2003), for which national surveys are used.

- Note 5 – To complement the European Union Labour Force Survey (Eurostat, 2002), which covers only European countries, national surveys were used: Statistics Canada (2002); Mexico's *Instituto Nacional de Estadistica Geografia e Informática (INEGI)* (2001); Korean Ministry of Education and Human Resources Development (2000); Korean National Statistics Office (2003); United States National Center for Education Statistics (2001).

● Note 6 – The Adult Literacy and Life skills survey (ALL) is an updated and improved version of the International Adult Literacy Survey, but it will not be used here except for establishing the value of the latter (Box 3.1). Too few countries (seven) were involved in the first round (OECD and Statistics Canada, 2005), the only one available at the time this book was being prepared.

ANNEX 3.A2

Additional Tables

Table 3.A2.1. **Participation in adult learning by type of learning, 16-64 years old, 1994-98 (%)**

	All learning		Job related learning	
	Total participation rate (female rate)	Mean number of hours per participant, taken as indicator for quality	Participation rate	Mean number of hours per participant, taken as indicator for quality
Australia	39 (40)[1]	264	33	206
Belgium (Flanders)	21 (20)	129	14	102
Canada	38 (42)	305	32	310
Chile	19 (27)	260	11	163
Czech Republic	26 (23)	168	21	118
Denmark	56 (63)	220	48	213
Finland	57 (67)	213	40	214
Germany[2]	–	–	–	–
Hungary	19 (21)	188	13	148
Ireland	24 (30)	332	19	323
Italy	(26)			
Netherlands	37 (39)	242	25	274
New Zealand	47 (51)	284	41	277
Norway	48 (50)	240	45	213
Poland	14 (13)	149	11	120
Portugal	14 (20)	–	–	–
Slovenia	32 (41)	211	25	186
Sweden	53 (53)	–	–	–
Switzerland	42 (41)	140	27	146
United Kingdom	44 (47)	214	41	189
United States	40 (42)	170	38	163
Average	35 (35)	196	30	178

1. For example, in Australia, 39% of the adult population has undertaken learning activities over the past 12 months (the rate is 40% for the female population).

2. Not comparable for Germany.

The countries are listed in alphabetical order. The countries in bold are involved in the OECD study.

Source: International Adult Literacy Survey (2000), processed by the authors.

Table 3.A2.2. **Proportion of the population at each literacy level (Prose), 16-64 years old, 1994-98 (%)**

	Prose literacy levels (distribution)				% of individuals still in initial education and training
	Level 1	Level 2	Level 3	Level 4/5	
Australia	17[1]	27	37	19	8
Belgium (Flanders)	18	28	39	14	12
Canada	17	26	35	23	–
Chile	50	35	13	2	11
Czech Republic	16	38	38	8	12
Denmark	10	36	48	7	17
Finland	10	26	41	22	22
Germany	14	34	38	13	1
Hungary	34	43	21	3	6
Ireland	23	30	34	14	7
Italy	34	31	27	8	9
Netherlands	11	30	44	15	10
New Zealand	18	27	35	19	5
Norway	9	25	49	18	24
Poland	43	35	20	3	12
Portugal	48	29	19	4	13
Slovenia	42	35	20	3	17
Sweden	8	20	40	32	–
Switzerland	19	35	37	9	6
United Kingdom	22	30	31	17	4
United States	21	26	32	21	8
Average/Total	*23*	*29*	*32*	*16*	–

1. For example, in Australia, 17% of the adult population is in the first literacy level.

The countries are listed in alphabetical order. The countries in bold are involved in the OECD study.

Source: International Adult Literacy Survey (2000), processed by the authors.

Table 3.A2.3. **Pathways into learning: first, second and third reported learning activities aggregated, 16-64 years old, 1994-98 (%)**

	Main pattern of the learning pathway					
	University or college qualification	Trade-voc or app. qualification	School qualification	Professional upgrading	Other	Mixed pathways
Australia	13[1]	16	8	42	10	9
Belgium (Flanders)	6	14	1	30	35	3
Canada	19	6	12	43	16	4
Chile	25	17	15	32	5	5
Czech Republic	1	25	24	17	25	6
Denmark	7	7	5	53	19	9
Finland	8	5	6	62	12	7
Germany	2	5	1	64	22	5
Hungary	9	6	2	46	26	7
Ireland	24	10	12	26	24	2
Italy	35	3	0	45	9	7
Netherlands	9	9	5	21	50	6
New Zealand	19	6	4	46	17	7
Norway	11	8	0	67	9	4
Poland	6	14	–	63	14	3
Portugal	–	–	–	–	–	–
Slovenia	13	4	14	56	5	8
Sweden	11	3	0	–	82	3
Switzerland	5	11	0	39	27	6
United Kingdom	8	7	5	17	53	10
United States	15	5	6	48	17	2
Average/Total	*14*	*6*	*6*	*43*	*23*	*5*

1. For example, in Australia, for 13% of the adult learners, the purpose of learning has a dominant in terms of "university or college qualification" for the three learning periods.

The countries are listed in alphabetical order. The countries in bold are involved in the OECD study.

Source: International Adult Literacy Survey (2000), processed by the authors.

Table 3.A2.4. **Aggregated reasons for undertaking learning activities (first, second and third mention), 16-64 years old, 1994-98 (%)**

	Reasons for undertaking learning activities			Number of learning spells reported in the sample (%)
	Qualification	Career upgrading	Other	
Australia	**47/22/14**[1]	**42/63/75**	**11/13/11**	**23/9/5**[2]
Belgium (Flanders)	**23/15/15**	**30/36/37**	**36/33/28**	**11/4/3**
Canada	40/22/28	43/62/57	17/16/15	21/7/5
Chile	60/24/7	33/67/86	7/9/7	21/5/2
Czech Republic	**53/43/26**	**17/17/16**	**28/23/20**	**14/6/2**
Denmark	**23/10/6**	**54/68/70**	**23/21/23**	**33/14/8**
Finland	23/11/11	63/73/73	14/16/16	31/14/8
Germany	**9/8/2**	**66/68/77**	**25/23/18**	**11/4/1**
Hungary	21/9/2	46/55/51	28/29/27	14/3/2
Ireland	**48/15/9**	**27/41/38**	**25/28/22**	**19/5/3**
Italy	**43/14/7**	**47/73/80**	**11/13/13**	
Netherlands (the)	**25/13/10**	**23/21/22**	**51/67/69**	**28/9/3**
New Zealand	**35/22/16**	**47/57/66**	**18/21/18**	**23/10/5**
Norway	22/8/5	68/82/86	10/10/9	26/13/6
Poland	21/15/6	63/78/81	16/5/7	11/2/1
Portugal	–	–	–	**15/2/1**
Slovenia	**39/6/5**	**55/82/80**	**5/10/9**	**28/8/3**
Sweden	6/31/–	–/–/–	93/64/–	31/7/0
Switzerland	**19/5/3**	**41/37/32**	**28/28/20**	**24/10/5**
United Kingdom	**27/11/9**	**19/23/27**	**5464/63**	**23/12/6**
United States	28/18/17	48/40/31	17/11/9	19/7/5
Average	*29/17/15*	*44/44/38*	*24/21/17*	*22/8/4*

1. For example, in Australia, 47% of the adults reported undertaking learning activities to obtain a qualification for the first reported learning activity, 22% for the second and 14% for the third.
2. 23% of the individuals described a first education and training period, 9 a second and 5 a third.
The countries are listed in alphabetical order. The countries in bold are involved in the OECD study.
Source: International Adult Literacy Survey (2000), processed by the authors.

Table 3.A2.5. **Level of educational attainment of the individual looking for a qualification, first reported learning activity, 16-64 years old, 1994-98 (%)**

	ISCED					Total
	0-1	2	3	5	6-7	
Learners seeking a qualification:						
University degree, diploma or certificate	0	2[1]	44	23	30	11.4
College diploma or certificate	1	31	39	19	9	4.5
Trade/vocational diploma or certificate	5	28	43	14	10	4.5
Apprenticeship certificate	5	39	42	4	9	2.3
Elementary or secondary school diploma	10	71	17	1	2	6.2
Learners seeking other than a qualification:						
Professional or career upgrading	2	12	35	16	33	43.7
Other	5	24	33	12	25	23.6
Total	3.6	19.5	35.3	14.6	27.7	98.7/96.2[2]

1. For example, among the learners seeking a university degree, 2% have attained ISCED level 2 upon leaving initial education and training.
2. Not necessarily 100% because of non-response.
Source: International Adult Literacy Survey (2000), processed by the authors.

Table 3.A2.6. **Motivation of individual undertaking learning activities according to level of educational attainment, first reported learning activity, 16-64 years old, 1994-98 (%)**

	Reasons for undertaking learning activities:							Total
	Learners seeking a qualification					Learners seeking other than a qualification		
ISCED:	University degree, diploma or certificate	College diploma or certificate	Trade-vocational/ diploma or certificate	Apprenticeship certificate	Elementary or secondary school diploma	Professional or career upgrading	Other	
0-1	0	2[1]	6	3	16	26	30	3.6
2	1	7	7	5	22	27	29	19.5
3	14	5	5	3	3	44	22	35.3
5	18	6	4	1	0	48	19	14.6
6-7	13	2	2	1	0	56	23	27.7
Total	11.4	4.5	4.5	2.3	6.2	43.7	23.6	96.2/98.7[2]

1. For example, among the individuals being ISCED 0 or 1, 2% are seeking a university degree, diploma or certificate.
2. Not necessarily 100% because of non-response.
Source: International Adult Literacy Survey (2000), processed by the authors.

Table 3.A2.7. **Logit simple, complete specification, 16-64 years old, 1994-98 (%)**

	Estimated parameter	Probability > |T|
Intercept	1.9**	0.00
Literacy score (the best of the three available scales: *Prose, Doc, Quant*)	0.002**	0.00
Income (reference: percentile 0-20):		
No income	0.06	0.48
Percentile 20-40	−0.42**	0.00
Percentile 40-60	−0.86**	0.00
Percentile 60-80	−1.37**	0.00
Percentile 80-100	−1.34**	0.00
Occupation (reference: white-collar high-skilled):		
White-collar low-skilled	0.06	0.25
Blue-collar high-skilled	0.18**	0.01
Blue-collar low-skilled	0.19**	0.00
Out of labour force	0.65**	0.00
Educational attainment (reference: ISCED 0 or 1):		
ISCED 2	0.12	0.26
ISCED 3	0.03	0.78
ISCED 5	0.2	0.08
ISCED 6 or 7	0.09	0.44
Industry (reference: agriculture, only the significant industries are kept):		
Mining	−0.52*	0.02
Construction	0.22	0.07
Communication	−0.22	0.08
Personal characteristics:		
Live with partner (reference: lives alone)	−0.38**	0.00
Gender (reference: male)	0.29**	0.00
Age	−0.07**	0.00
Engagement in the community (reference: often):		
Going to a library: barely	−0.58**	0.00
Going to a library: never	−0.87**	0.00
Going to a concert: barely	−0.07	0.22
Going to a concert: never	−0.1	0.15
Going to a sports event: barely	−0.04	0.28
Going to a sports event: never	0.05	0.25
Working in the community or NGOs: barely	0.16**	0.00
Working in the community or NGOs: never	0.19**	0.00

Table 3.A2.7. **Logit simple, complete specification, 16-64 years old, 1994-98 (%)** *(cont.)*

	Estimated parameter	Probability > |T|
Countries (reference: United States):		
Australia	**0.67****	**0.00**
Belgium (Flanders)	**−0.68****	**0.00**
Canada	0.13	0.17
Chile	−0.97**	0.00
Czech Republic	**0.75****	**0.00**
Denmark	**1.54****	**0.00**
Finland	−2.59**	0.00
Germany	**−0.67****	**0.00**
Hungary	−0.67**	0.00
Ireland	**−0.84****	**0.00**
Italy	**0.04**	**0.74**
Netherlands	**−0.2**	**0.09**
New Zealand	**−1.01****	**0.00**
Norway	−0.68**	0.00
Poland	−0.06	0.50
Portugal	**−1.11****	**0.00**
Slovenia	**−15.91**	**0.89**
Sweden	−0.14	0.17
Switzerland	**−2.68****	**0.00**
United Kingdom	**−0.31****	**0.00**

Likelihood ratio test: 0.00.

*/**: The number in the right-hand side column is the error that one should accept to reject the assumption that the estimated parameter is nil, *i.e.* to accept that it is statistically significant. It is usually accepted that estimated parameters are significant when the error is below 5% (0.05) – these are flagged with * – and very significant when it is below 1% (0.01) – there are flagged with **.

The countries are listed in alphabetical order. The countries in bold are involved in the OECD study.

Source: International Adult Literacy Survey (2000), processed by the authors.

Table 3.A2.8. **Logit simple, three aggregated variables and gender, 16-64 years old, 1994-98 (%)**

Dependent variable: "towards a qualification" (Items 1-5 in question F5)	Estimated parameter (and probability > |T|)			
Explanatory variables:	Very highly literate (4 and 5)	High-level job (white collar highly skilled and high income)	Highly educated (ISCED 567)	Gender (male)
Australia	**0.2 (0.00)****	**−0.9 (0.00)****	**−0.0 (0.94)**	**0.21 (0.00)****
Belgium (Flanders)	0.2 (0.36)	−1.6 (0.02)*	−0.9 (0.00)**	−0.2 (0.44)
Canada	0.2 (0.09)	−1.3 (0.00)**	−0.3 (0.00)**	0.5 (0.00)**
Chile	0.0 (0.97)	−2.2 (0.00)**	0.2 (0.18)	−0.3 (0.03)*
Czech Republic	**−0.2 (0.22)**	**−0.3 (0.09)**	**−0.4 (0.02)***	**0.3 (0.05)***
Denmark	**0.5 (0.00)****	**−1.8 (0.00)****	**−0.05 (0.00)****	**−0.1 (0.40)**
Finland	1.1 (0.00)**	−1.3 (0.00)**	−1.2 (0.00)**	0.1 (0.36)
Germany	**0.3 (0.37)**	**–**	**−1.6 (0.02)***	**−0.4 (0.31)**
Hungary	0.1 (0.58)	−0.3 (0.27)	−0.4 (0.10)	0.2 (0.25)
Ireland	**−0.0 (0.77)**	**−1.4 (0.00)****	**0.23 (0.24)**	**0.4 (0.02)***
Italy	**0.2 (0.22)**	**−2.8 (0.00)****	**−1.6 (0.00)****	**−0.2 (0.20)**
Netherlands	**0.6 (0.00)****	**−1.3 (0.00)****	**−0.2 (0.20)**	**0.4 (0.01)****
New Zealand	**0.3 (0.02)***	**−1.1 (0.00)****	**−0.2 (0.15)**	**−0.1 (0.23)**
Norway	0.0 (0.87)	−2.3 (0.00)**	1.2 (0.00)**	−0.2 (0.10)
Poland	−0.4 (0.22)	−0.2 (0.42)	−0.5 (0.13)	0.58 (0.02)*
Portugal	**–**	**–**	**–**	**–**
Slovenia	**0.7 (0.00)****	**−1.4 (0.00)****	**−1.1 (0.00)****	**−0.3 (0.00)****
Sweden	0.4 (0.20)	–	0.2 (0.38)	−0.3 (0.32)
Switzerland	**0.5 (0.00)****	**−1.4 (0.00)****	**−0.1 (0.35)**	**0.4 (0.00)****
United Kingdom	**0.3 (0.00)****	**−1.3 (0.00)****	**0.3 (0.00)****	**0.0 (0.90)**
United States	−0.0 (0.76)	−1.2 (0.00)**	−0.3 (0.03)*	0.24 (0.06)

*/**: The number in brackets is the error that one should accept to reject the assumption that the estimated parameter is nil, i.e. to accept that it is statistically significant. It is usually accepted that estimated parameters are significant when the error is below 5% (0.05) – these are flagged with *, and very significant when it is below 1% (0.01) –these are flagged with **.

The countries are listed in alphabetical order. The countries in bold are involved in the OECD study.

Source: International Adult Literacy Survey (2000), processed by the authors.

ANNEX 3.A3

International Adult Literacy Survey (IALS) Background Questionnaire

This annex provides the phrasing of the questions from which variables were derived for use in this chapter. Although the IALS was operated in different countries with different languages and cultural backgrounds, all the background questionnaires are similar. (They are available from *www.oecd.org/edu/literacy*.) The questions about "adult education" – from which the two questions below are extracted – were asked of all the individuals that have had periods of adult education in the 12 months preceding the interview. A maximum of three periods is described.

Section F, on "adult education"

Question F1:

"During the past 12 months [...], did you receive any training or education including courses, private lessons, correspondence courses, workshops, on-the-job training, apprenticeship training, arts, crafts, recreation courses or any other training or education?"

Question F5:

"Were you taking this training or education towards... (*read category/mark only one*)

1. a university degree/diploma/certificate?

2. a college diploma/certificate?

3. a trade-vocational diploma/certificate?

4. an apprenticeship certificate?

5. an elementary or secondary school diploma?

6. professional or career upgrading?

7. other."

References

Eurostat (2002), *European Union Labour Force Survey*, Eurostat, Luxembourg.

INEGI (Instituto Nacional de Estadística, Geografía e Informática) (2001), Census of Mexico.

Korean Ministry of Education and Human Resources Development (2000), Lifelong Education Survey.

Korean National Statistical Office (2003), *Social Indicators in Korea*.

Miyamoto K. and P. Werquin (2006), "Measuring Participation in Adult Learning", Working Paper, OECD, Paris.

OECD (2000), *From Initial Education to Working Life: Making Transitions Work*, OECD, Paris.

OECD (2003), *Beyond Rhetoric: Adult Learning Policies and Practices*, OECD, Paris.

OECD (2004a), *Education at a Glance*, OECD, Paris.

OECD (2005a), *Promoting Adult Learning*, OECD, Paris.

OECD and Statistics Canada (1995), *Literacy, Economy and Society – Results of the First International Adult Literacy Survey (IALS)*, Ottawa and Paris.

OECD and Statistics Canada (2000), *Literacy in the Information Age – Final Report of the International Adult Literacy Survey*, Paris (*www.nald.ca/nls/ials/introduc.htm*).

OECD and Statistics Canada (2005), *Learning a Living – First Results from the Adult Literacy and Life Skills Survey (ALL)*, Ottawa and Paris, *www.oecd.org/dataoecd/44/7/34867438.pdf*.

QCA (Qualification and Curriculum Authority) (2004), *Achieving the Lisbon Goal: The Contribution of VET*, edited by T. Leney, London.

Statistics Canada (2002), *Adult Education and Training Survey*, Statistics Canada, Ottawa.

United States National Center for Education Statistics (2001), National Household Education Survey. Werquin P. (1999), "Youth Labour Market Entry in France" in *Preparing Youth for the 21st Century: The Transition from Education to the Labour Market*, OECD, Paris, pp. 265-288.

Werquin P. (1999), "Youth Labour Market Entry in France" in *Preparing Youth for the 21st Century: The Transition from Education to the Labour Market*, OECD, Paris, pp. 265-288.

ISBN 978-92-64-01367-4
Qualifications Systems
Bridges to Lifelong Learning
© OECD 2007

Chapter 4

The Interaction Between Stakeholders and Qualifications Systems: Identifying Mechanisms

It is important to understand how qualifications systems influence lifelong learning, so that incentives for learning are improved in – and disincentives removed from – policy responses. Chapter 3 presented quantitative data showing the impact of national systems, but also pointed to the shortfall of such evidence. In this chapter an attempt is made to overcome that shortfall and look at qualitative evidence closely. The evidence here is drawn from country background reports and published research. Examples from different countries are included (indented between double lines).

If lifelong learning is to develop further in countries, the patterns of behaviour of individuals, employers and learning and qualification providers will need to change. Qualifications may play a role in bringing about that change, and this chapter analyses how by reviewing empirical evidence and the relevant theoretical literature.

Section 4.1 describes the scope of the review of evidence. This is followed by an evaluation of the drivers of change influencing lifelong learning and the barriers that confront individuals (Section 4.2), employers (Section 4.3) and learning and qualification providers (Section 4.4). The evaluation generates 20 mechanisms that can be used to optimise the impact of lifelong learning policies; these are presented in Section 4.5.

4.1. Stakeholders and country context

Who are the stakeholders in lifelong learning?

Lifelong learning is an activity carried out by individuals; therefore the motivation and capacity of individuals to take up further learning as influenced by the qualifications system[1] are at the core of this analysis.[2] The OECD has adopted a "cradle-to-grave" concept of lifelong learning embracing all learning activity undertaken throughout life that aims to improve knowledge, skills and competences within a personal, civic, social and/or employment-related perspective. Another major group of stakeholders are employers: they are both suppliers of learning and users of qualifications as quality assurance of skills. Employing organisations of all sizes create the opportunity for employees to learn during the process of work, both formally through on-the-job training and informally through observing and engaging with other, more experienced employees as the day's problems arise. Providers of learning and qualifications are numerous and include, for example, schools, colleges, employment sector learning centres and awarding bodies as well as firms. These providers, by means of their learning prospectus and their firm grip on high-stakes qualifications embedded in popular and political values, have an influence on opportunities for lifelong learning.

The community – this could be a social group based on locality, culture, ethnicity or sector – is another important stakeholder identified in several country reports. It is difficult to conceive of communities as stakeholders in the same sense as individuals, employers or providers: they are not generally direct users of qualifications in the same way. They are much more diffuse as an entity than, for example, employers – consequently they do not lend themselves to analysis in the same way as other stakeholders. Inducements and constraints acting on communities are included in Section 4.2.

The arrangements for governance of qualifications systems vary widely among countries and include a range of bodies (including government departments, government agencies with more specific tasks, private institutions, qualification awarding bodies and bodies responsible for providing information, advice and guidance to others). This group of governing or managing bodies is an extremely important stakeholder and while not a user of qualifications, it can have a direct and powerful influence on the operation and direction of development of qualifications systems. This book is aimed principally at that group. It does not address their inducements and constraints in the same way it does those of direct users of qualifications, but Chapter 6 does point to ways they could bring about changes in qualifications systems that would lead to better lifelong learning.

The effects on those stakeholders

As stated in Chapter 1, qualifications systems influence these three main groups of stakeholders – individuals, employers, and providers of learning and qualifications – in many different ways, and it is the nature, scope and intensity of these influences that are the focus of this chapter. The systems can act as a motivator for people to learn, give employers the incentive to recognise and develop qualifications, and act as the means for providers of learning and qualifications to respond to need and operate efficiently. For example, gaining recognition for learning can lead individuals to financial rewards as well as enhanced self-esteem and improved life chances. Regulating entry to the labour market through qualifications can drive up the skills supply for employers and create a strong market for providers. Qualifications systems can also act as an obstacle: fear of failing to reach the required standard leads some people to resist participation in learning for qualification, while others may be unable to express their skills through any kind of existing assessment. There are costs involved in qualification and these may inhibit some people and employers from participation – and that will have a knock-on effect on providers. This and other evidence indicates that a qualifications system can both motivate and discourage participation in learning.

Lifelong learning can be improved by increasing its quantity, quality, distribution and efficiency. Qualifications systems can influence the quantity of lifelong learning by, for example:

- Maintaining transparency for users (increasing confidence by reducing uncertainty).
- Publicising rewards to individuals with qualifications (increasing confidence in investment).
- Raising the quality of provision (increasing confidence in investment).
- Improving the range and relevance of qualifications (meeting needs).
- Easing access to qualifications through flexible qualifications structures (overcoming systemic obstacles).
- Minimising the cost of qualifications (for all stakeholders, more can be afforded).
- Encouraging employers to use qualifications in workforce development programmes (raising currency and providing incentives).
- Responding to the needs of learners, including specific groups (removing barriers to learning).

Quality of provision can be influenced by qualifications systems through:

- Developing diverse quality assurance systems (that are each tailored to purpose).
- Regulating the content, delivery and assessment of programmes (establishing standards).
- Clarifying the outcome of learning (making requirements clear).
- Improving training provision for teachers (raising the quality of teaching).
- Evaluating stakeholder perception to ensure needs are being met (making available sensitive feedback).
- Involving stakeholders in qualification design (increasing ownership).
- Regulating access to the labour market through qualifications (raising the quality by defining standards that must be met).

Equitable distribution of lifelong learning is influenced by qualifications systems through:

- Removing barriers to provision for specific groups (easing access).
- Recognising non-formal and informal learning (easing access for people with diverse learning histories).
- Reducing constraints on flexible approaches to learning for qualification (overcoming environmental barriers).

- Focusing on outcomes of learning whenever possible (communicating the purpose of learning clearly).

Efficiency of lifelong learning, in terms of governance, is influenced by qualifications systems through:

- Developing a single co-ordinated system of qualifications (efficiency of scale).

- Maintaining a clear structure of qualifications (avoiding wasteful confusion and repetition).

- Ensuring assessment, accreditation and certification processes are fit for purpose (as they are consumers of time and money).

- Maintaining stability in the system (change is expensive in a national system).

There are many other factors that enhance lifelong learning. The foregoing analysis and all that follows is solely concerned with the effects of qualifications systems. However it is extremely difficult to draw a line where non-accredited learning stops and learning for qualifications begins; the threshold is interesting territory. If qualifications systems are to draw in more learners, they need to increasingly embrace informal and non-accredited learning; yet this type of learning may be attractive to learners precisely *because* there is no formal assessment.[3] In other words learning has certain attractions for people and recognising this learning through qualification and certification may not be regarded as wholly desirable. The analysis therefore includes discussion of unintended consequences of formal recognition of learning.

Country and community context matters

Before moving on to consider the more specific influences, it should be noted again that qualifications systems are not independent of the social, economic and cultural conditions in which they exist. For example, the condition of the labour market – with its demands regarding volume and structure of work – translates into job opportunities and the necessity to acquire higher skills and (thus) qualifications. Innovation and new technologies provide another example: technological development requires workforce skill development and updating of qualifications. Institutional regulations can also lead to demand for qualifications; an example is the requirement in some countries to undertake vocational training in order to be entitled to unemployment benefits. The degree of compression of the wage structure and the general rate of labour turnover influence the possible returns of training for employers and (in turn) opportunities for individuals to train. Together with cultural values, these factors influence anticipated costs and benefits of qualification and are likely to differ between communities in a country.

Understanding the main stakeholder groups

None of the three main stakeholder groups can be viewed as a single entity with clearly defined behaviour. The paragraphs that follow nevertheless attempt description, since these groups are integral to the analysis. Recognising the diversity within them, the discussion will signal where possible the different effects qualifications might have on sub-groups. It is also important to acknowledge from the outset that: i) the three main groups may not embrace all stakeholders and ii) that there is no tight boundary between these groups – for example, employers are made up of individuals and employers often provide learning.

Individuals cannot be treated as a single homogeneous group of users with common needs and resources to commit to learning. Diversity within populations is obviously vast, and it would be useful to identify the main dimensions of variation that might be important from a qualifications point of view. The needs of younger people aiming to make an investment for later rewards are different to those who are near the end of working life and looking forward to retirement. Younger people using the school system have a different set of opportunities than a previous generation who now have access to adult learning provision. Women and men can have their aspirations for learning tempered in different ways by social and cultural differences. For example, in some traditions men are still firmly expected to be the main wage earner, although in other societies even a period of childbearing does not now seriously hamper career development for women. We know from countless studies that individuals who have qualifications are much more likely to be looking for further learning than those who are not qualified and, as work is often an important place of learning, those in work clearly have better chances of participating in learning than the unemployed. Finally, learning is often associated with communities – and those who are firmly established within the network of a community will know of information and opportunity sources, and may well find it easier to access services than newcomers. Even within some strong communities the general disposition to learn for qualification can vary from the strongly antagonistic and disapproving to the firmly supportive and encouraging.

Employers come from a diverse group of organisations. It is simplistic to view them as managers, bosses and leaders; an employer has functions that cover recruitment, training, business efficiency and development, and these dimensions among others interact with qualifications systems. Employees as a group (rather than as individuals) have a function to develop the organisation to provide greater rewards and stability of employment. The organisation may have a not-for-profit status and this may influence the type of learning that is encouraged within the organisation. The learning-for-qualification ethos in small employers is likely to contrast with that in multinational companies. Employers also vary in the general level of skills required for the central function of the company – some firms involve low skills and low technology, others high skills and high technology. Training needs will vary greatly, as could qualifications use.

The term *providers* has always been a "catch-all" to cover diverse interests in making training available and furnishing some kind of quality assurance process for users. All formal learning institutions are included in this group (for example schools, colleges, adult learning centres and training departments in firms), together with organisations that manage assessment procedures, awarding processes and certifications. These bodies may be publicly funded, charities (non-profit) or private firms. Funding agencies can also be considered providers. Some institutions deliver training, certifications and quality assurance, while others may focus solely on delivery or quality assurance. In some cases sectoral (professional) bodies may carry out these functions. Increasingly, management and electronic communication are transforming this kind of work, which is influencing the institutional structure.

Financing lifelong learning

The broad analysis presented here may provide an opportunity for policy analysts to consider who pays for qualifications system development. Much of the literature on benefits accruing from education focuses on the returns to individuals in terms of higher incomes, less unemployment and other positive outcomes. This suggests that individuals should pay for qualifications. However, there is also evidence that employers benefit from a more highly educated workforce, which would indicate that *they* should meet the cost of qualifications. Further evidence shows that there are substantial public benefits from higher levels of education, including lower social benefit payments and lower costs for the health and justice systems, and that suggests that the state should pay. There is a vast amount of policy-related work in the area of financing lifelong learning (OECD, 2000a, 2001a) and clearly this impinges on the financing of qualifications systems. While financing policy is fundamentally about influencing behaviour of all types of stakeholders, in this study the issue of funding is restricted to considering the cost of the qualifications system, and returns on investment in learning for qualifications.

The concept of a mechanism

Chapter 1 suggests that there exist mechanisms that link qualifications systems and lifelong learning outcomes. There is evidence supporting the idea of mechanisms in country background reports, and in discussions country experts have confirmed the usefulness of the concept. However, all of this evidence needs to be confirmed by logical argument addressing how these mechanisms function in terms of changing behaviour.

Before elaborating that argument, it may be helpful to review the central concept. A mechanism can be understood as a combination of two elements, a structural change and a conditional change. The two, which can act independently of one another, help identify the likely positive and negative effects a mechanism might have when applied in a particular context. Structural changes to national qualifications system might include the modularisation of qualifications or the introduction of new type of qualification. Changes to the conditions in which the system operates could include, for example, demographic changes, labour market factors, economic policy or the quest for a stable and culturally rich society. One mechanism may work for or against the effects of another mechanism; these interactions are explored in Chapter 6, as is the effect of social and cultural conditions on the ways mechanisms work.

This chapter now considers the ways stakeholder groups interact with their qualifications system and identifies how behavioural changes might arise. For each group, some broad background research is considered before looking closely at inducements to learn and constraints that reduce the quantity, quality, distribution and efficiency of lifelong learning. Some issues are specific to certain stakeholder groups; these are examined so that they might be better understood as policy is formulated. The evidence is used to create a list of mechanisms, which makes up Section 4.5 of this chapter.

4.2. Motivating individuals to learn

In lifelong learning, the individual is the primary "unit of activity". Consequently, lifelong learning implies diversity and individuality in learning patterns.[4] Government bodies (for example schools, national and local agencies, funding bodies, career guidance services, labour market research organisations) support learning processes by supplying information, infrastructure and incentives that may shape or influence the behaviour of individuals, families, communities and companies. Employers may do this as well. However, all bodies do not control the learning processes of individuals. Learners may have competing aspirations not resembling those of government or employers, and that may lead to a distortion of goals as individuals decide how to utilise learning.

Economic approaches to lifelong learning tend to assume the disposition of individuals as stable, equal for all, and mainly based on money. Sociologists place emphasis on different and changing lifestyle preferences. Generally speaking, in taking decisions, individuals try to optimise the benefits that range from personalised non-pecuniary rewards through to highly instrumental utility considerations. The subjective perception of alternatives, restrictions and possible benefits is influenced by the values the individual holds. It is these subjective expectations that influence the decisions. This means that their perception of possible benefits connected to the award of the qualification is a decisive factor, and this is influenced by evaluation of the chances of success and the risk of failure.

Inducements to learn

The ways qualifications systems motivate[5] or discourage individuals to learn are possibly the most critical aspect of this analysis. It is a single person that, when all else is done, makes the decision to learn or not to learn. Research has shown that motivation to engage in learning can arise from the wish to progress in work or study; an interest in the content or subject matter and/or a desire for personal development and fulfilment. Possibly less obvious is the motivation that can arise following a critical incident (such as the closure of a workplace) or during life transitions (such as leaving the family home or becoming a parent). Also not to be underestimated are peer pressure and the wish to be accepted and valued by a group of learners.

In order to view qualification as having value, the individual needs to be aware of the fact that knowledge, skills and wider competences can be acquired during all kinds of activity, and that sometimes they already have knowledge, skills and competences that they have gained during their life. The individual must then be able to identify the benefits of having their learning recognised, for example for entry to vocational or higher education, or improved job prospects. One implication of this process for policy makers is to accord priority to promoting an understanding of the nature of lifelong and life-wide learning, and illustrating how the harnessing of this learning can contribute to education and training and employment outcomes.

In France, about 8% of adult learning programmes lead to a qualification; that would seem to indicate that there is little interest in the qualification component of adult learning programmes as opposed to the learning component itself. However, it is not possible to conclude that people are not interested in a qualification. The recognition of any kind of prior learning (VAE, *Validation des acquis de l'expérience*) is growing in popularity as many more people seek to have their learning recognised. This is evidence that the qualification component seems to be attractive, and that for a qualifications system to be conducive to learning, it should enable individuals to have any prior learning recognised. This argument is supported by comparison with the former VAP (*Validation des acquis professionnels*), which recognised prior job-related learning and contained a significant learning component (Chiousse and Werquin, 2005). The French experience with VAE shows that by taking the first step in recognising learning, more people can engage in learning, which could lead to further qualifications.

Currency and returns to qualification

Among the motivations to learn is the belief in what being qualified will bring, such as higher earnings, protection against unemployment, a better job, and non-pecuniary rewards such as higher standing in the community. There is also the possibility of fulfilment and well-being that arises when a personal target is reached; this can lead to a greater belief in oneself and one's capabilities. The extent to which any of these returns motivates a person depends on the circumstances of the individual (including their capacity to discover and understand the benefits of qualification) and the prevailing social, cultural and economic context in their locality. For example, a person who lives in a country where entry to the labour market is tightly regulated and who is at the transition point from school to work will be particularly interested in learning for getting a job and what that may lead to. Someone nearing the end of their working life in a good job will be motivated to learn more about a personal pastime and may only want to have their learning recognised for reasons of reaching a personal target, or to improve their standing within a circle of like-minded enthusiasts.

The "currency" of a qualification probably cannot mean the same as the "rate of return" to a qualification. Clearly the latter influences the former: higher wages for qualified workers will raise the status of a required qualification. However, the term currency is probably more commonly understood to have a closer links to the social and cultural context of a country or community. For example, a factor in raising currency is the knowledge that few people actually achieve the qualification (Béduwé and Planas, 2003). The wider the ownership of a qualification, the less value it has for each individual. Currency is high when recruiters demand a specific qualification or when communities believe that a qualification has the potential to improve a person's status. In summary, it is likely that for maximum currency a qualification should:

- have clearly communicated links to labour market rewards;
- be clear about what learning is recognised;
- be part of a progressive track where one qualification can lead to another;
- be part of the process for regulating entry into occupations;
- be constructed so as to have the potential to provide credits towards other qualifications;
- be supported by socially accepted rules or norms.

The timescale over which benefits accrue from qualification is an important factor. Short-term gains such as labour market entry through initial qualification can lead to long-term gains in remuneration and job security. Evidence shows that initial qualification is likely to lead to more learning and (thus) higher qualification and the attendant higher returns (QCA, 2004). It also shows that full-time employment outcomes achieved by those who complete a qualification are significantly better than for those without post-school qualifications (Ryan, 2002). This confirms the high currency of initial qualification during upper secondary education – these qualifications are crucial for future prospects, both in the short term (labour market entry) and in the long term (prospects for further qualification).

Microeconomic evidence from Denmark for the period 1993-2001 confirms a significant positive relationship between the number of years spent in education and income. Male returns are found to be 6.5% per year of education, which is approximately 1% more than the equivalent female returns. Calculations of the internal economic rates of return to the individual and society of different types of education show that in general there is a positive return. The private rate of return is between 5% and 39%, while the social rate of return is between 3% and 17%.[6]

In Switzerland, there is a clear wage premium to be earned when qualified: wages rise with the level, and there is a significant premium for tertiary qualification holders. Overall benefits increase with the level of qualification attained: they are objective (employability, wage, job status and long-term returns) and subjective (personal satisfaction, willingness to undertake more learning activities). The holders of tertiary degrees from the newly created *Hautes écoles spécialisées* seem to do better than others in terms of these multiple benefits.

From a regulation point of view, in France, since the 1970s, collective agreements and wage grids resulting from collective bargaining among industry organisations and trade unions rely on qualifications achieved before joining the company. On the other hand qualification achieved after joining the company does not necessarily lead to a better wage or a career upgrade. In Belgium, this approach seems to have a longer history; qualifications have been a major factor in the regulatory determination of wages since 1945.

United Kingdom evidence shows considerable returns to qualifications when gained in initial education and training (*i.e.* to the age of around 25), but very limited wage increase returns to qualifications gained by adults over that age. This lack of evident economic return spans all levels of qualification. The principal exception was for those adults who had gained no qualification at all during initial education. For them, qualifications gained later in life were important in terms of access to jobs and higher earnings – in these cases, "second chance" qualifications seemed to attract some benefits usually associated with initial education.

There is substantial evidence to confirm the human capital[7] argument that individuals are inclined to sacrifice current resources in order to invest in education and training for future labour market returns (OECD, 2001a).

Currency of qualifications and job mobility

Modern economies are in flux, a fact reflected in the changing types and sizes of enterprises and sectors and in working practices within organisations. Levels of worker mobility are now consequently higher; new working practices generate the need for new skills, which means that more training is required for those in work than previously. Evidence indicates an increased demand for qualifications (Grubb, 2004), whereas previously job learning came through formal and informal observation, trial and error and networking. This is now much more likely to take place in a formal learning environment and lead to official recognition, as for example in Denmark, Germany and the United Kingdom (van Ravens, 2002). People move voluntarily between jobs because they have become more highly qualified and want to capitalise on their learning by seeking higher returns and more stability. They also move for new learning experiences. They might leave jobs and re-enter the labour market for personal reasons, such as a change in career, to raise children, or a move to another region or country. Qualification is also a safety element during such transitions. For example, a person returning to work after staying at home to look after children will be carrying proof of competence in the form of qualification. A system that maintains qualifications with high currency will facilitate movement of people and support a developing economy by capitalising on learning gained through many routes.

Traditionally, the link between a person's identity and the firm they work for has been a strong one. In recent years this link has weakened. Certainly for professional workers, identity is associated more with their track record of working experience, sometimes in different firms. In other words, it is more individually determined according to a person's own life design. A consequence of this process is that reputation and working achievements have to be recorded externally to the firm, and this is where the link between qualifications and occupational mobility becomes interesting. German evidence indicates that for half the people who changed occupation, their position had considerably improved – the higher the level of qualification, the more successful the change. The change in occupation had a particularly positive effect if it was determined by individual choice; if it fulfilled a job wish; and if the change was backed by systematic preparation for the new occupation through further education and training (Hecker, 2000a).

Employability

Increasing mention is made of the notion of employability (EC, 2004a, b; OECD, 2003); this refers to readiness for work and competence to function within a work environment. It is a dimension that is well established in some qualifications systems, notably and obviously those including apprenticeship. Employability often includes generic skills such as communication skills, numeracy, team-working and general information and communication technologies competence, but it can also include work-related technical skills. The need for employability is felt most strongly by young people and the long-term unemployed; how can qualifications systems help? Clearly where they can, the motivation to learn is enhanced. In many countries (*e.g.* Scotland) initial qualifications are being transformed to deliver these generic skills and should develop higher employability – if, as public pronouncements indicate, employers seek them and this is communicated to those who need them. Japan stresses the difference between *skills in specific types of work* and *specialised vocational ability*; the latter can be applied to a wide range of work. Qualifications attesting to skills that are more broadly applicable could lead to wider opportunities for employment and higher value for the qualification. In another example of the value of breadth (and therefore employability), over three-quarters of employed Greek seamen undergoing training considered that its most important benefits were the acquisition of additional skills useful for the company itself, thus providing some job stability. An equally large proportion believed the acquisition of skills useful in the wider labour market was more important because it increased employability and job mobility.

Changing occupation is much less of a problem if the knowledge, skills and wider competences learned during training can also be put to use outside the occupation generally for which a person has trained. In the case of qualifications gained in the German dual system, it was found that if the change in occupation was within a more narrow field in an economic sector, then in almost all sectors 42% of those making a change were able to apply "a great deal" or "a fair amount" of the skills and knowledge learned during training to their new job (Hecker, 2000b). There is obviously value of generic knowledge, skills and wider competences for individuals and communicating the nature and potential value to people who wish to develop their employability may result in greater incentive to learn.

Increasing employability is also an objective of benefit systems for the unemployed in many countries. Typically, in order to qualify for extended unemployment benefit, individuals are encouraged to undertake vocational training that could lead to a qualification. This is the case in Australia, England (New Deal) and France (*Contrat d'adaptation ou de qualification*).

Several countries have given examples or statistics regarding the better employability of highly qualified people as opposed to low-qualified ones. In Belgium (Wallonia) in 1999, hiring prospects were much better for individuals with highly technical upper secondary qualifications or with short-term tertiary ones. However, almost a third of employers did not state a clear qualification level needed for hiring. In Switzerland, the unemployment rate is higher at lower qualification levels. In 2002, the overall unemployment rate was 2.9%. For those with no more than compulsory schooling, it was 4.5%; for tertiary degree holders, it was 2.2%.

In France, the Ministry of Labour stresses the notion of quality when designing a qualification. Employability is a clear concern in this process, and quality is viewed as a way of ensuring currency of qualifications in the labour market and possible progression in the education and training system. Notions such as visibility and portability are at the heart of the work carried out by five commissions in charge of creating or amending a vocational qualification.

Progression

One of the benefits people seek when they learn for qualification is that it puts them on the starting grid for another qualification that will itself yield benefits. Indeed the next qualification may be a personal goal and represent returns that are neither pecuniary nor job – related. This stepwise approach is becoming more explicit in qualifications systems, as seen in the development of national frameworks and other attempts to make systems transparent. In some countries the progressive nature of qualifications is a fundamental architectural element in new systems: sometimes qualifications are named in a sequence that signals an established common route.

Qualifications frameworks are a new international phenomenon (Young, 2003). The goals of national frameworks are challenging and wide-ranging. They focus on making progression (vertical and horizontal) clear, increasing flexibility in future qualification routes, facilitating credit transfer, extending recognition of some qualifications, clarifying linkages between qualifications, eliminating to the extent possible barriers to access, and providing some kind of quality assurance. A summary of the OECD Thematic Group's report on this phenomenon is included as Annex A. The report provides full details of how frameworks aim to facilitate progression from one qualification to another. New proposals within the Danish and English systems offer the individual student lifelong multiple horizontal and vertical pathways at all qualification levels, through credit transfer mechanisms and recognition of prior learning, regardless of context. In each of these countries an ambitious and integrated national framework for clarification and assessment of competences has been prepared and is being considered for implementation. The blueprint for the new national framework of qualifications in Ireland includes specific policies and strategies to improve access, transfer and – a key element – progression for learners.

While clear progression tracks are likely to motivate learners to seek qualification, people's preferences change over time; during a lifetime new opportunities develop and new demands emerge. A person might be motivated to set out on a long programme leading to qualification but, for a variety of reasons, the programme may itself become a disincentive to learning as time passes. Thus there is the likelihood that flexibility within qualifications systems, such as stepping off points or opportunities to specialise, can maintain motivation. This flexibility may be particularly important to people at the early stages of building a career since opportunities and constraints are likely to be more common as they grow into a work environment. Older people also need to feel they can learn for a qualification in a manner sufficiently flexible to be accommodated within current routines. This situation has been recognised in Germany (as well as in other European countries following the Bologna Process), where university provision is geared primarily to young people below the age of 30. Dual study courses designed for working adults, which have shorter learning programmes and recognise vocational learning achievements, are not common. However, the introduction of defined cycles (or levels) within which qualifications reside may provide additional incentive to take up a new, successive course of study. Short programmes within a cycle allow qualification requirements to be met more flexibly, while potentially offering more vocational orientation; thus they facilitate new interdisciplinary links and the pursuit of studies while in employment.

In Denmark the latest amendments to Reform 2000 and the other adult education and training reforms will increase options for obtaining a qualification recognised in the labour market. Qualifications are expressed as one level within a broader overarching qualification with multiple levels. An example is Information and Communication Technology support, a recognised qualification in the labour market. It is also a step towards the qualification *Datafagtekniker* (Data technician). This offers the individual increased options for re-entering the educational system at a later stage as an adult, either in adult vocational training or in the further education system for adults to obtain a higher level of qualification.

In French-speaking Belgium, Bruxelles-Formation and the Walloon Bureau for Vocational Training and Employment (FOREM), public bodies in charge of adult vocational training, deliver training programmes to unemployed people and offer guidance before, during and after the training spell (information and counselling). These programmes are oriented toward the labour market (supply, demand and firms' needs) and are free. Their aim is to ease the transition to employment of jobless people. More broadly, there is clear evidence in Belgium (Wallonia – Brussels) that some qualifications more often lead to additional qualification(s). For instance, in the 7th vocational grade, it is possible to obtain an upper secondary qualification (*CESS, certificat d'enseignement secondaire supérieur*) that allows for entering the tertiary non-university system (after a 6th vocational grade that is).

In Switzerland, recent developments have led to better vertical bridging and more frequent opportunities for progression within the education system for individuals engaged in vocational tracks. Examples include the creation of the vocational *matura* (*maturité professionnelle*) at the end of upper secondary education and the creation of the Universities of applied sciences.

Similarly in France the creation of the vocational baccalaureate (*baccalauréat professionnel*) in the mid-eighties is probably the major reform carried out over the last

30 years in order to facilitate upward progression of individuals engaged in vocational tracks. Those holding a vocational baccalaureate, like those who have the general baccalaureate, have direct access to tertiary education.

There is however evidence (Raffe, Howieson and Tinklin, 2005) that while a "climbing frame" of qualifications can be designed, not all learners progress without difficulty. Failure rates are high even though weaker learners can join the frame at an appropriate level and climb at their own speed. It is likely that this is at least partly due to the assessment methods used in certain qualifications.

Learning programmes and assessment

The outcome of a qualification is not the only factor that can determine motivation to learn. The internal structure of learning programmes and assessment practices are also important. Students with different backgrounds have different forms of "cultural capital", reflected to greater and lesser extents in qualifications. The constructs of knowledge used in qualifications and rewarded in assessment systems favour certain forms of learning, such as abstract conceptualisation compared to concrete experience or active experimentation (Kolb, 1984). Furthermore, they favour certain forms of intelligence, notably logical-mathematical intelligence compared with bodily-kinaesthetic intelligence (Gardner, 1993).

Learners take a positive view of modular learning programmes – which, while they may not always meet learning needs, do match learning habits. (For example, learners are given some scope for self-organisation in the learning process). Modularised curricula enable the education provider to respond quickly to changes in job requirements due to new technologies or caused by the restructuring of work organisation in companies (Steinhäuser, 2002). The fact that people have preferred learning styles is well documented (Kolb, 1984), and it is clear that if a programme is not structured according to their preferred learning style, people will fear underachievement. The dimensions of choice are numerous and include what is to be learned, how it is to be learned, with whom it is to be learned, where it is to be learned and the time frame for learning, including the pace and sequence of learning episodes. Each of these dimensions can be subdivided further and a landscape of enormous variation can develop. This is, however, the learner view, and learning providers have to develop programmes that are manageable. Thus the match between learner preferences and institutional offering becomes an influence on motivation. In Switzerland, all *matura* schools have now introduced a new curriculum: learners have a role in fashioning their programme by choosing among many optional courses.

The method of evaluation or assessment of learning that is employed can have a particularly powerful influence on the motivation to learn for a qualification. A fear of failure and frustration can sometimes arise from a sense of knowing and being able to do things that cannot be recognised through some assessment regimes. In Germany one of the factors likely to discourage pupils from going on to the upper secondary level with the aim of achieving the *Abitur* is the performance-based entrance requirements. In Greece, Second Chance Schools aim to re-engage learners; a combination of a personal portfolio and systematic monitoring of student performance is meant to identify gaps in learning at an individual level. The monitoring involves a written assessment that is suspected of being a serious deterrent to participation in second chance schooling. Research evidence supports this suspicion; in response, the active involvement of tutors and learners in feedback processes is known to improve retention and raise achievement (Black and William, 1999; Torrance and Coultas, 2004). Learners across all sectors prefer coursework assessment and practical competence assessment to final exams. But coursework and practical assessments are not without problems: both can lead to bureaucratic processes for students and tutors especially when assessment outcomes are used for third parties for quality assurance processes and accountability of institutions.

One of the issues for assessment models is the extent to which they can recognise the breadth of desirable characteristics developed in individuals. For example, in Japan the ability of the individual worker can be seen as consisting of the following three elements: i) latent specific knowledge and skills that are necessary for performing work; ii) co-operativeness, positiveness, and other attributes when performing work; and iii) latent personal attributes such as motivation, personality, temperament, beliefs and values. This range of qualities is extremely difficult to assess effectively and efficiently. One of the tools the Japanese are exploring is an initial diagnostic stage of self-assessment and simulations for complex skills that are difficult to assess in other ways.

At the post-school level the major challenge has been to develop qualifications that meet the needs of the full range of types of learners. Evidence of increased individual demand for vocational education and training in Australia suggests that the flexible nature of vocational qualifications and their assessments has increased demand from individuals and employers for vocational education and training. Vocational qualifications are now recognised nationally and are clearer about outcomes. In some countries the goal of flexibility has resulted in the central control of the system being eased, possibly at the cost of coherence at the national level. There is a balance to be struck between tailoring provision to a range of learners and maintaining a system that looks and works in a coherent fashion.

In Germany the state has traditionally organised (in some detail) the acquisition of qualifications in schools and higher education institutions. There is a correlation between, on the one hand, age and level of qualification and training and, on the other, the degree of independence and individual responsibility granted to learners to determine what, how and where they learn. Opportunities are now available for various groups of learners to exercise more self-determination and personal responsibility. Grammar school students are allowed a degree of choice of courses and examination subjects in relation to their age and level of education. Learners at full-time vocational schools can choose between different learning paths, ranging from prevocational training, basic training and the achievement of a vocational qualification, to the achievement of a double qualification. In recent years, the structuring of training under the dual system in compulsory and optional units has also increased the freedom of the individual to decide what he or she would like to learn. However, the question of which optional units are actually available also depends on the individual training company. On the whole, these measures offer greater flexibility and are thus appropriate for encouraging learners to assume more personal responsibility and self-determination in the process of lifelong learning. Nevertheless, the aim remains the achievement of full qualification as proof of the individual's ability to study and/or take up skilled employment.

The United Kingdom National Vocational Qualification system is comprised entirely of modules; this is true also of the *Open College Network* system of validated courses and the Scottish *Higher Still* structure. Experiences differ, however. While in Scotland it is common for people to undertake an aggregation of modules without undertaking the particular combinations laid down in standard qualifications (called grouped awards), in England it would seem that fewer than 20% of those taking National Vocational Qualifications do so to gain units without full qualification; often this is because they have had to cut short their studies for reasons beyond their control.

Portability of qualifications is a key issue for motivating users and it is highlighted in the OECD publication on improving the financing of lifelong learning (OECD, 2001a). Cross-sectoral recognition of qualifications is seen as crucial in this optimisation process. In order to achieve portability, it is suggested that the knowledge skills and competences embodied in qualifications as learning outcomes need to be explicit and clear to recruiters. In some countries (*e.g.* Denmark) the system of recording credits or partial qualification is seen as a positive step towards cross-sectoral recognition of achieved qualification.

France has had different experiences of improving portability of qualifications. Those delivered by some employment sectors have limited currency (CQP, *Certificat de qualification professionnelle*). On the other hand, practices resulting from the new law on the recognition of prior learning (VAE) are a good example of where inter-institutional co-operation can lead. In this latter case, wage earners can have access to qualifications that are portable throughout three different institutions: the Ministry of Education, the Ministry of Labour and the Commerce and Distribution Industry. The experiment was piloted in two regions in 2002 with the aim of developing a tool for bridging (*passerelle*) qualifications. New information and communication technologies have been intensively used and a fourth partner, the Ministry of Agriculture, was involved for a subsequent experiment in 2003. The whole experience seems to be a success, but the main conclusion is that without a sound analysis of what each individual can do, it is not possible to create bridges between qualifications.

Some learning is gained through experience and non-formal means. It is interesting to note the motivations people have for wanting this learning to be formally recognised. Although there is much evidence arising from learner surveys about reasons for learning, it is more difficult to find evidence related to the desire for qualification (Chapter 3). This is the subject of a new OECD study.

The fact that countries are taking steps to ease the influence of formal assessment may signal that demand for qualification, as opposed to learning, is less important for some people. In Australia practitioners have been reluctant to introduce award-based qualifications for reasons of cost and because the formal assessment requirements might act as a deterrent to learners who lack confidence and have had bad experiences with formal learning. Nevertheless, as the sector has grown, some states have introduced new qualifications designed to provide re-entry routes into education pathways or progression routes. One recent example is the Certificate of Tertiary Education introduced in Victoria, Australia, in 1999. Its pilot phase indicated a high level of articulation into subsequent types of education and training.

In Ireland, Kelly (1994) surveyed the learning provision and qualifications needs of adult learners in non-formal, community-based situations. She found that some adults who had left formal schooling with no qualifications valued highly any kind of qualification, however informal. Other people in the community may also value qualifications, so that the learner is consulted in the decision making process in the community. Therefore they experience support and gain affirmation from other learners and from tutors. Examining the factors that lead non-formal learners to seek qualifications, she found that a high proportion does so for reasons of quality/credibility, as against progression opportunities (21%) and jobseeking (32%).

In summary, while evidence shows that assessment for qualification, especially by more formal means, might be a deterrent to learning. However, for the more confident learners, assessment can have positive effects in terms of building up and sustaining self-esteem and self-confidence, spurring participants on to further learning (Schuller *et al.*, 2002).

Shortening the transition from initial education and training to working life

For people leaving schooling and entering work there is a well-documented period (QCA, 2002; OECD, 2000b) during which motivation is volatile. Self-doubt, poor knowledge of options and personal and social factors make decision making for the longer term difficult and commitment unreliable. For some people, the relevance of some learning programmes is at odds with immediate personal needs. Thus a time of instability develops when people need learning to satisfy both pecuniary and non-pecuniary ambitions. Effective support and provision of well-communicated options are likely to shorten this period of instability and provide some individuals with the confidence to commit to learning, possibly for qualification.

In Switzerland, there is evidence that individuals' qualification(s) impact on the school-to-work transition. In short, the higher the qualification the faster the transition into employment will take place after leaving the initial education and training system (Buchmann and Sacchi, 1998). In addition, the job obtained (status, wage) is more influenced by the type of qualification(s) held than by the number of years of schooling.

In France, surveys carried out on the school-to-work transition by the *Centre d'études et de recherche sur les qualifications*, Céreq, signal that an individual who has failed to obtain a qualification, even if they reached the final examination, has lower employability. The transition from school to work is much easier for those who have a qualification. It is even the case that in terms of labour market performance, the gap between those who hold and do not hold qualification(s) is widening.

Personal fulfilment and the wider perspective

The immediacy of personal development, financial rewards and high self-esteem in motivating people to learn for qualification is well established; however there may be much wider social goals that encourage individuals to learn even if it does not lead to a qualification. For example, people may see learning as offering themselves and others a sense of inclusion and engagement in the development of society, leading to healthier lifestyles, lower propensity to commit crimes, higher levels of trust, richer social networks, and greater levels of participation in volunteer organisations and democratic institutions. In a longitudinal study of the social benefits of higher education, Bynner and Egerton (2001) showed that graduates (as opposed to people with ISCED level 3 qualifications) were more likely to be:

- In managerial jobs.
- Protected from unemployment.
- Involved in further learning.
- Assessing themselves as healthy in body and mind.
- Safe from accidents.
- Parents of children with no educational problems.
- More likely to be involved in civic activities.
- More likely to be egalitarian and have faith in the political process.

This represents a clear series of wider benefits. What is still to be confirmed is the precise way higher education qualifications lead to these benefits.

Research with older learners (aged 50-71) identifies a wide range of motivations to learn, of which only two have a direct bearing on qualifications as a motivational factor (Dench and Regan, 2000). Whilst almost all the people surveyed accepted that "you need qualifications to get anywhere these days", it is clear that also qualifications play a role in achieving a personal goal.

Constraints to learning

Certain constraints on learning could be lessened through the qualifications system. These constraints include psychological reactions to and attitudinal positions about learning, the flow of information and advice and its complexity, lack of time, costs, and lack of physical support facilities such as transport or a crèche. Mechanisms need to deal with these constraints if lifelong learning is to be enhanced. A useful and comprehensive review of barriers to learning (although not specifically learning for qualification) is presented by Rick, Valckenborgh and Baert (2003) in their work on "learning climates".

Early experiences of learning

There is extremely strong evidence that if a person has not successfully embarked on learning for qualifications soon after leaving compulsory education, they are not likely to do so later. It seems that people form negative views of formal learning through their initial experiences of school, and these are resistant to change. It is difficult to resolve from the evidence whether the negative attitudes are held towards institutionalised formal learning, to assessment of learning, or to both.

> In Australia, recent analysis of factors influencing participation in further education and training, using data from household surveys, reported that irrespective of the type of study or training there was a higher probability of participation for those with higher levels of prior educational attainment. Participation in study leading to a qualification was 27% for those whose highest educational attainment was upper secondary education, compared to 60% for those who held a postgraduate qualification.

Research into the independent effects of qualifications suggests that the risk of unemployment is substantially lower for those who obtain post-school education and training qualifications. In a study of the effects for individuals of different qualifications,

Ryan (2002) found that full-time employment outcomes achieved by those who complete a qualification are significantly better than those of persons without post-school qualifications. Throughout the world, countries have been attempting to break down these constraints on early achievement. Some of the more promising approaches are described in the next section.

Psychological barriers

Some individuals, particularly those with low self-esteem, may not recognise the potential value of the knowledge, skills and wider competences they have gained through non-formal and informal learning. People with low formal educational attainment are sometimes fearful of reliving what for them had been a negative and painful experience (Bryce, 2004). Individuals may feel that assessment for qualification is likely to focus on a lack of competences; fear of further failure is a disincentive.

A survey undertaken by Australian National Training Authority (ANTA, 2000) under its National Marketing Strategy for Skills and Lifelong Learning found that about 22% of Australians appear to face strong attitudinal barriers to learning. They have usually not undertaken any study or training for some time and have often achieved the level of learning they need for their current job or see no reason for further learning. Some in this group do not see education and training as relevant to themselves. Others do not see a need for learning. Most lack confidence in their own learning abilities and therefore do not participate. Among the non-participants, many are early school leavers and formed negative views of formal study and learning through their initial experiences of school or further study.

Cost

It is likely that for some people, costs also limit participation in learning. These costs go beyond the fees needed to pay for courses, assessment and the award of a qualification; they include the time that needs to be set aside and the impact that has on lifestyle. There are also opportunity costs associated with time demands, since it is possible that learning will take the place of earning in the short term.

In Sweden, education throughout the national school system, from pre-school to university, is free of charge for the individual. In conjunction with a well-developed study support system, this means that many people have reduced financial constraints to study. The study support system is the most common way of financing adult studies. It consists of two parts, a grant and a loan, and together they cover living expenses during full-time studies. Study support is generalised in the sense that everyone learning for the same study duration and pace receives the same amount of money regardless of age, family situation or place of residence. Additionally, all employees in Sweden have the legal right to leave of absence to study as long as they have been employed for at least six months with one employer. Employees themselves determine the kind of education in which they will participate. The employer has the right to postpone granting leave of absence for a maximum of six months. Employees have the right to return to work when they wish.

Co-financing strategies include those that reduce the risk to individuals of investing in learning through shared investment. One example is the tertiary tuition loan model, where repayment is income dependent. This was first introduced in Australia in 1989 as the higher education contribution scheme. Under the scheme, students are entitled to take a loan to cover tuition fees. They are liable for repayment in the form of a 3% tax on income once their income reaches a threshold (approx EUR 14 000 in 2002/3). Thus, while the expected average returns for a tertiary qualification may be substantial, under the scheme the government assumes the risk for those individuals whose postgraduate earnings prove exceptionally low. In 2002 the government extended the logic of income-contingent repayment loans to enhance lifelong learning by establishing the Postgraduate Education Loans Scheme.

Subsidy to individuals is one way to reduce cost, but there are other possibilities based on more flexible provision leading to shorter periods of learning. These include approaches such as assessment of prior learning and more flexible modes of delivery (for example, modularisation), which are seen as a means to greater efficiency. These possibilities merit further consideration as ways of improving the benefit-to-cost ratio and thus helping resolve financing issues.

It is difficult to estimate the proportion of people who are put off learning because of cost. A survey in Germany revealed that of all those eligible for higher education, 8% gave cost as the reason for their decision not to choose higher education courses.

Students who accept financial responsibility and continue with their studies and endure financial hardship may be more motivated to look for high quality in their learning provision. In New Zealand, students pay a significant amount of their course costs (which range from 0% to 70%, average about 30%), and consequently some feel the need to express concerns about the quality of the education they receive.

Formal qualification does not always lend added value to learning. The cost (and perceived bureaucracy) involved in accreditation of learning that is not greatly valued in external markets may deter potential learners. Decisions about whether and how to accredit learning need to take into account the balance to be struck between the benefits of practical external recognition and the additional costs and constraints on learning. It is likely that different degrees of rigour in accreditation will be appropriate to different types of learning, and to different groups of learners.

While significant amounts of vocational learning take place through paid work, it is increasingly common for learners to be workers and for these two activities to be entirely separate. Full-time learners are often part-time workers, in an effort to fund studies.

Information flow

It is unlikely that detailed information regarding long-term benefits arising from specific qualifications is communicated to potential learners. They are far more likely to receive a rather general message of the value or currency associated with types of qualification. The latter is important, but more people might be inclined to study for qualification if the rates of return were better communicated. However, there is a view that details of actual returns to qualification is a second-order problem when information about qualification needs of recruiters for specific occupations is not communicated well, even to those who might be interested in working in occupations where recruitment is difficult. The problems that need to be solved have to do with the availability of accurate information about qualification needs, the returns to qualification and their accurate communication, and the availability of advisory services (OECD, 2003). Sometimes the careers advisory services themselves have training requirements, and when these are not met they hinder effective work (OECD, 2004). In Japan the provision of vocational information and career guidance is an important part of the development of a labour market that is independent of large corporations – interestingly the two dimensions, information and counselling, are considered separate systems.

In a review of information, advice and guidance services in Europe (EC, 2004a), it was concluded that their role, quality and co-ordination should be strengthened so that they support learning at all ages and in a range of settings, so as to empower citizens to manage their learning and work better. The report also stated that due account should be taken of individual requirements and the needs of the different target groups.

In French-speaking Belgium, Bruxelles-Formation and the Walloon Bureau for Vocational Training and Employment (FOREM) – public bodies in charge of adult vocational training – place a great deal of emphasis on information and guidance. Among their missions, two are of particular importance in this regard: 1) interfacing between the education, vocational training and employment worlds; and 2) providing information and guidance to learners and potential learners (with priority clearly given to unemployed people). Several countries have mentioned the particular situation of vocational training, held in low esteem except for high-level technical training. In Belgium there are many attempts to raise the attractiveness of vocational qualifications and the corresponding programmes. One of them has been to communicate their benefit more often and more positively, and this is certainly a way forward even if it is believed that much remains to be done to change this perception.

Flexibility matters

Already highlighted above is the desire individuals have for flexible delivery of learning. A study of how flexibility in vocational education and training is conceptualised across 31 European countries revealed that it is a "fluffy" concept; there is no consensus on meaning (QCA, 2004). Modularisation is reported as the most common policy to enhance flexibility – nearly all European countries are developing modularised curricula. A few countries are increasing flexibility by establishing national qualifications frameworks and credit transfer systems (including the award of partial qualifications) that together can contribute to better horizontal and vertical progression routes through vocational education and training systems. The realisation of an individualised pathway through these systems is less common.

Recognition of non-formal and informal learning (see the summary of the thematic group's report at Annex A) is an issue on the policy agenda of nearly all countries. Currently the lack of systems for recognition is possibly constraining motivation to learn, since individuals thus lack a qualification that would signal respect for their learning (and therefore identity). Such systems also offer the possibility of exemption from some learning requirements and so reduce the cost involved.

In April 2004, the Flemish government approved a decree concerning formal recognition of non-formal and informal learning related to work experience. This decree focuses on validating meaningful, profession-related competences obtained in daily experience inside and/or outside the workplace. Individuals can step into a recognition procedure and

---

obtain a "certificate for work experience". The decree grants formal recognition to people who can prove they have the skills and knowledge needed for a particular occupation.

Following the European developments on the structure of bachelor's and master's degrees for higher education, the Flemish government installed the Decree on Flexible Learning (April 2004). This means that higher education institutions can grant exemptions within certain study programme units and even grant a degree if the outcome of assessment concludes that the competences are indeed held by the applicant.

In most countries there are very few qualifications available that require short periods of learning and have limited numbers of learning outcomes. Where these "small" qualifications exist they seldom have any significant national currency. In a lifelong learning context, more such awards will be needed to provide recognition for the variety of learning achievements likely to be involved in a diverse range of qualifications. Obviously, it should be possible to amalgamate "small" qualifications into "bigger" ones – at which point we see the value of accumulation of credit. Awareness of the potential of "small" qualifications to encourage learners is possibly the reason for so many countries expressing interest in credit systems.

In France, the action plan "learning differently" (*Se former autrement*) specifically focuses on preparing people to enter the knowledge society, through reform of vocational training. One aspect of this plan is delivered by the Division for Employment and Vocational Training (DGEFP) of the Ministry of Labour in the form of a module of initiation to the Internet. It lasts 14 hours on average and focuses on navigation, communication and information gathering. It leads to a certificate from the Ministry of Labour; the aim is to have as many individuals as possible entering education and training programmes, especially those sent by the main adult learning organisation (AFPA) or the public employment service (ANPE). Since the module's introduction in October 2002, 150 000 unemployed people have received this certificate.

Credit transfer processes offer flexibility by allowing individuals to have learning recognised when programmes are only partially completed, and enabling them to gain exemption from future learning by being able to "cash in" their credits upon enrolment in new programmes. Experience of working national credit systems appears to be limited to New Zealand, Scotland and Sweden, with firm plans in place in other parts of the United Kingdom. However, the European Commission has a substantial programme under way to provide the infrastructure for a European system for credit transfer (EC, 2004b) for vocational education and training (ECVET) that will synchronise with the European Credit Transfer System (ECTS) already operating in some higher education institutions in Europe.

While qualifications frameworks, recognition systems for non-formal and informal learning and credit transfer systems are becoming recognised as having the potential to support lifelong learning, they need more widespread practical application if greater flexibility is to develop.

Motivating individuals to learn – some issues

The literature on lifelong learning makes it clear that economic advantage allows other benefits to be afforded. An issue arises from this: there may be a mismatch in the way qualifications systems are developed for economic purposes on the one hand and the advantage of individuals on the other. Clearly though, any development of the economy is likely to be of advantage to a country's population. The issue centres on the diversity of needs and interests of individuals, and the much more limited and focused needs of a country's economy. For example, investing in the development of qualified information technology specialists might not serve the best interests of individuals who need to raise their levels of basic literacy.

Using economic argument to increase learning often involves devolving responsibility for learning to individuals, since they will be the beneficiaries. One of the approaches used is to move away from state-designed and state-funded provision and to place responsibility on individuals to pay for their professional development. The effectiveness and equitable nature of this policy depend on the availability of the required provision, so that the individual can exercise the responsibility they have (Billett, 2001). Thus funding probably needs to be shifted to supporting individuals when sufficient learning opportunities are available.

Inequality is resilient

Creating equality of opportunity does not guarantee equity in terms of who takes advantage of that opportunity. There are consistent findings within and between countries that the distribution of learning – in the form of qualifications – is strongly related to measures of social inclusion (Bynner and Parsons, 2001). Deeply embedded trends underlie social groups' use of provision. The groups identified as resistant to learning for qualification are adult learners; people with disabilities; learners from socio-economically disadvantaged backgrounds, more particularly those living in disadvantaged communities or remote districts, members of minority ethnic groups including travellers and refugees. Many factors combine to bring about under-participation by these groups, including availability of financial support, the level of supply of learning provision and community values. It is difficult to identify here the part played by the qualifications system in promoting or inhibiting access to learning. In some countries policy has established equal opportunity for men and women; however, qualification outcomes remain better for men and are the most acute at lower levels, although there are signs that this pattern is reversing (Murray and Steedman, 1999).

In Switzerland, many disparities between the genders still exist. Nevertheless it seems that the gap in terms of achievement and progression in the qualifications system is closing, except perhaps for the very high levels, still dominated by men: only 45% of university qualifications go to women and the proportion is even lower for doctorates (34%). Women are largely outnumbered in terms of vocational qualifications and almost absent in *Hautes écoles spécialisées*, the recently created highly performing university vocational system.

Higher aggregate individual participation does not necessarily signal equal access among these disadvantaged groups.

In Australia, groups have very low access. For example, in 2001 only 1.2% of domestic students were from an indigenous background, although indigenous people constitute around 2.7% of the population aged 15-64. Students from the lowest socio-economic status quartile of residential locations represent only about 15% of total enrolments – a proportion unchanged over the past decade (though absolute numbers have risen over this period in line with the overall increase in student numbers). Regional differences in participation are also marked; these often intersect with indigenous status and/or low socio-economic background.

Monitoring is necessary

There are many national and international surveys of skill needs and learning provision. Responding to individuals' needs by making qualifications fit for purpose typically requires acting on knowledge of those needs, as well as ambitions and constraints, individuals feel. Strategic actions can only be taken if information sensitive to personal attitude changes towards learning for qualification is collected and analysed. That raises issues about the status, sensitivity, style and capacity of monitoring and evaluation exercises countries use. An effective monitoring system will signal where a shift of policy and resources might be advantageous.

Belgium (Wallonia-Brussels) and France have in common the job directory (ROME, *Répertoire opérationnel des métiers*) that lists and describes all the existing jobs. This monitoring, updated continually, can be seen as a possible way to motivate employers to fund qualifications and use them.

Governance of qualifications systems

In many country reports the qualifications system is described as a top-down, centrally controlled provision that varies considerably in the way social partners use it. The question arises as to what extent regionalisation and greater involvement on the part of key stakeholders would enhance lifelong learning. In many countries, control of the qualifications system is being adjusted to meet policy objectives. For instance, Switzerland has prepared and adopted a new Law on Professional Education. Its aims include widening access to qualifications and progression paths for individuals, as well as changing accreditation and awarding processes, in order to enhance flexibility and so meet the future demand for skills. In Ireland legislation is the basis for a major reform of the qualifications system, including new centralised structures for the design and maintenance of the system and a streamlining of the range of bodies empowered to award qualifications.

The evidence indicates that qualifications frameworks are increasingly used as a policy tool. The report from Thematic Group 1 (Annex A) makes clear that there are many perceived benefits to government of producing a central declaration of qualification types and the linkages between them in the form of a framework. These advantages include increased transparency and flexibility, higher participation rates and increased mobility of learners. However, Young (2003) also identifies qualifications frameworks as instruments of accountability for educational institutions and a basis for international comparisons of national systems. In some countries the national qualifications framework is a tool for regulation and quality assurance; admission to the framework is a prize for qualification providers. This use of the frameworks may reinforce central control over provision and restrict the expansion of individualisation and regionalisation. Thematic Group 3 (Annex A) also identifies the tendency for governments to retain tight control over framework development while acknowledging the gains to be made by involving a wide range of stakeholders.

Over-qualification

There is growing concern in research and policy as to whether and to what extent workers are overqualified for their job and whether or not a "skills gap" exists between skill profiles and job requirements (Tessaring, 1999). Reports from several European countries indicate that a considerable share of workers cannot fully utilise their skills at work and are thus regarded as overeducated or overqualified. These findings question the pressure some qualifications systems apply to increase learning for qualification. They instead suggest systems focus more on recognising and using knowledge, skills and wider competences that already exist in individuals. Of course, young people who have acquired high and broad skills may have been better trained than is necessary to perform a first job, and they may feel themselves overqualified during their first working years. However the training they have received will probably prepare them better for coping with future and unpredictable job demands and for occupational mobility.

There is evidence of increased over-qualification in Switzerland. When comparing a cohort of young people who entered in the labour market in the early 1980s and another one that did so ten years earlier, it seems that the latter received less benefits than the former, when qualification is kept equal. The explanation could come from a slow depreciation of qualifications with the overall improvement of the levels of qualification attained.

Summary of inducements and ways of overcoming barriers to learning for individuals

The purpose of this chapter is to identify mechanisms that link qualifications systems with lifelong learning. The following summary points are provided to show how the evidence above on inducements and barriers to learning by individuals lead to the mechanisms listed in Table 4.1.

Individuals will be more likely to learn if the qualifications system:

- Enables progress in jobs.
- Enables progress in learning programmes.
- Allows prior learning to be recognised.
- Provides a degree of choice within qualifications.
- Makes explicit good returns to qualifications.
- Makes explicit good currency for qualifications.
- Provides numerous routes to the qualification of choice.
- Includes the opportunity to carry forward credits for another qualification.
- Ensures that qualifications are portable to new settings.
- Includes qualifications that are a condition for labour market entry.
- Includes qualifications that recognise competences that make individuals more employable.
- Includes tracks or frameworks of qualifications.
- Ensures that the content of qualifications is transparent.
- Promotes modern pedagogies and structures of programmes.

- Ensures adult learning is different in style from initial education.
- Promotes effective assessment methods.
- Makes available good and accessible advice on decisions about qualifications.
- Is cost effective (money, time and opportunity).
- Is based on flexible programmes (size, time commitment, credit based).
- Includes well co-ordinated qualifications management.
- Includes opportunities for feedback on experience of qualification value.

4.3. Encouraging employers to use and support learning

The idea of qualification is extremely important to employers. It signals what employers seek in terms of skills supply, and it is a means of filtering the supply of skills itself so that they get what they want during recruitment. The latter is possible if qualifications provide reliable signals as to the likely productivity of the qualified worker (Spence, 1973). Both these processes have been described in the sequence: employment/labour market → qualifications system → learners. However it is also possible that the qualifications system allows people to develop the skills that employers come to value.

It is important to recognise that even in highly regulated labour markets there are few hard rules to describe the interaction between qualification and the needs of employers (Béduwé and Planas, 2003). The idea that people learn relevant knowledge, skills and wider competences over a certain period of time and that this "qualification" then prepares them for entry to a job is a social construct. It is a kind of standard that helps the learner, communities, employers and learning providers make sense of the fuzzy relationship between qualification and the labour market. The expectations of all the partners of the "standard" represented by qualification must be met most of the time, otherwise this system would collapse. Evidence in country background reports suggests that the trend recently has been to further strengthen the notion of qualification standards in the minds of all partners.

In Spain, after the passing of the Act 5/2002, the management of continuing training subsystem has been modified in order to adapt training to the qualifications framework (diplomas or certificates) and establish a new funding model with the aim of simplifying and accelerating the administration procedures, thus facilitating the involvement of small and medium enterprises.

The needs of employers – even needs based on an aggregate of all employers – are not the same as those of the economy. The former are likely to be immediate and generated by modernising work practices and changing trading conditions. Many of these needs will be short term in nature, as the driving forces behind them have themselves been generated in the short term. The needs of the economy, on the other hand, will be influenced by the longer-term goals of maintaining an infrastructure that continues to generate a foundation of skills supply and satisfying broad national social and economic policy, as well as responding to changes in trading conditions. Part of the infrastructure of the economy is the network of learning providers, which requires steering during periods of growth and contraction and therefore requires a longer-term view of priorities. Since competency requirements seem to evolve very quickly, it has become difficult to anticipate the future needs of the labour market, even in the short run. It becomes especially difficult when considering any change to the qualifications system, since updating the national registers and describing all the qualifications – and sometimes a framework of qualifications – takes time. The situation is therefore complicated because three different processes coexist in the labour market: the training process, the qualifying process and the production process. (The latter is defined as the time a qualified individual takes to become a productive worker.)

In many countries the supply of skills (i.e. the number of people entering the labour market at their varying levels of qualification) is set to become an issue. A demographic downturn is expected in the next generation and the level of completion of upper secondary education seems to be reaching a plateau (Béduwé and Planas, 2003). This will mean that in some countries employers will be seeking to recruit from a shrinking pool of qualified people. The role of employers in enhancing lifelong learning is therefore likely to become increasingly pertinent.

The OECD's large-scale study of adult learning (2003) highlighted the role of the employer as provider of professional upgrading. While this survey did not focus specifically on learning for qualification, it did point out the extent of unmet demand for learning among workers. Taken with other, more general evidence of the rise in the need for qualification as described above, this could indicate an unmet demand for qualification.

Inducements to use and support qualifications systems

Involvement in qualifications development

One of the pressures that could induce employers to make more use of qualifications and provide more resources for learning toward qualification is their direct involvement in qualifications development. There is a full report on the rationale and the issues involved in stakeholder involvement in the report of Thematic Group 3 (Annex A). Here, some further issues are raised that relate particularly to steps in involving employers more fully.

Employers already play key roles in qualification development and management. These range from being the lead partner in initiation of new qualifications to intervening strongly when it comes to the issue of the reliability/validity of awarding processes. Often, central agencies appoint employers (including employee representatives) to head committees governing the qualifications system or some of its features. There are many examples.

In French-speaking Belgium, the Community Qualification and Occupations Committee (*Commission communautaire des professions et des qualifications – CCPQ*) aims at raising the profile of technical and vocational training programmes. The idea is to check the match between the qualifying training and (current and future) occupational needs. This requires that adjustments be made, and in order to do so a legislative framework for the worlds of work and education to meet was created to foster partnerships in the establishment of "training profiles".

In Germany, the social partners and the federal government work closely together in the development and adaptation of qualifications offered in the dual system of vocational training. Representatives of employers, unions, the federal government and the *Länder* work together within the Board of the Federal Institute for Vocational Training (BIBB). Qualifications are developed through a procedure approved by all the parties. Both the interests of the sector-based associations and the umbrella organisations of industry are co-ordinated, and the basic syllabuses for the part-time vocational schools are aligned in terms of schedules and programmes with the regulations for in-company training.

In Denmark, there is tripartite co-operation between government, employers and employees. These social partners decide on the aims, content, duration and final status of the individual programmes. Within the framework of this distribution of tasks and authority, which is laid down by law, programme development and innovation take place with tripartite consensus. This co-operation ensures that the education and training effort appears unified to individuals, colleges, employers and administrative authorities. It is also intended to ensure coherence between education and employment possibilities. In accommodating education and training policy, qualification requirements of the labour market, and individual skills and needs, the co-operation ensures programme relevance and quality.

Until 1992 the social partners did not play any role in developing vocational training in Greece. The state was the main actor for planning and implementing vocational training and education measures. In 1998 it became involved in the administrative boards of organisations involved in doing the planning. In Ireland, the social partners are key stakeholders in the process of developing a national framework of qualifications, and their involvement carries legal status. Both the employers' and trade unions' national organisations make nominations to the memberships of the Qualifications Authority and each of the Awards Councils. Employers and unions are also involved in some aspects of structuring the qualifications system, particularly in the development and monitoring of apprenticeships. Many employers are involved at programme level in local partnerships with providers of education or training.

In Korea, the roles of industry, including the labour unions, in the qualifications system are minimal. Demands are growing for more active participation in the establishment of new qualifications and the elimination of old qualifications and testing procedures. This limited role is due to the fact that economic development has been the outcome of a rapid process of government-led industrialisation; human resource development was initiated by the government.

In New Zealand, employers are key participants in Industry Training Organisations (ITO), helping to build industry ownership of training and training infrastructure. New legislation requires these bodies to develop arrangements for the collective representation of employees in the governance of the ITO.

In Australia, the vocational education and training system has undergone a decade of continuous reform that has used industry leadership. The system now consists of mainly industry-developed and -validated qualifications, which provide for nationally recognised competences.

In Slovenia, ties between national qualifications and the employment system have been strengthened by the participation of employer and employee representatives in all phases of the development of qualifications; this should guarantee their relevance for the labour market, with no need for additional recognition procedures by social partners.

In France, vocational training competence is shared among four partners: the state, employee representatives, occupational sectors and employers. Qualifications are defined by *Commissions professionnelles consultatives*; employers are represented in these *Commissions* (committees), together with the other social partners. Employers are also involved in the definition of some curricula, such as for the "*Licence professionnelle*", and the delivery of some part of the training in that they provide placements for learners. Some sectors have created certificates called CQP (*Certificat de qualification professionnelle*). Employers are involved in a jury for examining applicants' achievements for recognition as formal qualifications, such as the mainstream vocational education and training qualifications, the vocational baccalaureate (*Baccalauréat professionnel*) and the two-year technician degree (*Brevet de Technicien Supérieur* – BTS).

In Japan, the legal status of social partners has been incorporated in a process wherein the government determines the level of skill and associated knowledge needed in order to pass each grade for each trade, and ensures consistency in the technical levels required. In doing so, it consults expert reviewers. Test criteria are updated and test questions prepared by experts on technical matters who are recommended by co-operating organisations in industry and appointed by the Japan Vocational Ability Development Association.

In Spain, the regulation and co-ordination of the National Qualifications and Vocational Training System as a task of the General State Administration is done through the General Council of Vocational Training. The Council is a consultative body for institutional participation by the public Administrations, General State and Autonomous Communities and social partners.

In Switzerland, professional associations (often social partners together) are developing qualifications of the vocational education and training system in addition to their role as providers of qualifications in advanced vocational education and training.

In the United Kingdom, a Skills for Business Network has been developed that, through its various employment-related partners, has a central role in developing and maintaining national occupational standards and therefore in influencing the qualifications that flow from these standards. The newly formed Sector Skills Councils have a key role in skills-need analysis for sectors and in forming a range of qualifications that meet these needs.

Having established that there are substantial returns to employers for providing training, Billett and Smith (2003) suggest that involvement with qualification development is a productive way of persuading employers to invest more in employee development.

Raising employer demand for qualifications

Employers are more likely to focus on qualifications during recruitment, and more likely to invest in qualification-related training, if qualifications offer value for money in recognising workplace competence and the potential to work at specific levels in employment. Employer surveys generally reveal the desire for the system to be responsive to their needs in terms of the content of qualifications and the administrative arrangements necessary to validate learning. They pinpoint the key quality of relevance to their working practices, and the need for confidence that recruits or trainees with certain qualifications will consistently prove themselves as capable workers. This confidence takes time to establish and at least partly explains why employers' views of qualifications development can be rather conservative.

Returns to qualifications for employers have been consistently strong (OECD, 2001b). Most evidence suggests that returns to general or academic qualifications tend to be better than to vocational qualifications, although this is by no means clear-cut. The nature of the signalling function is much debated and varies across countries, regions and types of qualifications and their related labour markets. Nevertheless, where there is reliable evidence of strong returns to employers, for example in certain sectors or at certain qualification levels, that needs to be communicated to employers and their representative organisations.

In a Belgian (Wallonia) survey of employers, a preference in terms of level of qualification is expressed in 70% of the cases. A similar United Kingdom survey of employers produced the same result and it was apparent that there had been a significant rise in employers' qualifications requirements, particularly at degree level. In the United Kingdom survey there was also limited evidence of credential inflation – employers would demand a qualification level from job candidates, but the qualification would not actually be necessary to carry out the job in question (see over-qualification above). This applied to around 30% of jobs that required qualifications. The figure of 70% of qualifications-based recruitment is further confirmed in a German survey of training managers in small, medium-sized and large companies. Seventy-seven per cent of them are of the opinion that successful participation in company-based continuing education and training measures should be validated. Sixty-seven per cent of them believed that it should also be possible to certify the skills that staff acquired as part of their work (Grunewald and Morall, 2001).

This suggests that both recruitment and training have a firm basis for using qualification. It also indicates that for employers this is not a one-way street but a two-way process – the discovery of skills development in employment has revealed skills that need to be recognised, which in turn has repercussions on the design of the qualifications system itself. The French experience is important here: professional organisations of employers are often at the origin of a new qualification, or making a case for modernising an existing one. This kind of intervention might arise from a demand for a special skill or from the need to adjust the level of qualification demand. Sometimes large employers require a qualification to serve their own purposes.

In Japan the greatest area of concern is how to eliminate mismatches between labour supply and demand. (The issue of needs analysis is discussed later, but here the focus is on getting employers to use qualification as a tool for skills development.) Building a system to evaluate workers' vocational ability as a social framework is expected to play an important role in facilitating labour mobility (as well as eliminating mismatches) and the role of trade skill tests has consequently increased. Though implemented on a limited scale at present, these tests play an important role in stabilising employment, facilitating re-employment, and improving the social status of workers. Nonetheless it is not the case that a high proportion of employers regard a pass in a trade skill test as a judgmental factor in recruitment processes, however they are a factor in judging the employee's motivation or ability to meet challenges, rather than a benchmark for judging vocational ability.

Although the majority of Australian employers agree that people qualifying after vocational education and training do possess the skills appropriate to employers' needs, employers indicated some lack of clarity in what a qualification tells them. In 2001, about three in four employers with recently qualified employees said that it is difficult to tell what a person can actually do from their vocational education and training qualifications (NCVER, 2001). This was a larger percentage than two years earlier, when only 68% of employers held this view. It suggests that some Australian employers do not view qualifications as a reliable source of information.

Jobholders, as opposed to employers, offer a different perspective about what qualifications are needed for their jobs (Felstead, Gallie and Green, 2002): while 29% of United Kingdom jobholders, for example, thought that qualifications were important, that factor was considerably outweighed by experience (49%) and motivation (35%).

The demand for an in-firm qualifications system is growing, especially in very large international companies. In countries such as Korea, the means to acquisition of skills required in work is not readily available to potential recruits; the process needs to take place within the companies. The Korean Ministry of Labour has been providing budget support to employers who have excellent in-firm qualifications systems in place. Some large Slovenian firms and services have started to develop their own systems of qualifications, competences and training delivery. However, these qualifications usually supplement national qualifications. In such cases national qualifications are what mainly serve as an indicator of "trainability" of newly hired workers. In New Zealand, McDonald's offers employees training that can lead to certificates and diplomas registered within the national qualifications framework, rather than offering its own qualifications. One reason for its doing so is the role of McDonald's as a "first employer" that needs to offer training that will be recognised within New Zealand by future employers of its current staff.

Increasingly, employers are using qualification as a means of meeting regulatory requirements that protect the consumer or worker; here, qualifications are an assurance that firms have fulfilled their obligations (Selby *et al.*, 2004). Large firms are becoming in effect regulators of a sub-contracted labour force. Previously they were contracting out, but held accountable by customers for the quality of the work that they managed. Thus they needed a system for licensing those who worked on their projects, even though they did not have direct-line management control. Qualifications are an obvious way of doing this. Employers who feel they need to guarantee the quality of the work of sub-contractors therefore have an added interest in making sure the demand for learning for qualifications is maintained.

Eliminating the gap between qualifications and skills needs

A major concern for many countries is understanding the future needs of the labour market. Good management of the qualifications system is certainly an instrument for upskilling of the labour force. Workers' competences have also become a key asset of employers who rely on human capital more than any other input to maintain high added value and productivity.

The role of qualifications as an indicator of potential for learning is confirmed in research: employers see qualification as a kind of guarantee of a worker's greater and faster adaptability to changing work practices (Béduwé and Planas, 2003). The changing demand for competences reflects wider changes, such as the opening up of the world market, the international mobility of workers, the globalisation of trades, the worldwide use of the new information and communication technologies, and the pervasiveness of the knowledge economy/society. What kind of qualification is desirable in this changing labour market? Will high-level general education qualification become more desirable at the expense of qualification in highly specific technical skills? In Germany the forecast is that, despite the already high proportion of skilled workers in the working population, global demand for employees with vocational education and training qualifications will rise further. Demand for highly qualified employees in the service industry has risen considerably; unemployment among skilled workers with vocational qualifications in these occupations is lower than in manufacturing jobs.

In Denmark, the outsourcing of functions to other countries, relocation of knowledge-intensive international firms within the country, technological advances, sector convergence, emerging new markets and customer preferences have driven developments in education and training. For example, in the electronics industries and the high end of the textiles industry, there are examples of new models of supply and strategic partnerships. These build on networking using a one-stop-shop principle, with close school-firm and inter-firm local collaboration. Education and training are commonly understood by providers to be part of the broader context of innovation and institutional specialisation; providers take a less institutional approach to education and training. On the supply side, education and training providers respond to the demand for qualifications that contribute to increased productivity and product and process innovation. They have contributed to local and/or sectoral economic growth or restructuring, firm re-localisation and net job creation within sectors that are under heavy global competitive pressure.

In Australia, some large-scale reforms have attempted to improve the match between qualifications and employers' skill needs. For example, the introduction of national training packages to meet current and emerging skill requirements is a development aimed at ensuring that vocational qualifications are industry-based, and assessment is geared more towards skills and knowledge acquired under workplace conditions. Another example is the inclusion of generic skills and competences in the frameworks underpinning the senior secondary certificate (upper secondary level) in most states and territories.

National surveys of employers of vocational education and training graduates (1995, 1997, 1999 and 2001) provide information on employers' views on levels of satisfaction with the skills of vocational education and training graduates (NCVER, 2001). The proportion of employers who viewed the system as providing graduates with skills appropriate to employers' needs increased by about 13% between 1995 and 1999 (to 70%). Employers' overall satisfaction with the quality of people with qualifications has remained stable since 1997, with around four out of five satisfied. Compared with 1995, a larger proportion of employers in 2001 agreed or strongly agreed that the vocational education and training system is providing qualified people with skills appropriate to their needs. The proportion who agreed or strongly agreed that training pays for itself through increased productivity has remained stable.

This high level of satisfaction is not evident in Korea. There, the view is that what is taught through the vocational training curriculum is not what is required in the workplace; consequently, the training offered at education institutes or schools is the subject of great dissatisfaction on the part of industries, causing the latter to turn their back on qualifications. One of the reasons vocational training falls below par in quality is that there is an absence of co-operation between education institutes or schools and onsite workplaces, between the central government and regional governments, and among the relevant government ministries. The problem is compounded because the competitive environment itself acts as a disincentive to co-operation.

Several studies have noted the shortage of specific vocational skills in the Irish workforce; some also note that this shortage has not been corrected by in-work training programmes (O'Connell and Lyons, 1995). Irish employers use various means to identify gaps or emerging trends, at both national and local levels. For example, at national level the Expert Group on Future Skill Needs undertakes periodic studies of the Irish labour market. Its third report (2001) investigated the employment and training needs of the construction industry 2001-06; it recommends that the number of apprenticeships be increased, and suggests accelerating the training of some apprentices. The Expert Group attempts to quantify skills needs in terms of both occupation and qualification level. It is notable that the new Standards Based Apprenticeship followed an analysis of future skill needs, and that trade employers are directly involved in the monitoring and ongoing development of this qualification to ensure its continued relevance to the particular labour market sectors concerned.

The emphasis on initial recruitment of generalists by employers in Ireland has resulted in a considerable participation in programmes that lead to "add-on" qualifications. For example, the Master of Business Administration and other business-oriented qualifications are often acquired by non-specialists recruited into management levels of organisations, and specialist graduates (such as engineers) who were recruited as specialists but have been promoted into management or organisational development positions. In Portugal the increasing demand for middle management is a result of emerging forms of employer organisation where the demand for a higher production specialisation relies on qualified workers at middle management level. The priority accorded the middle management qualification may be considered a strategic measure within a modernisation process deemed necessary for the competitiveness and development of the national economy.

Easing recruitment processes

Employer use of qualifications in recruitment is under-researched and little substantive literature exists. The general message from small-scale studies is that qualifications are used primarily as a screening mechanism prior to interview. This is particularly the case for the recruitment of first entrants to the labour market. If qualifications were perfectly matched to the needs of employers and future skills needs were identified systematically, employers would increasingly use qualification in recruitment and, in so doing, could increase the demand for learning for qualification. There are three points of interest to employers here: i) can the quality of the qualification be relied upon; ii) does the qualification title make clear the content and level of knowledge, skills and competences involved; and iii) are there enough potential recruits with the qualification for it to be used as a sifting mechanism?

An important issue is the amount of detail employers need in qualifications for purposes of recruitment. In New Zealand the National Certificate of Educational Achievement is intended to provide learners and employees with more information about what a person has actually learned from education. The qualification provides a fuller picture of achievement by reporting it against national standards. Some employers avoid being too restrictive in defining qualification requirements: they ask for alternative levels of the same qualification, where the lower level can be compensated by greater work experience. Qualification is also often defined fairly broadly in recruitment literature, for example "higher education in an appropriate subject". This provides employers with enough room for considering additional criteria when hiring new workers. There is an assumption that certain services (above all financial and business) regard tertiary level qualifications as an indicator of general skills and abilities while field-specific qualifications are developed on-the-job or in specially designed training organised by the employer.

Some qualifications, especially those linked with secondary education, do not set out to recognise work-specific skills and competences but concentrate on broad and transferable occupational skills. Naturally these qualifications are open to the criticism from employers that they are not relevant to the workplace, as young people are not capable of applying knowledge obtained from school in practical circumstances. In countries where this is the case (e.g. Slovenia, the United Kingdom), employers usually require some form of work experience in addition to formal qualification.

In some countries there are legal requirements to use qualification in recruitment. In Slovenia, competent employment sector bodies are legally obliged to define the qualification requirements to pursue these jobs. Qualification requirements are defined in terms of levels and fields of formal education. However, employers are not obliged to stick to the existing national qualification structure. In France, having a qualification is key to successful recruitment because it is held in very high esteem. In heavily regulated labour markets, such as those based on qualification through dual systems, the recruitment process is dominated by the information arising from the qualification process. The vocational education and training qualification in Germany leads to three complementary certificates: the examination certificate from the relevant chamber of commerce; the certificate from the vocational school; and the training certificate awarded by the company. A survey (BIBB, 1998) found that almost all companies in Germany rate the training certificates awarded by companies as "very important" or "fairly important", second only to the job interview. Almost all companies agree that this certificate provides the most information as far as specialised knowledge, practical skills, care and precision in work, and comprehension of the occupation are concerned. Other information sources, such as grades in the final examination at the chamber, were far less frequently rated as "very important". The examination certificate awarded by the chambers provides information about learning ability with regard to more theoretical questions and about intellectual skills rather than about proficiency in the occupation. Accordingly, only 23% of the companies in the surveys agreed with the statement, "The examination certificate provides valuable information about proficiency in the occupation".

Keating et al. (2004) report that employers' understanding of (and reliance on) qualifications is relatively subjective. The secondary role of qualifications after work experience in selection is thought not to be about lack of trust in qualifications; rather, it is related to employers' view of what better prepares recruits, together with the high value placed on reducing risk. Most employers acknowledge that qualifications signal greater potential for learning and skills acquisition, but they see them as weaker signals for more immediate competence because of the limited learning experiences for which they testify.

Evidence suggests a need to build on the screening role of qualifications and on their role as indicators of potential for learning and skills acquisition. Were employers to view them as cogent indicators, they would use them more systematically, which would act as an incentive for learning for qualification.

Portability of qualifications and fluidity of the labour market

Job mobility and, to a lesser extent, geographical mobility seem to be an issue in many of the countries involved in the OECD study. From an employer perspective, the opportunity of having employees move from one company site to another can be useful. Notwithstanding social, cultural and linguistic considerations, qualifications could make this process easier. The qualification in question must be transparent in terms of the knowledge skills and competences to which it attests and, as stated above, this may be a serious limitation. However, even if such transparent qualifications were available in every national system, there would still be the problem of equating national qualifications from different countries. Some international companies have developed qualifications that can be regarded as international (organisations such as Microsoft, Cisco, Novell, and 3 Com). Likewise, many international bodies offer accreditation and certification services for specific occupational needs. An international market for qualification and learning has been developing for some years in higher education. Indications are that this type of international business in qualifications will continue to expand.

There is an international framework of education and training (OECD, 1999) that offers the possibility of matching national qualifications from different countries. However, it is formulated around generalised statements about programme design and sequencing rather than qualification. The system is especially poor for comparing vocational education and training qualifications. Countries in the European Union have embarked on developing a qualifications framework for Europe (EC, 2005), explicitly designed to cover vocational education and training as well as higher education qualifications. The endeavour builds directly on the Bologna Process, which brings some international transparency to university qualification levels. A specific and detailed analysis of qualifications frameworks and levels was commissioned by CEDEFOP (Coles and Oates, 2004) in order to define reference levels for facilitating transfer of information from one national system to another.

Besides full qualification, there is an opportunity to bring about more learning if partial qualifications are recognised in other countries. An employer would be able to move people with specific skills in their own company workforce abroad and consequently would be raising the currency and support for partial qualification. The CEDEFOP reference level study was directly linked to a vocational credit transfer system being developed by the European Commission. This system is geared to enabling people with learning achieved in one country receive qualification in another. Many countries (*e.g.* Belgium [Flemish Community], Denmark, New Zealand, the United Kingdom, and Sweden) have developed or are exploring the development of credit transfer systems; these will be useful for employers in terms of not only managing deployment of their workforce but also increasing flexibility in other ways, such as recognising training episodes and making it easier to modernise qualifications incrementally. In Denmark a system of credits for partial qualification is used to forge a link between initial vocational education and training, and continuing vocational training.

Collective agreements

Some countries report the use of qualification as part of the collective bargaining process linking wages to work levels. That connection can be a strong influence on the ways employers use and sponsor the development of qualification, and consequently on the demand for learning for qualification.

Greece has a system of payments directly linked to qualification level, from school-based qualification through to doctorates. Slovenia has arranged jobs/posts into nine wage-related categories, ranging from simple jobs to jobs requiring the employee to hold a doctoral degree. This kind of linkage between qualification and wages may bring increased relevance and efficiencies. However, in countries where there is no such link, it will be argued that it increases the bureaucracy and costs of a process that needs to be flexible, adaptable and cost-effective at all times. Employers can nonetheless benefit from being involved in such schemes, and that involvement raises the interest of employers in qualifications.

Monitoring the system

From the employer point of view, interaction with the qualifications system is likely to be dynamic. The processes of expansion, contraction, modernisation, cost-cutting, relocation, merging with other companies, human resource development, recruitment, remuneration and many others can have an effect on and be influenced by qualifications. This dynamic interaction demands a monitoring system sensitive to trends in employers' use of qualifications and their desire to see new elements of qualification.

Many countries regularly conduct specific employer and labour force surveys; international organisations also monitor employer views (CVTS, Eurostat). However, these services are for the most part weak in dealing with changes in demand for qualification. In some cases data on qualification are not compatible with useful information from other surveys (EC, 2004a).

Some countries have the tradition of the *Observatory*, where experts from different interest areas join together to commission and review research into (*inter alia*) the employer/qualification interface. In Portugal the OEVA (Observatory of Entries into the Working Life) is a mechanism for permanent observation of the transition from school to work. The mechanism provides detailed and updated information on the relationship between training and employment and continuing education.

As Smyth *et al.* (2001) have pointed out, monitoring of education and training systems has not yielded comparable transnational data on the point of transition from school to work.

Constraints on using the qualifications system

Constraining influences – the barriers to raising employer expectations of qualifications – include perceptions of poor matching of existing qualifications with employer needs, and the consequential effects of low currency and credibility for employers. One of the possible reasons for these perceptions is the inevitable tension between the management of an education system for social purposes such as citizenship education and health education, and more explicit employment-related functions. A further tension arises for qualifications systems when the needs of employers become firm-specific and the interests of individuals and communities are inevitably wider and longer term. The diversity of needs of both employers and individuals can lead to complexity in the form and types of qualifications available – and this is itself a constraint.

Costs of supporting qualification

Most obviously, costs can constrain the involvement of employers in qualification development. Billet and Smith (2003) discuss the motivations for employers to invest in training (not specifically learning for qualification) and conclude that the motivations are mostly subject to cost/benefit analyses that yield mixed results in terms of providing incentives. However, quoting the research of Smith (2001), they stress that better methods of appraising returns to companies need to be used; when they are used, returns are impressively high – which could lead employers to contribute more willingly. (See Wolter and Schweri [2003] for some evidence from Switzerland). Switzerland has an ongoing programme of special initiatives to encourage the enterprises to offer apprenticeship places to young people. These are backed by legal arrangements put in place in 1996 and 1999.

Smaller employers have a basic resource constraint on becoming involved in qualifications development. The Belgian and Slovenian reports signal that larger companies are much more likely than small ones to become involved in a range of labour market, employment and qualification-related activities.

Research in Slovenia, however, indicates that funds of employers are by far the most important source of direct financing of participation in training. Employers finance 65% of employee training while individual employees themselves cover about 25% of the costs. According to these data the share of training financed by employers is increasing with the size of the employers. In organisations with up to 20 employees, the employer funds approximately 50% of the training of the employed, and in large organisations (500 and more employees) about 80%.

One of the main ways companies contribute to qualification development is through direct involvement in training. These schemes are subject to fluctuations typical of HRD and recruitments needs.

In Denmark an analysis carried out in 2003 seems to indicate that the reduction in overall number of apprenticeship places is a reflection of company changes. International takeovers seem to have a negative effect on companies' willingness to take in apprentices. Other types of in-firm training schemes, both for social or re-employment purposes and for raising educational levels, also seem to have a negative effect, as do major organisational changes and outsourcing from the public sector to the private sector; conditions concerning apprenticeship places do not seem to be a part of the outsourcing contracts made with private firms.

The OECD study on adult learning (OECD, 2003) concludes that employers, while serious contributors to learning provision, are sometimes buying high-level skills though consultancy rather than investing in the long-term development of skills through training.

Encouraging employers to use and support learning: some issues

Credential inflation

If lifelong learning policies meet with real success, a high proportion of the population could be qualified to high standards and investment in learning considered a good risk by many people. That situation would have implications for a qualifications system. For example, where qualifications operate in a free market, their currency can be derived from more than, say, a good match with recruiters' requirements. The relative value of a qualification can depend on the availability of people with that qualification. An abundance of such people will devalue the qualification, and a shortage will raise its currency. Over-qualification, sometimes known as "credential inflation", is a phenomenon witnessed when many people seek to be recruited with the same qualification. Recruiters begin to raise qualification requirements in order to make the recruitment process manageable, while acknowledging implicitly that the higher level skills are not likely to feature in the work expected of the person eventually hired. Several countries, including Australia, Belgium (Wallonia – Brussels), France and Korea, raise the issue of credential inflation. For example, the Australian report states that the high levels of school retention reached in the late 1980s and maintained (after some decline) over the next decade occurred during labour market change and industry restructuring that weakened the employment value of the senior secondary certificate. Many school leavers obtained jobs for which they would have been regarded as overqualified in earlier years (Teese and Polesel, 2003).

Korea has attempted to measure the effect of over-qualification. One study shows how well educational background and skills levels are aligned with current jobs. The results reveal that workers receive more education than their current jobs require.

The Australian report also points out that credential inflation can reflect upward shifts in the required skill levels and competences associated with economic and technological change. One of the ways to deal with this issue has been to develop a national framework for recognition of competences acquired in different learning settings, to ensure transferability of learning. This creation of national standards for occupations is becoming a more common activity across countries. Once the framework is developed, all qualifications can be mapped against these standards and any further credential inflation can be understood independently of the employers' demand for higher skills.

Summary of inducements and ways of overcoming barriers to learning for employers

The purpose of this chapter is to identify mechanisms that link qualifications systems with lifelong learning. The following summary points are provided to show how the evidence above on inducements and barriers for employers to use qualifications leads to the mechanisms summarised in Table 4.1.

Employers will be more likely to use and support a qualifications system that:

- Facilitates the recruitment process.
- Refers to standards that are clearly understood by learners and providers.
- Includes qualifications that are up-to-date and recognise the skills needed in the economy and enterprises.
- Makes explicit competences developed in qualifications.
- Inspires confidence that qualifications will support the modernisation of work practices.
- Makes explicit the level of return for investing in training and qualifications.
- Encourages employers to be involved in the design of qualifications and the management of the qualifications system.
- Includes qualifications that are quality-assured and -regulated.
- Includes a well understood framework.
- Includes qualifications that combine technical competences with general employability competences.
- Includes qualifications that are comparable to others and enable mobility of employees from one location to another.
- Permits partial qualification or modular systems that enable more precise coverage of workplace skills.
- Includes clear and reliable links with collective bargaining and wage scales.
- Monitors skill needs in enterprises.
- Is less costly to maintain.
- Ensures that pedagogies are modern and efficient.

4.4. The qualifications system and the role of learning and qualifications providers

From the discussion above of changes in the behaviour of individuals and employers, one can conclude that providers are considering ways to widen their client base. This means finding ways to engage new types of learners and responding to the need to develop more efficient and effective education and training methods to deliver to employers the qualified people they seek. Whether private or publicly funded, providers are probably working to meet these needs with little extra in terms of financial support. Provision is changing accordingly; the spectrum of learning includes all different forms – organised, virtual and workplace, as well as non-formal learning. In addition to organisation, providers fill a wide range of functions that include assessment. These functions cover the following three processes:

- Recording of existing knowledge, skills and competences – the process of personal identification of the competences obtained previously.

- Validation of knowledge, skills and competences – the formal process linking existing achievements to predetermined standards based on content and level.

- Certification – a process that confirms the validated competences obtained in formal, non-formal and informal contexts.

It is necessary here to keep in mind the contribution of the less formal providers of learning, since these are often small and have as one of their strengths the lower status of formal recognition. The following example from Australia is typical.

Adult and community education in Australia owes much to the informal settings in which courses may be offered. A typical example is the "neighbourhood house" converted to a suite of classrooms, with a kitchen and play areas for children. Adults who come to classes in these settings are not under the kinds of academic pressures faced by senior secondary students or by those in university lecture theatres or the classrooms of vocational education and training institutions.

One reason this kind of provision is important is because it is likely to serve as a bridge to formal learning. People with poor expectations of themselves or experiencing some transition in their life may be reluctant to engage in full scale learning programmes, and this kind of non-accredited learning offers an alternative.

Providers are beginning to feature more strongly in the debates on lifelong learning; OECD (2003) provides a useful summary of the issues involved. There is increasing evidence (QCA, 2004) that a significant means to drive up lifelong learning is to support innovative practice in terms of pedagogy. The new practices often develop in enterprises and in new learning arenas – some of them virtual in nature. The challenge is to research and develop training programmes so that practitioners and providers can judge the benefits of developing new ways of delivering what individuals and employers want. Practitioners can then extend their influence and guide learners who might be deterred from traditional pedagogies. Distance learning and the use of new information and communications technologies offer major advantages as well as difficult challenges for providers.

Inducements

Provider involvement

As with employers, a key inducement is to involve all stakeholders – students, parents, local community representatives and labour-market partners – as closely as possible in the learning organisation. This facilitates a close match of provision to need and a sense of ownership that can foster expansion of learning provision. Countries (*e.g.* Belgium [Wallonia – Brussels], Denmark and the United Kingdom) report that this is often currently the case, with some variation in the involvement of different stakeholders according to the national context. In France, building of *référentiels de diplômes* is increasingly based on consultation with social partners. In Switzerland, the success of the reforms of the upper secondary level (*Maturité professionnelle*) and the preparation of the law on vocational training owe much to a process that involved all stakeholder groups. In Denmark, students' rights are embodied in student councils and, primarily in their right to be consulted on matters pertaining to the organisation of teaching, choice of themes in single subjects, and choice of teaching and working methods. Linked to the idea stakeholder involvement is the forming of partnerships among the range of agencies that can present a more co-ordinated approach to provision. This is discussed in detail later in this section.

In Belgium (Wallonia), some of the training delivered by the Walloon Bureau for Vocational Training and Employment (FOREM, *Office wallon de la formation professionnelle et de l'emploi*) is organised in partnership with other providers of learning and/or with industry sectors. This is also the case for Bruxelles-Formation, the public French-speaking body in charge of adult vocational training in Brussels. Bruxelles-Formation works through partnerships with the branches, the non-profit organisations for social and occupational integration, the teaching programmes for social advancement education, and the Brussels French-speaking service for the disabled. These partnerships allow different groups of the population to be reached and delivery of vocational preparation in different fields. Qualifications achieved range from basic literacy to marketing techniques for graduates.

Recognition of prior learning

A key area for improving the take-up of learning provision is the extent to which existing learning outcomes, however achieved, can be recognised as contributing to a formal qualification. This encourages more learning by opening up access to learning programmes by lowering costs (through exemption) for some parts of learning programmes or assessment processes. However, the bridge between formal qualification and recognition of non-formal learning is not straightforward (Bjørnåvold, 2002); there is very little research evidence of benefits arising from learners translating non-formal learning into learning for formal qualification. In France and Japan, where the opportunity to have learning recognised for formal qualifications has already been introduced, growth in use of the system suggests the market for recognition is very strong (Chiousse and Werquin, 2005). Recognition of non-formal and informal learning is covered in detail in the report of the Thematic Group 2 (Annex A). It is important to note that the membership of Thematic Group 2 was particularly wide, which is to say that many countries see the recognition of non-formal and informal learning as having the potential to meet social and economic needs. These needs are also described in detail in the annex. Most of the 31 countries offering advice on progressing towards developing vocational education and training in order to meet the European Union's social and economic goals also identified progress or solid plans to develop recognition systems to encompass non-formal and informal learning.

In Spain the assessment, validation and recognition of non-formal and informal learning has been the object of an experimental project aimed at establishing a link to the new National Catalogue of Vocational Qualifications. The idea is to evaluate and accredit occupational skills acquired through on-the-job experience or non-formal training channels – units of competence form the basis, so as to facilitate cumulative partial accreditation leading to a diploma or certificate upon completion of training. The experimental project has been applied in six vocational areas and in various contexts, so as to gather more extensive evidence about procedures, social processes implied and the costs involved. The project takes into account European and international experiences, and has been implemented under criteria guaranteeing the evaluation's reliability, objectivity and technical standards.

Quality assurance processes

Learning providers need to be able to show their customers that provision matches or exceeds criteria governing quality of provision. This is especially important when private providers are responsible for small-scale specific training. There is possibly an optimum size for quality assurance systems; if these systems are small in scale it might not be possible to establish widespread trust; if they are too large they might become bureaucratic and insensitive to the styles of local provision. In Switzerland the diverse and rather incoherent system may have created the need for an umbrella organisation for ensuring quality and the EDUQUA system that is a relatively inexpensive quality assurance system that providers can use (Pont and Werquin, 2003). It is important to note that EDUQUA does not meet certain well-known international standards; if they did, some small-scale providers might not be able to comply. Thus a balance needed to be struck between required levels of quality assurance and provider resources.

Central determination of quality assurance processes is common. Countries have developed systems of regulation by publishing documents setting out the criteria or protocols for offering qualification.

The introduction of a competitive training market in Australian vocational education and training has led to a greater diversity of providers obtaining registration, and hence to the potential for uneven quality. The development of a deregulated system, occurring at the same time as the introduction of the Australian Qualifications Framework, has required progressive strengthening of quality assurance mechanisms in the vocational education and training sector. The national quality assurance framework is in its third generation following the National Framework for the Recognition of Training and the Australian Recognition Framework. Now the strengthened Australian Quality Training Framework provides the means to ensure the quality of and provide for a truly national vocational education and training system. Implementing a national system of awards has boosted the employment value of nationally recognised vocational programmes and facilitated progress through different levels of the system.

In 2002 in France a new national Repertory of Certifications was introduced with the aim of creating an all-encompassing architecture of vocational education and training qualifications. Eligibility for registration in the repertory requires meeting two basic conditions: qualifications must be accessible not only through training but also through the accreditation of prior experience (VAE); and it must be shown that the social partners were involved from the start in the design of the qualification in question. In conformity with the common currency principle, all qualifications registered in the repertory must be structured in terms of units of competence. The purpose of this new co-ordinating system is to bridge the recognition gaps between the various systems of qualifications while also imposing common quality criteria on all providers.

Improving co-ordination of provision

There are advantages to be gained by co-ordinating the learning provision of the various institutions involved. These advantages derive more from increasing efficiency and ensuring a breadth of provision than from searching for economies of scale. Countries with federal systems of government report that there are issues to be addressed arising from regional differences in administrative arrangements. The Dutch experience summarises the gains to be made from good co-ordination.

In the Netherlands, the old institutions for the various types of vocational education and adult education in a region are merged into one single administrative and organisational unit, the Regional Vocational College. These new institutions include colleges of intermediate vocational education, schools for part-time instruction as part of the apprenticeship training route, and schools for basic adult education and day/evening education. With decentralisation, these institutions have a large measure of administrative and financial autonomy. Regional Vocational Colleges are considered to have a variety of advantages. Combining various types of education and expertise makes it easier than before to provide tailor-made programmes for specific groups of learners, and the wishes and needs of regional trade and industry are taken into account more fully. The Regional Vocational Colleges look set to become the central network of principal regional actors, for example by making common learning arrangements with local trade and industry.

In Switzerland the need for further co-ordination is clearly acknowledged, especially at the upper secondary level. The purpose is not to create a singular route or a singular form of upper secondary qualification; the necessity to keep separate tracks is clear. Nevertheless, there is a growing awareness of a need to co-ordinate actions at the upper secondary level to help young people achieve their goals. Therefore, a pilot project – *Projet secondaire II* – has been initiated to help the dialog between the different actors (CDIP, 1996; CDIP, OFFT/EDK and BBT, 2000). Its main purpose has been to create a centre of competences (*Centre de compétences*) for upper secondary education at the national level.

Outcomes-based qualification

One method of developing transparency in learning programmes (including assessment and certification) is to build the programme on expected outcomes of learning rather than input measures such as a learning programme specification. Even long-standing, large-scale programmes can be clearer to learners when outcomes are used to describe the learning. In addition to setting standards (in terms of outcomes) and presenting the opportunity to ensure quality of provision, outcomes allow individuals and employers to use the qualification to meet several objectives.[8] The French report points to the advantages for providers themselves, who are able to streamline provision and enjoy efficiency savings.

Where a credit transfer system is available the opportunity to use a range of credits to initiate a new area of learning or reduce unnecessary repetition of learning is a high prize.

In Denmark many adult vocational training courses give adults a formal right to credit transfer from an initial vocational education and training programme. This may result in a reduced study programme. Together with credit transfer, the option of recognition of non-formal and informal learning (especially work-based) opens up flexible pathways for the unskilled worker towards a nationally recognised qualification as a skilled worker. Education programmes that are relevant to the participant depend not only on their educational background (level and vocational field), but also on their needs or aspirations for vocational progression as a supplement to the original educational background. Equally important are the more flexible possibilities at the basic education level of being able to use their credit and thus shorten study/training programmes in youth vocational education and training. That gives adults a "second chance" to acquire higher-level qualifications.

Korea has developed a "credit bank system" that allows individuals to accumulate credits from all sorts of institutions, including universities and non-formal education and training institutions. A student can receive a higher education degree, depending on the number of credits accumulated. Since non-formal education and training institutions were previously not allowed to issue credits, it was difficult for university dropouts, employed/unemployed adults and inactive adults to accumulate human capital leading to a degree recognised in the labour market. For non-formal educational/training institutions to issue certified credits, they need to be formally accredited by the Ministry of Education, which involves complying with standardised curricula and syllabuses developed by the Korean Educational Development Institute. The Korean labour market puts high value on formal degrees. The credit bank system is thus a key initiative that allows individuals of all ages and skill levels to invest in human capital, to be more productive, and to be valued in the labour market. Since the "priority" groups are the very people that would benefit most from skill upgrading and degree acquisition, the credit bank system is a key scheme to support lifelonglearning among these groups.

In Switzerland, it is possible to obtain a Federal Certificate of Capacity (CFC, *Certificat fédéral de capacité*) without taking formal tests. The Certificate was first introduced in 1999. Assessment is not based on participation in formal programmes but rather qualification procedures created *ad hoc* . It is the country's first step toward recognition of prior learning.

Progression and partnerships

Evidence from around the world suggests institutions are now more active than ever in creating bridges into formerly external sectors. Secondary schools in particular have introduced or expanded vocational elements within upper secondary programmes. Universities have become more open to vocational education and training students, and inter-sector provision of qualifications has become more common. Australia is seeing the development of articulation and credit transfer arrangements between schools and Registered Training Organisations (RTOs), and between Registered Training Organisations and universities. During the past few years in Denmark, more young people have made a transition to a vocational education and training programme after having completed a general academic or mixed upper secondary programme. A growing number of students in vocational education and training thus obtain a dual qualification through credit transfer from another upper secondary programme.

The workplace as a learning site

Workplaces represent a major site of formal, non-formal and informal learning. Non-formal learning may be found in the delivery of structured programmes not recognised for qualification – such as induction programmes for new recruits, graduate trainee programmes, workshops in skills development, and so on. In many cases however, course components compare with those of recognised qualifications in both presentation and learning outcomes. They are of significance in documenting the knowledge, skills and wider competences of a worker and providing assurance that training has taken place to a requisite level and are of particular significance in signposting career pathways within an organisation. Recognition of the workplace as a learning site for qualification-based learning could lead to a major enhancement of lifelong learning: OECD research (2003) indicates unmet demand. Recognition of less formal work-based learning is already a major initiative in many countries.

Special provision

The country background reports contain details of many special initiatives focused on learning provision for a particular social group, or that describe a particular kind of relationship between learning providers and employers. Some of these initiatives are summarised briefly here.

In Greece, certain shortcomings in education have been covered by the establishment of Second Chance Schools that aim to reintegrate adults into the formal education system or into non-formal education and training. A new law gives Greek citizens aged over 18 who did not complete their compulsory education the opportunity to attend an 18-month programme and acquire a certificate corresponding to completion of lower secondary level education. Second Chance Schools are aimed at adults who, save in very few cases, do not make use of the right to enter formal education in joint classes with children of school age. Social circumstances are taken into account for entry and special weighting is given to former prisoners or former drug users, but cases of individuals who have difficulty adapting or with mental disabilities are not accepted. Studies are completely free and include teaching material and stationery. In many cases the municipal authorities support the programme by providing participants with means of transport and youth clubs for children.

In Japan, the University of the Air was established in 1985 by the national government to promote lifelong learning. It accepts – without examination – those aged 15 or above with no certificate of senior high school completion, as students to take a range of courses. Depending on their academic performance, University of the Air students can enter a bachelor's degree programme at a university.

In Korea, the Self-Study Degree Award System provides opportunities to acquire degrees through self-instruction or self-study. When a new law was introduced in 1990, the Korea Institute of Curriculum and Evaluation began holding certified humanities courses and exams for the first time; at present, the Korea National Open University runs the Self-Study System. In order to acquire the degree, the candidate needs to pass four rounds of exams. The first is the basic general humanities to evaluate the general competence of the candidate. The second deals with knowledge and technical issues across each of the majors necessary for studying the respective major. The third is an upgraded exam that evaluates whether the candidate has specialist knowledge and technical competence in their major. The last exam is the bachelor's degree acquisition exam; this evaluates a candidate's overall ability, and whether the candidate possesses the appropriate specialised knowledge and technical know-how for a bachelor's degree.

In New Zealand, the growth of private training establishments (PTEs) is an education reform initiative that links to the qualifications system by providing a new form of delivering qualifications to learners. A law allowed private provision of tertiary education, and established a mechanism for use of public funds. Private training establishments have to be a corporate body with goals and purposes that relate primarily to education and/or training. Some PTEs have been established for profit, but not all. Some are established to serve the interests of local community groups. In 2001, the New Zealand Qualifications Authority (NZQA) estimated that 64% of private training establishments were limited liability companies, 14% were trusts and 22% were incorporated societies. Most learners attending PTEs are engaged in education and training after compulsory education, but for some senior secondary learners these establishments offer an alternative education to secondary schools. The impact they will have on lifelong learning depends on the goal of a particular private training establishment and the courses it is delivering.

Constraints on providers

Complexity of the range of providers

As indicated above, several countries specify the problems encountered by employers and individuals when there are too many providers of very different types within the system. The quest for transparency may force the managers of provision to co-ordinate the programmes they offer. While the goal is clear, there may be local issues that prevent this process from happening. There appears to be a move in some countries (such as the United Kingdom and France) to decentralise control and allow more local interpretation of effective provision. Vendor qualifications from international companies may grow in popularity as this more diverse provision becomes established. The main issue for learners when provision is complex may not be making sense of what is on offer, as much as having confidence that the learning for qualification carries good currency in the labour market and has the potential to lead to a further qualification.

Costs

Almost all countries identify costs as a constraint in developing learning provision to meet needs. Some of these constraints relate to the providing institutions; others relate to individuals and employers but have a serious effect on providing institutions. This issue also affects adult education more generally, where funding is insufficient and requires increased investment from both private and public sources (OECD, 2003).

Several countries identify measures to help individuals and employers bear the cost of learning for qualification. Examples of these measures are individual learning accounts, career development loans, small firm training loans, support for trade union activities, facilitating flexible working arrangements and structural learning funds (including covering part of the cost of installing ICT equipment).

In some countries (*e.g.* New Zealand and the United Kingdom) there is public concern that the cost of tertiary education, including the cost of student loans, may act as a disincentive to post-compulsory study. The universal access to the student loan scheme has maintained participation rates in post-compulsory education among sections of society that were previously not well represented in higher education.

The qualifications system and providers: some issues

The main issues for providers of learning have been raised above. These relate to the following:

- Managing the systems so that overall provision is co-ordinated and efficient while allowing for local diversity so that specific needs can be met.
- Monitoring the use of the system in terms of the extent to which it meets the needs of users, the quality of provision and the efficiency with which resources are used. Lack of monitoring information renders strategic decision making less robust.
- Allowing for growth in the capacity of institutions and practitioners to develop new pedagogies that can have an impact on the learning careers of individuals and the development of employers.

The Portuguese report describes the following three key elements of pedagogy:

- The basic features of the educational model are based on the thematic organisation, duration and sequence of the modular system, the qualification of teachers and trainers, and an environment that stimulates learning in accredited organisations.
- The flexible and non-constraining model of attendance leaves the responsibility for achievements to students. Public funding, which assures zero cost, should be sufficiently motivating for individual efforts of active citizenship.
- The range of training options must be flexible but, at the same time, avoid complexity. The funding system should be selective so that it does not hinder local promoters from undertaking the training initiatives they find most suitable.

There is also the need to build the expertise of trainers in assessment processes that provide motivating feedback to learners. Negotiating learning objectives and recording outcomes are growing in importance in non-formal settings; this holds promise for other sectors, especially work-based learning (Torrance and Coultas, 2004).

Summary of inducements and ways of overcoming barriers to learning for providers

Providers will be more likely to engage with a qualifications system that:

- Includes qualifications that allow for use of modern pedagogies and new technologies.
- Encourages involvement in the design of qualifications and the management of the Qualifications system.
- Includes qualifications that use fit-for-purpose quality assurance processes.
- Allows for the recognition of prior learning.
- Includes entry paths to qualifications programmes that are flexible.
- Makes explicit the competences developed in qualifications.
- Provides a sense of well co-ordinated qualifications management.
- Enables positive links with employers and other providers.

- Allows for the development of provision to meet specific needs of learners and employers.

- Reduces costs of qualifications.

- Monitors the network of providers to ensure co-ordinated provision.

- Monitors the demand for qualifications so that only those clearly demanded are offered.

4.5. Mechanisms affecting behaviour

The analysis so far makes it clear that the learning behaviours of individuals, employers and providers of learning for qualifications are directly and indirectly influenced by the kind of qualifications system operating in the country. The analysis points to specific modifications in terms of structure or operating conditions, which will change the likelihood of each of these groups participating in, using and providing qualifications. These change agents have been labelled mechanisms in Chapter 1 and it is now possible, using the evidence in this chapter, to concretise the theoretical idea and set forth 20 mechanisms for consideration as tools to strengthen policy responses for improving lifelong learning. Table 4.1 lists the 20 and describes how each might work.

By reviewing all the evidence about the ways of behaviour of the three main stakeholder groups (individuals, employers and providers) it has been possible to derive the 20 mechanisms that could improve policy responses so that qualifications systems play their part in enhancing lifelong learning. While each mechanism has the potential to support policy making in relation to qualifications systems, it is the way that these mechanisms interface with policy responses to lifelong learning that is important. Chapter 5 examines this interface between policy responses and mechanisms in depth.

Table 4.1. **Potential mechanisms**

Mechanism	Short examples of how the mechanism might work
1. **Communicating returns to learning for qualification**	The incentives are based in the qualifications system itself and hinge on the reward and returns (financial and otherwise) for gaining qualification. The process of communicating the advantages of learning for qualification may inspire individuals to seek out learning. *Individuals* would be motivated to learn for qualifications with good returns. *Employers* would have a greater skills market to draw on and may see investment in learning as more secure if learners seek learning in work. *Providers* would be involved in communicating returns to increase demand for their programmes.
2. **Recognising skills for employability**	For some people the barrier to further learning is that they cannot find quality work that enables work-based learning. Their general skills level is low. For these people, providing training that includes the experience of work and that focuses on employability skills may be a breakthrough to further learning. *Individuals* with poor general skills levels might be inclined to learn these skills and then go on to further learning later. *Employers* would need to make available training in the experience of work and possibly training in employability skills; they could gain from a wider skills supply. *Providers* would need to develop learning programmes in this area and would be meeting client needs.
3. **Establishing qualifications frameworks**	Qualifications frameworks can make progression routes clear, remove dead ends and bring coherence and quality assurance to qualifications systems. *Individuals* might be motivated to learn if they can be guided towards appropriate qualifications for their aspirations. They might also have confidence in nationally approved qualifications. *Employers* will find a framework helpful in setting out qualification requirements for a job and in relating an applicant's qualification profile to a standard reference point. It may help rationalise training provision. *Providers* might find a framework of qualifications useful for promotional material as they can market qualifications according to a well-known structure and, like recruiters, they might feel more secure in the knowledge that certain qualifications are national benchmarks.

Table 4.1. **Potential mechanisms** (cont.)

Mechanism	Short examples of how the mechanism might work
4. Increasing learner choice in qualifications	This mechanism is about the exercising of personal responsibility. Qualifications should be designed so that there are clear exit points (with credit) for those who have a change of plan. Choice may be more about options within qualifications than options between qualifications, although crossing points between qualifications may be seen as advantageous.
	Individuals may be motivated by the freedom to make decisions about their future learning.
	Employers may find that the increased complexity of qualifications complicates recruitment and planning. However, they may come to see that exercising choice becomes an aspect of a candidate's identity and so could make selection more effective.
	Providers will come under pressure to differentiate course offerings in response to more selective demand, for example by creating awards delivered through both sectors, double degrees, and courses in new cross-disciplinary or more specialised fields.
5. Clarifying learning pathways	The mechanism ensures that the qualifications system creates career and learning opportunities through the definition of tracks or routes that appeal to learners' interests and ambitions, providers' structures and recruiters' needs. The existence of crossroads where individuals can change track without penalty is an important feature.
	Individuals may find the security of a designated qualification track appealing, although lack of choice may be a disincentive to learn.
	Employers too may feel confident in a simple system with an established track, and they may feel that candidates who have remained on track are more committed to their chosen field than those who decided to change track at some stage.
	Providers may find management of more flexible programmes more difficult and more costly, and therefore may increase investment in defined tracks.
6. Providing credit transfer	Credit transfer processes will provide flexibility for individuals and employers. They will also be a means of counting an individual's existing skills and learning toward further qualification, thus cutting the cost of repeating work. It will ease the burden of time or financial commitment to learning. It might also act as an incentive for job progression if credit counts in different job environments.
	Individuals may be motivated by the way they can cash in credits earned earlier and gain credits for a range of future options. The flexibility may overcome some kinds of personal constraints.
	Employers may see a unitised system as overly complex and, while they can recruit people who have specialised in units of particular relevance to the firm, the recruitment process itself will be more complicated. It offers them a chance to tailor training to their specific needs.
	Providers may be more ambivalent about credit systems because they might add to administrative costs – but the engagement of many more people on unit-based programmes will be an incentive.
7. Increasing flexibility in learning programmes leading to qualifications	This mechanism focuses on the ways learning programmes are responsive to the learning styles of the individual – qualification processes can limit the flexibility of programmes.
	Individuals will be motivated by programmes that match their learning and assessment preferences. If the qualifications system has options within it for providers to tailor programmes to these preferences, then participation may increase.
	Employers may view flexibility in assessment for qualification as an attractive option, as it may be perceived as fit for purpose.
	Providers will find flexibility attractive as it will allow them to respond to the market as they see it. Flexibility, however, may bring with it complexity and cost implications.
8. Creating new routes to qualifications	Reasons for non-participation in learning are numerous and diverse, and overcoming non-participation demands that a range of entry points be available and that specifications for entry point prerequisites be clear and minimal. The mechanism needs a clear linkage between non-award-bearing programmes and award-bearing programmes. Funding regimes and quality assurance processes need to be differentiated so that they are minimal for low-stakes qualifications.
	Individuals with low self-esteem, low confidence or a poor record of education achievement will find unnecessary obstacles in introductory or entry programmes removed, thus facilitating non-threatening access.
	Employers may need to create flexibility so that workers seeking further learning are encouraged to participate in it. This may have cost implications.
	Providers will need to create new routes and may create stronger markets in this area.
9. Lowering the cost of qualification	Cost is a key inhibitor to qualification for certain groups. Both time and money are included as there are direct costs (of programmes, of assessment) and indirect costs (opportunity costs, personal time costs). The individual is the prime focus for cost but providers and employers pass on costs in one way or another, and so costs to them are important.
	Individuals will be less inhibited by lower costs, costs spread out over time, and costs where payment is deferred until later. They will be motivated by any support to minimise opportunity costs.
	Employers will be motivated to use qualification-based learning if impact on production costs is low. Flexibility in the system (for example credit transfer, recognition of prior learning) is likely to reduce employers' costs.
	Providers will strive to ensure systems are efficient to reduce costs to individuals and employers. Therefore, system maintenance costs (quality assurance, international benchmarking, and qualification development) will be important areas for efficiency savings.

Table 4.1. **Potential mechanisms** *(cont.)*

Mechanism	Short examples of how the mechanism might work
10. Recognising non-formal and informal learning	Recognition systems for non-formal and informal learning make explicit the value of learning that is not assessed as part of a formal learning programme. This kind of recognition can act as a safety net for those who have not yet fully engaged with learning. *Individuals* with relatively low levels of formal achievement might be motivated to enter programmes and continue learning if their knowledge, skills and wider competences acquired through experience can be recognised and used to reduce the costs of qualification. *Employers* may see wider skills supply if more learning is recognised in the workforce. On the other hand, this might lead to a reduction in commitment to formal training programmes. *Providers* may be encouraged to widen access to programmes if quality-assured recognition systems are in place. There may however be increased direct and indirect costs involved in recognising non-formal and informal learning.
11. Monitoring the qualifications system	This mechanism represents a feedback loop for the qualifications system. The outcome of the data analysis will allow the managers in the qualifications system to gauge how well it is responding to the needs of individuals, providers and recruiters. *Individuals* will benefit if the monitoring process is sufficiently sensitive to identify their needs in terms of learning for qualification. *Employers* will find information on skill needs useful if it is reliable and sensitive, and if trend data can be produced. *Providers* can use information to develop programmes to better meet the needs of their clients.
12. Optimising stakeholder involvement in the qualifications system	The likelihood of qualifications meeting needs is enhanced if all users are genuine stakeholders and play a part in modernising qualifications. Inclination to use qualifications will be higher if a sense of ownership exists. Agreements between the stakeholders on developments to the qualifications system may be more stable. The stakeholders might operate in a more co-ordinated way and communicate more coherent messages about the qualifications system. *Individuals* will be more inclined to learn for qualification if it is evident that the learner voice has been heeded in qualification design and delivery. *Employers* need to be sure qualification meets their needs, and genuine involvement is a way to do this. *Providers* need to know their clients' needs and will wish to be clear about new methods of delivery and the cost implications of new developments.
13. Improving needs analysis methods so that qualifications are up to date	If there is a systematic way of reviewing qualifications against labour market and economic needs, qualifications based on these processes will be perceived as relevant and worth investment. The methods used must also prepare for future skills needs. *Individuals* will be encouraged by the value placed on up-to-date qualifications by employers. *Employers* will appreciate the value of people qualified in theory and practice, and the currency of qualification reflecting this will be raised. *Providers* will be confident in marketing modern qualifications to clients.
14. Improving qualification use in recruitment	Recruitment processes that use qualifications to sift and discriminate potential recruits will develop higher currency for the qualifications used. *Individuals* will be inclined to learn for qualifications if the latter are widely used in recruitment and for ensuring progress in careers and learning. *Employers* will be motivated to use qualification in recruitment processes if it is useful as a proxy for knowledge, skills and wider competences of the jobseeker and if they can be sure of the standards and content recognised by the qualification and that it is delivered and assessed effectively. *Providers* will be inclined to support programmes where there is strong demand for qualification by employers because the latter are a major client.
15. Ensuring qualifications are portable	By allowing qualifications to be used to make easier transitions between jobs or learning programmes, the value of learning for qualifications will be raised. *Individuals* would be more inclined towards participation if they could use their qualification to progress across educational or occupational sectors as well as within a sector. *Employers* may find the process of dealing with many different qualifications confusing and inefficient. *Providers* would be able to promote qualifications with high portability.
16. Investing in pedagogical innovation	Efficient and effective teaching will, over time, contribute to the value placed on the qualification that recognises this learning. Good delivery of education and training lowers costs for qualification-based learning. *Individuals* can be highly motivated by good-quality teaching. *Employers* will see a reduction in training costs and better matching of training to needs. *Providers* will need to assure teaching quality and deliver the training for teachers and trainers. There will be cost implications.

Table 4.1. **Potential mechanisms** (cont.)

Mechanism	Short examples of how the mechanism might work
17. Expressing qualifications as learning outcomes	Making clear to learners, providers and recruiters what the outcomes of the qualification are in terms of knowledge, skills and wider competences leads to firmer expectations.
	Individuals can be motivated by clarity of learning outcomes and the possibility of gaining credit for learning already acquired.
	Employers will be able to specify their recruitment needs more clearly and have more confidence when using qualifications in the process of matching candidates to jobs.
	Providers will find the outcomes-based approach easier for co-ordinating different learning programmes. They might also be more confident in explaining to clients the value or currency of a qualification based on outcomes.
18. Improving co-ordination in the qualifications system	The mechanism produces a clear infrastructure of qualifications and the institutions delivering them.
	Individuals are motivated by clear and consistent interactions between all the agencies involved in funding, delivering and awarding qualifications.
	Employers will see gains in receiving consistent information and may be more motivated to provide and use qualifications.
	Providers may find cost savings from increased coherence in the way the agencies interact, as demands on them will also be co-ordinated.
19. Optimising quality assurance	The levels of quality assurance processes applied to the development and operation of qualifications affect the way people view qualifications. High levels of quality assurance might increase the value ascribed to qualifications; on the other hand it might develop constraints on the ways qualifications can respond to different user needs.
	Individuals are likely to be motivated to learn for qualifications of guaranteed quality. They will find attractive the cost reductions gained from reduced bureaucracy requirements for providers.
	Employers will be motivated by the increased confidence they can have in quality-assured provision, but will require maintenance of minimum effective quality-assurance procedures.
	Providers will be confident in marketing of qualifications of guaranteed quality, and will benefit from cost savings.
20. Improving information and guidance about qualifications systems	Effective information, advice and guidance services using communications technologies could increase the quantity and distribution of lifelong learning.
	Individuals may overcome some barriers to learning if guided through the qualifications information maze.
	Employers would benefit from a one-stop-shop for qualifications information.
	Providers may benefit from being able to market qualifications through information, advice and guidance centres, and from obviating the costs of relocating learners who made poor initial choices.

Notes

1. Often, it is actually the process of qualification rather than the whole qualifications system that has an effect on lifelong learning. For the purposes of this study, a specific qualification is considered part of the qualifications system, and therefore the system can be said to be responsible for the effect.

2. Before a more detailed discussion of linking mechanisms is undertaken, it should be pointed out that many factors influence lifelong learning and that qualifications systems may be just one of them. It is also important to accept the view that increased formal recognition of knowledge and skills is not always a good thing for individuals as will become clear later in this volume.

3. The OECD is currently considering how to investigate this issue.

4. This is intended not to challenge the notion of learning as a social activity, but rather to focus attention on the individual as the decision maker about whether to learn.

5. The word motivation is taken to cover a range of an individual's behaviour: the way they initiate things, determine the way things are done, perform an activity with intensity and show perseverance to see that activity through to the end.

6. The private rate of return is a measure of the profitability of an investment in education. It is interesting because it accounts for lifetime earnings (not just starting earnings) and the costs of undertaking a qualification (Borland, 2001). In the Danish example, the private rate of return is calculated as the lifetime income (after tax) minus (loss of potential income while studying plus direct costs of a programme).The concept of social rate of return extends the notion of private rate of return by considering social costs and benefits. The social rate of return measures the net benefits to society of educating its citizens. If education is treated by a society as an investment in its people, then the society will be made better off by an increase in educational investment as long as the social rate of return is higher than that for other public investments (Junankar and Liu,

2003). In the Danish example, the social rate of return is calculated as the lifetime income of all individuals (before tax) minus public expenses for education.

7. Taken to mean: the knowledge, skills, competences and attributes embodied in individuals that facilitate the creation of personal, social and economic well-being.

8. See Adam (2004) for a full evaluation of the purposes of using learning outcomes and a review of developments in this field in European countries.

References

Adam, S. (2004), "Using Learning Outcomes – A Consideration of the Nature, Role and Implications for European Education of Employing Learning Outcomes at the Local, National and International Levels", United Kingdom Bologna Seminar, Herriot Watt University, Scotland.

ANTA (Australian National Training Authority) (2000), ANTA Marketing Strategy for Skills and Lifelong Learning: Market Segmentation Report, Brisbane.

Béduwé, C. and J. Planas (2003), Educational Expansion and Labour Market: A Comparative Study of Five European countries – France, Germany, Italy, Spain and the United Kingdom – With Special Reference to the United States, CEDEFOP, Office for Official Publications of the European Communities, Luxembourg.

BIBB (Bundesinstitut für Berufsbildung) (1998), Bundesinstitut für Berufsbildung: Referenz-Betriebs-System, Aussagekraft von Prüfungen, Information No. 12, BIBB, Bonn.

Billett, S. (2001), "Learning Throughout Working Life: Interdependence at Work", Studies in Continuing Education, Vol. 23, No. 1.

Billett, S. and A. Smith (2003), "Compliance, Engagement and Commitment: Increasing Employer Expenditure in Training", Journal of Vocational Education and Training, Vol. 55, No. 3.

Bjørnåvold, J. (2002), Lifelong Learning: Which Ways Forward?, D. Colardyn, ed., College of Europe, Kennicentrum EVC, Utrecht.

Black, P. and D. William (1999), Inside the Black Box, King's College, London.

Borland, J. (2001), New Estimates of the Private Rate of Return to University Education in Australia, University of Melbourne, www.melbourneinstitute.com.

Bryce, J. (2004), "Different Ways Secondary Schools Orient to Lifelong Learning", Educational Studies, Vol. 30, No. 1, Carfax Publishing.

Buchmann, M. and S. Sacchi (1998), "The Transition from School to Work in Switzerland: Do Characteristics of the Educational System and Class Barriers Matter?" in Y. Shavit and W. Müller (eds.), From School to Work: A Comparative Study of Educational Qualifications and Occupational Destinations, Clarendon Press, Oxford, pp. 407-442.

Bynner, J. and M. Egerton (2001), The Wider Benefits of Higher Education, HEFCE (Higher Education Funding Council for England), London.

Bynner, J. and S. Parsons (2001), "Qualifications, Basic Skills and Accelerating Social Exclusion", Journal of Education and Work, Vol. 14, No. 3, pp. 279-291.

CDIP (Conférence suisse des directeurs cantonaux de l'instruction publique) (1996), Projet secondaire II, Dossier 43B, CDIP, Bern.

CDIP, OFFT/EDK and BBT, eds. (2000), Le secondaire II à venir, Rapport final du groupe de projet secondaire II, Études et rapports 9, CDIP/EDK, Bern.

Chiousse, S. and P. Werquin (2005), "They Must Be Mo-ti-va-ted: Qualification to Make Adults Learn" in J.L Guyot, C. Mainguet and B. Van Haeperen (eds.), La formation professionnelle continue: enjeux sociétaux, Collection Économie, Société, Région, De Boeck, (in French).

Coles M. and T. Oates (2004), European Reference Levels for Education and Training: Promoting Credit Transfer and Mutual Trust, CEDEFOP Panorama Series 109, Office for Official Publications of the European Communities, Luxembourg.

Dench, S. and J. Regan (2000), Learning in Later Life: Motivation and Impact, Research Report RR183, Department for Education and Employment, London.

EC (European Commission) (2004a), Education and Training 2010: The Success of the Lisbon Strategy Hinges on Urgent Reform, European Commission, Brussels.

EC (2004b), Maastricht Communiqué on the *Future Priorities of Enhanced European Co-operation in Vocational Education and Training* (VET), European Commission, Brussels.

EC (2005), Towards a European Qualifications Framework for Lifelong Learning. Commission Staff Working Document, Brussels, 8 July 2005.

Felstead, A., D. Gallie and F. Green (2002), *Work Skills in Britain 1986-2001*, Department for Education and Skills, London.

Gardner, H. (1993), *Multiple Intellegencies*, Basic Books, New York.

Grubb, N. (2004), *The Education Gospel: The Economic Power of Schooling*, Harvard University Press, Cambridge (Massachusetts) and London.

Grunewald, U. and D. Moraal (2001), *Betriebliche Weiterbildung* (eds.) Bundesinstitut für Berufsbildung. Der Generalsekretär, Forschung Spezial Heft 3, Bielefeld.

Hecker, U. (2000a), *Berufliche Mobilität und Wechselprozesse*, in: (eds.) Dostal u.a., Beiträge zur Arbeitsmarkt- und Berufsforschung, Band 231, p. 67-97, Nürnberg.

Hecker, U. (2000b), *Berufswechsel – Chancen und Risiken. Ergebnisse der BIBB/IAB-Erhebung 1998/99*, in Berufsbildung in Wissenschaft und Praxis, 29. Jg. Heft 4, p. 12-17.

Junankar P.N. and J. Liu (2003), "Estimating the Social Rate of Return to Education for Indigenous Australians", *Education Economics*, Vol. 11, No. 2.

Keating, J., T. Nicholas, J. Polesel and J. Watson (2004), *Qualifications Use in the Australian Labour Market*, NCVER (National Centre for Vocational Education Research), Adelaide.

Kelly, M. (1994), *Can You Credit It? – Implications of Accreditation for Learners and Groups in the Community Sector*, Aontas/Combat Poverty Agency, Dublin.

Kolb D. (1984), *Experiential Learning*, Prentice Hall, New Jersey.

Murray, A. and H. Steedman (1999), "Growing Skills in Europe: The Changing Skill Profiles of France, Germany, the Netherlands, Portugal, Sweden and the United Kingdom", 3rd International Conference, Researching Vocational Education and Training, Bolton Institute, England.

NCVER (2001), "Statistics 2001: Survey of Employer Views on Vocational Education and Training", National Report, Adelaide.

O'Connell, P. and M. Lyons, (1995), *Enterprise-Related Training and State Policy in Ireland: The Training Support Scheme*, ESRI (The Economic and Social Research Institute in Ireland), Dublin.

OECD (1999), *Classifying Educational Programmes: Manual for ISCED-97 Implementation in OECD Countries*, OECD, Paris.

OECD (2000a), *Where Are the Resources for Lifelong Learning?*, OECD, Paris.

OECD (2000b), *From Initial Education to Working Life: Making Transitions Work*, OECD, Paris.

OECD (2001a), *Economics and Finance of Lifelong Learning*, OECD, Paris.

OECD (2001b), *The Well-being of Nations: The Role of Human and Social Capital*, OECD, Paris.

OECD (2003), *Beyond Rhetoric: Adult Learning Policies and Practices*, OECD, Paris.

OECD (2004), *Career Guidance and Public Policy – Bridging the Gap*, OECD, Paris.

Pont B. et P. Werquin, 2002. "L'apprentissage des adultes en Suisse et dans d'autres pays de l'OCDE. Une perspective comparative". *Schweizerische Zeitschrift für Bildungswissenschaften/Revue suisse des sciences de l'éducation/Rivista svizzera di scienze dell'educazione*, 24 (2), pp. 279-307.

QCA (Qualifications and Curriculum Authority) (2002), *Research Review: Reasons for the Drop-Out of Young People from Education, Training and Work at School-Leaving Age*, T. Leney (ed.), London.

QCA (2004), *Achieving the Lisbon goal: The Contribution of Vocational Education and Training*, T. Leney (ed.), London.

Raffe D., C. Howieson and T. Tinklin (2005), "The Introduction of a Unified System of Post-Compulsory Education in Scotland", *Scottish Educational Review*, Vol. 37, No. 1, pp. 46-57.

Ravens (van), J. (2002), *Lifelong Learning: Which Ways Forward?*, D. Colardyn, ed., College of Europe, Kennicentrum EVC, Utrecht.

Rick K., K. Valckenborgh and H. Baert (2003), "Towards a Conceptualisation of 'Learning Climate'", EURONE&T Workshop Paper, Implementing a Learning Society in an Enlarging and Integrating Europe, Stirling, University, Scotland.

Ryan, P. (2002), *Individual Returns to Vocational Education and Training Qualifications: Their Implications for Lifelong Learning*, NCVER, Adelaide.

Schuller, T., A. Brasset-Grundy, A. Green, C. Hammond and J. Preston (2002), *Learning, Continuity and Change in Adult Life*, Centre for Research on the Wider Benefits of Learning.

Selby, C., L. Smith, K. Hummel and C. Cheang (2004), *The Valuing of Qualifications by Australian Employers*, NCVER, South Australia.

Smith, A. (2001), *Returns on Investment on Training: Research Readings*, NCVER, Adelaide.

Smyth E., M. Gangl, D. Raffe, D. Hannan and S. McCoy (2001), "A Comparative Analysis of Transitions from Education to Work in Europe", Final Report to the European Commission, ESRI (The Economic and Social Research Institute in Ireland), Dublin.

Spence, A. (1973), "Job Market Signalling", *Quarterly Journal of Economics*, Vol. 87, pp. 355-379.

Steinhäuser, K. (2002), *Modulare Nachqualifizierung im Zeichen moderner Bildungsökonomie. Ein Fallbericht*, unveröff. Dissertation, Marburg/Laan (Druck in Vorbereitung).

Teese, R. and J. Polesel (2003), *Undemocratic Schooling: Quality and Equity in Australian Secondary Education*, Melbourne University Press.

Tessaring, M. (1999), *Human Resource Potential and the Role of Education and Training*, CEDEFOP, Thessaloniki.

Torrance, H. and J. Coultas (2004), *Do Summative Assessment and Testing Have a Positive or Negative Effect on Post 16 Learners' Motivation for Learning in the Learning and Skills Sector?*, Learning and Skills Research Centre, London.

Wolter S. and J. Schweri (2003), *Coût/Bénéfice de la formation des apprentis pour les entreprises suisses*, www.bbt.admin.ch/berufsbi/publikat/f/wolter_f.pdf.

Young, M. (2003), "National Qualifications Frameworks as a Global Phenomenon: A Comparative Perspective", *Journal of Education and Work*, Vol. 16, No. 3, London.

ISBN 978-92-64-01367-4
Qualifications Systems
Bridges to Lifelong Learning
© OECD 2007

Chapter 5

Putting Mechanisms to Work Supporting Policy Responses

Having considered countries' policy responses for developing lifelong learning via qualifications systems (Chapter 2), the discussion moved on to examine the various influences on stakeholder behaviour and identified 20 mechanisms that could improve understanding of how those policy responses work and possibly render them more effective (Chapter 4). While the rationale for policy responses may vary and their effects might not be fully understood, the mechanisms have been identified on the basis of research evidence of their effects on stakeholders in the qualifications system. This chapter looks more closely at the dynamic connection between mechanisms and policy responses.

In Section 5.1 the quantitative and qualitative evidence from Chapters 3 and 4 are linked together in an effort to explain discrepancies. Each policy response is then examined by considering the mechanisms that might support it (Section 5.2). An attempt is made to judge the potential strength of influence each mechanism has on relevant policy responses. Short case studies reveal how countries have fared with the practical application of some mechanisms. Section 5.3 offers a kind of "useful" ranking of mechanisms based on the power and versatility of each.

5.1. Linking quantitative and qualitative evidence

The evidence for linkages between national qualifications systems and lifelong learning has been gathered together in Chapters 3 and 4. Chapter 3 attempted to examine the link with quantitative indicators. The exercise proved to be difficult, but some evidence can be derived: interesting correlations between proxy indicators for national qualifications systems and proxy indicators for lifelong learning. As stated several times however, these correlations are neither systematic nor always strong. They indicate the existence of a complex set of relationships between the many components that can describe or structure a qualifications system, and the many others than can describe or structure lifelong learning. It is therefore not surprising that the qualitative evidence in Chapter 4 is useful for examining these complex sets of relationships. In fact, quantitative and qualitative evidence do not necessarily link very well with each other. There are several reasons for this and it is useful to review them.

On the quantitative side, a few interesting correlations can be established between different indicators. There seems, for instance, to be a link between the existence of a dual system in a country and the proportion of adults undertaking learning activities. More generally, even if it does not appear that high levels of motivation to achieve qualifications are necessary for achieving high levels of lifelong learning – and even if data do not show which features of a qualifications system are likely to encourage or discourage greater lifelong learning – there is evidence that those who have not achieved a qualification at ISCED 3 or above and/or who have low levels of literacy are interested in the qualification component of learning. It may be that the offer of a credible "second chance" qualification plays an important part in motivating such people to learn; they are the common target group for policy makers, as can be judged by the adult learning programmes recently set in motion in most OECD countries (OECD, 2005a).

It should be remembered that the evidence given in Chapter 3 is based on assumptions, such as if a large number of learners are interested in a qualification this could mean that the system is conducive to learning for a qualification and/or that qualifications are useful for entering the labour market/achieving personal objectives. The existence of assumptions like this one indicates how difficult it is to establish robust correlations. There is barely any direct measure of the concepts used to describe qualifications systems.

This also holds true within data sources in each country; not even the background reports prepared for the study display quantitative data or indicators that directly support the qualitative arguments they contain. The typology of system features is an example of attempts to overcome these problems and establish correlations that could be linked to the qualitative evidence. There seems to be consensus about which general elements structure a qualifications system (Table 3.1), but these elements are conceptual constructs that do not necessarily translate well into quantitative indicators. It was not possible to find quantitative counterparts and only proxy variables could be used. One apparent exception that does measure well is the existence of a dual system in a country, if the measurement is the fraction of a cohort entering an apprenticeship with shared responsibility between an educational institution and a firm. Far more difficult is assessing whether a country has a straightforward credentialist system, and that indicator has proved unsatisfactory. There are cultural issues involved in defining a credentialist system, and more research needs to be done.

The data reviewed and analysed in Chapter 4 are substantial and, while the derivation of the 20 mechanisms is based on good evidence, the elements of the mechanisms could have been grouped in different ways. Quantitative correlations would have been a useful guide to effective groupings.

One solution to some of the problems described above about linking qualitative and quantitative evidence would be to organise review visits to countries, so as to include some form of ground research. Another is to refine the link between the mechanisms emerging from qualitative investigations and existing and future quantitative data. This would also entail a revision of the typology with additions/removals of some general elements and the addition of new countries to broaden the scope and provide additional variation. Qualitative elements seem to dominate the quantitative ones, though the latter are a very interesting first step. For now, it is necessary to move forward and look at the role of the 20 mechanisms to promote lifelong learning, for they could well form the basis of a new typology to describe qualifications systems – one that would have policy usefulness built into its design.

5.2. Policy responses and mechanisms

It is useful to examine each policy response and consider which mechanisms could be active and strongly support a policy response, and which ones might offer some useful support but not have a decisive effect. This is summarised in Table 5.1, where an attempt is made to allocate mechanisms to policy responses using two categories: a strong role, and a supporting role. For example, the mechanism *increasing learner choice* is likely to be effective within the policy response *increase flexibility and responsiveness*, and therefore have a strong role to play. However, the mechanism *lowering the cost of qualification* is likely to provide weaker but nevertheless important support for the *increase flexibility and responsiveness* policy response. It is possible for any mechanism to be strong in the context of one policy response, have a supporting role in another, and be absent from a third. The boundary between strong and weak is inevitably arbitrary and in some contexts it is likely that the power of a mechanism could be stronger or weaker than is outlined in Table 5.1. The table is therefore a suggested broad guide to the relationship between mechanisms and policy responses. In this chapter each mechanism is considered as acting alone, free from the influence of other mechanisms. This situation is hardly likely to be encountered in practice, and Chapter 6 considers interactions between mechanisms in detail. Table 5.1 is offered as a toolbox of useful devices for enhancing lifelong learning, and represents a significant outcome of the study.

The paragraphs after Table 5.1 offer a brief explanation of how the mechanisms support each policy response. For each response, strong effects are given in the first paragraph and supporting effects in the second.

Table 5.1. **A broad guide to the relationship between mechanisms and policy responses**

Policy responses	Mechanisms with a strong role	Mechanisms with a supporting role
Increase flexibility and responsiveness of the qualifications system	Increasing learner choice in qualifications. Providing credit transfer. Increasing flexibility in learning programmes leading to qualifications. Creating new routes to qualifications. Recognising non-formal and informal learning. Optimising stakeholder involvement in the qualifications system. Improving needs analysis methods so that qualifications are up to date. Ensuring qualifications are portable. Expressing qualifications as learning outcomes.	Establishing qualifications frameworks. Lowering cost of qualifications. Monitoring the qualifications system. Investing in pedagogical innovation.
Motivate young people to learn for qualifications	Communicating returns to learning for qualifications. Recognising skills for employability. Increasing learner choice in qualifications. Clarifying learning pathways. Providing credit transfer. Increasing flexibility in learning programmes leading to qualifications. Creating new routes to qualifications. Lowering cost of qualifications. Investing in pedagogical innovation. Optimising quality assurance. Improving information and guidance about qualifications system.	Establishing qualifications frameworks. Optimising stakeholder involvement in the qualifications system. Improving qualification use in recruitment. Ensuring qualifications are portable. Expressing qualifications as learning outcomes.
Link education and work through qualifications	Recognising skills for employability. Establishing qualifications frameworks. Clarifying learning pathways. Providing credit transfer. Increasing flexibility in learning programmes leading to qualifications. Recognising non-formal and informal learning. Optimising stakeholder involvement in the qualifications system. Improving needs analysis methods so that qualifications are up to date. Improving qualification use in recruitment. Ensuring qualifications are portable.	Creating new routes to qualifications. Monitoring the qualifications system. Investing in pedagogical innovation. Expressing qualifications as learning outcomes. Maximising co-ordination in the qualifications system. Improving information and guidance about qualifications system.
Facilitate open access to qualifications	Providing credit transfer. Creating new routes to qualifications. Lowering cost of qualifications. Recognising non-formal and informal learning. Improving information and guidance about qualifications system.	Establishing qualifications frameworks. Increasing flexibility in learning programmes leading to qualifications. Monitoring the qualifications system. Optimising stakeholder involvement in the qualifications system. Increase the use of outcome-based assessment methods. Maximising co-ordination in the qualifications system.
Diversify assessment processes	Providing credit transfer. Recognising non-formal and informal learning. Expressing qualifications as learning outcomes.	Increasing flexibility in learning programmes leading to qualifications. Monitoring the qualifications system. Investing in pedagogical innovation. Optimising quality assurance.

Table 5.1. **A broad guide to the relationship between mechanisms and policy responses** *(cont.)*

Policy responses	Mechanisms with a strong role	Mechanisms with a supporting role
Make qualifications progressive	Establishing qualifications frameworks. Clarifying learning pathways. Providing credit transfer. Creating new routes to qualifications. Expressing qualifications as learning outcomes. Maximising co-ordination in the qualifications system.	Increasing flexibility in learning programmes leading to qualifications. Recognising non-formal and informal learning. Monitoring the qualifications system. Optimising stakeholder involvement in the qualifications system. Ensuring qualifications are portable. Optimising quality assurance. Improving information and guidance about qualifications system.
Make the qualifications system transparent	Establishing qualifications frameworks. Clarifying learning pathways. Optimising stakeholder involvement in the qualifications system. Expressing qualifications as learning outcomes. Maximising co-ordination in the qualifications system. Optimising quality assurance processes.	Communicating returns to learning for qualifications. Monitoring the qualifications system. Ensuring qualifications are portable. Improving information and guidance about qualifications system.
Review funding and increase efficiency of the qualifications system	Providing credit transfer. Lowering cost of qualification. Recognising non-formal and informal learning. Monitoring the qualifications system. Optimising stakeholder involvement in the qualifications system. Improving needs analysis methods so that qualifications are up to date. Ensuring qualifications are portable. Improving co-ordination in the qualifications system. Optimising quality assurance.	Communicating returns to learning for qualification. Establishing qualifications frameworks. Clarifying learning pathways. Creating new routes to qualifications. Investing in pedagogical innovation. Expressing qualifications as learning outcomes.
Better manage the qualifications system	Establishing qualifications frameworks. Monitoring the qualifications system. Optimising stakeholder involvement in the qualifications system. Improving co-ordination in the qualifications system. Optimising quality assurance.	Providing credit transfer. Creating new routes to qualifications. Improving needs analysis methods so that qualifications are up to date. Improving information and guidance about qualifications system.

Policy response 1: Increase flexibility and responsiveness

Flexibility in qualifications systems is supported by all mechanisms that increase choice – for example, in widening the range of qualifications available and increasing the number of routes to them. Credit transfer offers flexibility within and between programmes, and can lead to partial qualification that will ease stepping out of a qualification programme and stepping back in sometime later. Recognition of non-formal and informal learning will also support the policy response through enabling flexible entry into qualification programmes. Portability of qualifications opens up options for people who revise their career plans or see a different opportunity to learn for qualification. Responsiveness to the needs of employers will be aided by these flexible measures, but perhaps more important to the stakeholders will be improvements in the ways skill needs are included in qualifications. By involving learners as stakeholders in qualification design and management, the qualification itself might become more learner-centred. Employers and providers will find qualifications that are outcome-based clearer to use and understand. The involvement of stakeholders generally will help maintain the pressure to respond to needs.

There are mechanisms that support customisation by creating more flexible outcomes for learners, but they do not play a direct role. For example, qualifications frameworks illustrate opportunities to transfer from one qualification programme to another. Lowering the cost of qualification means people can afford more and therefore have more choice. Another aspect of this learner orientation might be improved by monitoring the qualifications system to make sure that their needs are met. While pedagogy is not directly part of qualification, diversity in pedagogy could create a sense of customisation for the learner.

In Sweden, the Adult Education Initiative is part of a reform in adult learning. The intention was for all education and training that took place within the Initiative to be governed in form and content by the needs, wishes and capacity of the individual. The idea is that those adults most in need of education should be given a chance to catch up and add to their stock of knowledge and perhaps gain qualifications.

Approximately 800 000 adults, almost 20% of the workforce, were given a chance to supplement their previous education and training during a five-year period. Many of those taking part in the Adult Education Initiative were people who would probably otherwise never have had the chance to continue studying and gain qualifications. The broad recruitment was successful partly thanks to generous, earmarked funding as well as outreach activities carried out by trade-union organisations and organisations for the disabled.

The municipalities and the state were jointly responsible for the Adult Education Initiative. Financing took the form of state grants but each municipality was individually responsible for organising, planning and implementing the education and training.

During the Spring of 2001 the Swedish government presented goals and strategies for the development of adult learning based on the needs of the individual in a Bill (Adult Learning and the Development of Adult Education [prop. 2000/01:72]). The Bill sets out a strategy for support from the state and the municipalities for adult learning based on the needs of the individual. The focus is shifted from teaching in school-like forms to more flexible ways of providing support for the individual's learning. The individual should be the focal point and education and training should as far as possible be steered by the demands of users. Outreach activities, guidance, validation, accessibility and study support may be said to constitute the cornerstone of an infrastructure for lifelong learning. Responsibility for ensuring that all the elements of this structure are in place – with the exception of study support – rests with the municipal councils.

This flexibility must be developed on the basis of local conditions in each municipality. The municipalities play an important role as educational organisers, but should also develop their role as co-ordinators of information measures, counselling and education and training opportunities. This involves building up networks, creating forms and channels for co-operation and co-ordination between municipal administrations, state authorities and institutions, popular adult education, education and consultancy companies, partners on the labour market, organisations representing handicapped persons and other actors involved.

Policy response 2: Motivate young people to learn

The key mechanisms for motivating young people to learn are those that create clear benefit for getting a job. Young people will also be motivated to learn if they receive advice and guidance on the returns to qualifications in different careers. More choice also motivates young people, such as in range of qualifications available, different learning pathways, and flexibility in learning programmes, including pedagogical innovation. More choice through flexibility, for example by providing credit transfer, should lead to stronger motivation to learn for qualifications. Another kind of mechanism that could motivate people to learn is the way qualification generates employability and increases the perceived quality of the education and training on offer as well as the qualification that results from learning. If high costs of qualification (both in money and opportunity to earn) are likely to demotivate young people, lowering costs might have the opposite effect.

Motivation may also rise if recruitment processes make more use of qualification from secondary education and explicit use of the clarity resulting from use of qualifications frameworks and outcomes-based assessment methods. If more qualifications are seen as portable across the boundaries between types of job and types of learning programme, they may be seen by people as more desirable. Motivation to learn for qualification may be higher if the key stakeholders (learners, employers and learning providers) are involved in the management of general education.

In the United Kingdom the dropout rate in the school-to-work interface has been uncomfortably high for some years. Recent reports and comparative studies signal that this is an issue that needs attention. The participation rates of 16-year-olds in full-time education have remained relatively static at about 70-72%, and at 58-59% for 17-year-olds. The government set up an enquiry into 14-19 education that had the objective of reforming the qualifications process for young people in England: shifting the balance of incentives would lead to a greater proportion of young people prepared to commit themselves both to staying on and to making further progress in the education and training system compared to previous cohorts. The enquiry has led to the production of a White Paper.

The reforms will begin with a review of the curriculum experienced before age 14, on the basis that providing a sound foundation for what follows after age 14 is needed to help prevent disengagement. The level of prescription in the curriculum of 14-year-olds will be reduced to allow room for greater concentration on the functional elements Maths and English. Curriculum (and qualification) relevance is to be achieved by providing choice and flexibility, in particular by introducing more coherent and better-quality vocational provision. Young people who currently leave at 16 will be encouraged to stay in learning if they can tailor the vocational curriculum to their needs and aspirations but in a way that provides them with clear progression opportunities in the future; tailoring will include the option of combining vocational elements with more general learning. Interlocking diplomas at different levels has been proposed; young people will be motivated to enter a system where they can see the path ahead and gain credit for what they are doing. All stakeholders will be involved in developing the diplomas, which are intended to become established as a clear and valued alternative to the traditional academic qualifications route for vocationally oriented young people. For the most disengaged 14-to-16-year-old learners, a special pilot programme based on the existing post-16 scheme "Entry to Employment" will be developed.

Policy response 3: Link education and work

Many mechanisms strengthen the link between education and work. The inclusion of work experience in general education programmes, possibly as vocational tracks, is likely to be helpful. Programme content that leads to higher employability also helps, as will systematic analysis of skill needs in enterprises. The latter will ensure qualifications are up to date and encourage employers to use them in recruitment. Education and work can also be strongly linked by setting up a system for recognising non-formal and informal learning so that learning in the workplace can be used in further qualification, and learning gained outside work be recognised in work settings. Establishing qualifications frameworks that clearly show the links between qualifications that are generally vocational and academic in nature will help; similarly, portability of qualifications can bridge the gap between education settings and work settings. Credit transfer arrangements can also enable this bridging. Then there is the involvement of stakeholders such as employers who might appreciate the opportunities arising from better use of qualifications in recruitment processes and workplace development.

Supportive mechanisms will include investment in pedagogical innovation that will enable work-based learning to become more attractive to learners and providers, and the provision of new routes to qualifications. If qualifications use outcome-based methods, the additional clarity might make work applications clearer to employers. Sometimes existing qualifications serve the purpose of linking education and work, but the information available to learners may be weak; ensuring that the information is up to date and relevant is a supportive mechanism. Monitoring the response of learners to qualifications provision will allow co-ordination of the different elements to be optimised for linking education and work.

In Germany from the mid-1990s onward, four new IT qualifications were created for training at skilled worker level, and in 1997 they were recognised nationally. The main characteristic of the qualifications developed is that they are based on new structural models for initial vocational qualifications. They consist of a relatively stable core of vocational knowledge, skills and wider competencies, which make up the mandatory units. These are linked to optional units, which – depending on the occupational field – account for between one-third and half of the overall qualification.

Building upon these four qualifications, a system of "continuing education and training" with three career levels and a total of 35 qualifications was defined by the Federal Institute for Vocational Training (*Bundesinstitut für Berufsbildung*, BIBB) on behalf of the Federal Ministry for Education and Research, accompanied by an expert advisory panel appointed by the leading associations of the two sides of industry. On the first level are "specialists", on the second "operative professionals" and on the third "strategic professionals". The first level is made up of 29 specialist profiles (customer advisor, software developer, technician, etc.). They are accessible to holders of the four skilled worker qualifications and to learners from outside the profession. The individual profiles or qualifications are clearly defined by their fields of work (no substitution is possible); these can be used as entry qualifications for the next level up (operative professional level). Qualification and certification should take about one year. There are no examinations: the qualification is certified by an accredited private organisation. However, the operative professional exam is open to those who can make a convincing case that they have acquired the skills that justify admittance. This means that formal learning can be replaced by certification of work experience.

In a second step, four qualifications at the second career level of the system and two qualifications at the third were defined. For both levels a public exam in accordance with the Vocational Training Act is envisaged. The second level (operative professional) covers the following areas of qualification: IT skills, staff leadership/management, budget management, technical engineering, process engineering, project management and marketing. The staff leadership/management section is recognised as part of the trainer eligibility exam. At the third career level (strategic professional) the qualifications relate to the development of business policy and to planning resources, product lines or investments. The middle level of the system is considered equivalent to a Bachelor of Engineering, the highest level is equivalent to a Master of Engineering; the tasks at this level are currently for the most part carried out by university graduates.

In order to facilitate transition between the systems for vocational training and academic studies, the education and economics ministries and the social partners have advocated a system for counting vocational qualifications towards higher education qualifications, along with regulations for continuing education and training in IT. The Standing Conference of Ministers of Education and Cultural Affairs was called upon to allow such qualifications to be counted towards further studies in the case of the new IT qualifications by applying a points system as practised within the framework of the European Credit Transfer System.

Policy response 4: Facilitate open access to qualifications

Strong mechanisms include the development of new routes to existing qualifications that might be more attractive to some learners. This includes the transfer of credit for achievements from previous learning. Lowering the cost also means access to more expensive qualifications will become possible. Any mechanism that makes requirements of qualifications clear through better information and guidance systems will support this policy response, as will the opportunity to have prior learning recognised for a qualification.

Flexibility in learning programmes might engage learners who were not inclined to qualification-based learning, and a qualifications framework will make opportunities clearer to learners. Using learning outcomes to describe qualifications and learning programmes has the potential to clarify the necessary preparation for qualification-based learning and consequently open more routes. Any monitoring that uncovers obstacles to learning for qualifications will be useful for providers to consider. Involving a wide range of stakeholders might develop stronger trust in the access routes to qualifications that are often blocked. However, more open access and closer involvement of a range of partners will call for closer co-ordination of the parts of the qualifications system involved.

In Switzerland modularisation contributes to opening up access to qualifications. During the 1990s policy debates focused on increasing flexibility by introducing a modular system, especially into higher vocational education and training. Some professional associations started work on a scheme for professional and higher professional examinations under the auspices of the Federal Office for Professional Education and Technology. One of the outcomes has been the common development of similar curriculum modules for different professions (e.g. accounting, SME management), thus widening access.

During a first period of experimentation this system was well received by the professional associations, as there were positive effects on the professional outcomes for many modules. On the basis of these positive experiences the Swiss Parliament decided to strengthen the legal base for a general introduction of modularisation in the Swiss vocational education and training system via a new federal law on professional education (accepted by Federal Parliament at the end of 2002). One important element of the regulation is the dissociation of curriculum and qualification procedure.

The most important goal of the modularisation is to allow individuals to choose individual curricula, especially in terms of date, localisation of the module and composition/ structure. By recognising partial qualifications, this system meets the requirements of permeability and flexibility and increases the mutual recognition of modules.

The Federal Office is in charge of further developing modular education, assuring information on modular vocational education and training, and co-ordinating the mutual recognition of modules, curricula and pathways between different curricula. In order to achieve these goals, the Federal Office produced guidelines for modular vocational education and training at the end of May 2002. (*Cf. www.bbt.admin.ch/berufsbi/projekte/ modula/f/index.htm*, in French.).

Policy response 5: Diversify assessment processes

Strong mechanisms for this policy response include the introduction of credit transfer; different modes of assessment will need to be compared before transfer can take place. The same may be true for systems recognising prior learning. Outcome-based methods may also require the development of more diverse modes of assessment based on use of criteria.

Supporting mechanisms involving changes to learning programmes, through response to learner choice or due to innovation in teaching methods, will contribute more diverse methods, as will the need to ensure that assessment methods are fit-for-purpose and fulfil requirements of quality assurance methods. Monitoring developments in diversification of assessment methods will also be necessary to maintain confidence in the qualification outcomes resulting from these new approaches.

In Mexico attention has been paid to diversifying assessment processes through the use of three initiatives.

a) *Setting up systems to recognise non-formal and informal learning*

Working people and those who are unemployed may aspire to having their occupational competence certified, regardless of how it was acquired. They are encouraged to use the services of new assessment centres (*Centro de Evaluación*, CE) – these may be enterprises, chambers, enterprise associations, educative institutions, or unions. Around 1 400 centres are accredited to carry out assessments.

Persons possessing an occupational competence certificate may have that competence recognised within the academic and vocational routes. It will be possible to establish assessment credit criteria that link occupational competence certificates with programmes in the different educative cycles, levels and careers of the national educative system. The agreement includes the possibility for people who acquired learning outside the mentioned routes and who do not have any certificate to take tests to obtain recognition of their previous learning. New regulations stipulate that beneficiaries may gain recognition through certificates, records, diplomas or titles; learning accreditation is by subject matter, grades, cycles, levels or careers. Through the new regulations, 32 637 individuals have received the upper secondary education certificate (3C level, ISCED) and 656 have achieved a bachelor's degree in one of 24 occupations.

b) *Increasing the use of outcome-based assessment methods*

This mechanism is an intrinsic part of the standards-based development of vocational education and training. The assessment method used is outcome-based, according to criteria established in the national agencies. In other words, learning evidence is evaluated with respect to the performance criteria and application fields established to determine if a person is competent.

c) *Providing credit transfer*

Academic credit recognition and transfer is an issue of great importance for the 138 public and private institutions of higher education, affiliated to the National Association of Universities and Higher Education Institution (*Asociación Nacional de Universidades e Instituciones de Educación Superior, ANUIES*). Some inter-institutional programmes have begun to be implemented around credit transfer. For example, graduates from Aguascalientes Technological University (*Universidad Tecnológica de Aguascalientes*) on two-year study programmes may continue bachelor studies and embark on graduate studies at the Aguascalientes Autonomous University (*Universidad Autónoma de Aguascalientes*), by means of recognition and credit transfer.

Policy response 6: Make qualifications progressive

The key mechanisms all have to do with increasing coherence of the qualifications system – for example, developing a framework of qualifications or defined learning pathways that could include new routes to qualifications. Outcome-based methods and the operation of a credit transfer system will allow a clearer idea for all stakeholders of how one qualification builds or leads to another. The infrastructure of the qualifications system also needs to be well co-ordinated.

This policy response is supported by any action to make qualifications systems flexible and having achievement in one qualification count in another through, for example, recognition of non-formal learning or making qualifications portable. The involvement of stakeholders will help to ensure that unnecessary barriers to progressive qualification are identified and removed and that information and guidance clearly shows the progressive nature of qualifications. In addition to quality assurance measures this policy response will be informed by systematic monitoring of how people progress (or do not progress) through the qualifications system – with quality assurance, providers must ensure that qualifications are clearly progressive in practice.

The Associate Degree was added to the Australian Qualifications Framework in 2004. It is a new sub-degree qualification of two years' duration, positioned at an equivalent level to the Advanced Diploma (a mainly vocational education and training qualification).

In the past, some universities under their autonomous powers offered an associate degree as a local award accredited against local criteria. Now that the Associate Degree is a national qualification title with nationally agreed criteria and guidelines, it can be offered on a consistent basis *across sectors* by a range of providers able to meet the relevant government requirements for higher education qualification. These include public vocational education and training (*e.g.* Technical and Further Education institutions –

TAFEs) and private vocational education and training as well as higher education institutions.

The Associate Degree illustrates the flexibility inherent in the sectoral structure of the Australian Qualifications Framework. Because Australian qualifications are clearly sector-specific in their outcomes and quality assurance requirements, they can be offered by these different providers in all sectors without loss of clarity or certainty in respect of their particular sector-specific quality and standards. The capacity for a single institution to offer qualifications across sectors is an important aspect of the responsiveness of the system to local needs for a diversity of learning pathways.

The Associate Degree is also a progressive addition to the Australian Qualifications Framework in the following respects:

- It is a short-cycle degree particularly suited to the newer evolving knowledge-based, multidisciplinary occupations for paraprofessionals in fields such as biotechnology and nanotechnology.

- As such, it is responsive to the diversity of the international market and the globalisation of knowledge.

- It offers an alternative pathway to a related bachelor's degree, and an early exit point, as well as being a qualification in its own right.

- It is a stimulant to creative re-design of bachelor's degrees where an articulated pathway with full credit is required.

- It offers a learning alternative to the Advanced Diploma, with greater emphasis on the knowledge base of the academic discipline and on generic rather than specialist employability skills.

Policy response 7: Make the qualifications system transparent

Many mechanisms work to increase transparency. Qualifications frameworks and learning pathways are usually designed for this purpose. Making clear the learning goals of qualifications through the use of learning outcomes will help make the qualification clear to learners and more useful to recruiters. Coherence in management of all the wider aspects of qualifications systems (including the use of quality assurance processes) and having a range of agencies involved in qualification design and delivery will be important. Involving stakeholders in qualification development will help detect areas where the system requires clarification.

In addition to these strong measures, the portability of a qualification across settings may also support this policy response. The same benefit could arise from systematic monitoring of learner views of qualifications and the linkages between them. Sometimes the qualifications available and their requirements need to be explained more clearly to potential users, *e.g.* the potential returns to individuals for achieving a qualification.

The Spanish vocational education and training system has been reformed to make it more transparent for all users. The goal was the creation of an overall system of vocational training, qualifications and accreditation, in co-ordination with active policies for employment and fostering worker mobility and lifelong learning. The creation of a national system of vocational qualifications was part of the national programme of reform (1998-2002); one of its aims was the integration of subsystems of vocational training. Among the measures proposed was the creation of the National Institute of

Qualifications. In 2002 a new law on qualifications and vocational training became the basis for a qualifications framework. It also introduced the concept of occupational qualification, which is understood as the set of job-specific skills that can be acquired through formal and non-formal/informal processes that are subject to quality assurance.

The establishment of the vocational education and training qualifications framework allowed identification of the tools of transparency: the procedure for the recognition, evaluation and recording of occupational qualifications; the roles for information and guidance in vocational training matters; the restructuring of the network of vocational training centres; and the reordering and continuous updating of the vocational training offers linked to the vocational education and training qualifications framework. With these tools and through the study of equivalences between vocational training subsystems and the procedures for credit attribution in formal and non-formal learning – and through the monitoring, evaluation and improvement of its quality and workings – the national framework for vocational qualifications made a major contribution towards transparency.

The framework comprises the National Catalogue of Vocational Qualifications, which are modular in structure, arranged in 26 vocational families and ordered in five levels; the Catalogue is now in an advanced process of elaboration.

A recent document on education and training matters ("*Una educación de calidad para todos y entre todos*", *Ministerio de Educación y Ciencia, debate educativo.mec.es*, 2004) reaffirms the will to advance with the progressive integration of subsystems, recognising some of the more pressing and historical problems involved. The document is now open to a process of social and political debate.

Policy response 8: Review funding and increase efficiency

Efficiencies and cost reduction will arise from making qualifications count for more – through portability, transfer of credit, recognising existing learning and raising the awareness of employers. These mechanisms can be supplemented by others that ensure that qualifications are fully meeting the needs of stakeholders. They include making sure that needs analysis methods are accurate, a process that may be helped by involving key stakeholders. Quality assurance methods and monitoring procedures can be used to ensure that the qualification process itself is efficient and minimises the cost of individual qualifications. Finally, measures to increase co-ordination will directly affect the efficiency of a qualifications system.

Certain mechanisms will support this policy response, notably the effective communication of returns to learners. Frameworks, new routes to qualification and pedagogical advances might also reduce costs and make qualification more efficient. Outcome-based assessment, which has the virtue of transparency, might reduce inefficiencies while raising the level of coherent operation of the system.

In Denmark, *Individual Competence Clarification* (IKA or Individual *Kompetenceafklaring*) has been legally linked to adult vocational training as an option since 1997. Its aim is to clarify the individual's personal and professional competencies and eventual further training needs, and to prepare them for participation in adult vocational training. In 2002 approximately 22 000 people participated in an individual competence clarification programme. Compared to figures from 1999 this represents an increase of 13 776 persons, corresponding to an increase of about 168%.

If the applicant does not meet the admission requirements, the college is required to inform the student about those requirements. Counselling forms an integrated part of the application and assessment procedure.

On the basis of the assessment process mandated by legislation, a personal educational plan is drawn up for the applicant. The plan has a validity of six years. The flexible duration allows adults to work while obtaining a vocational qualification corresponding to the initial vocational education and training level. From a system perspective this is a way to increase efficiency. From an individual perspective it may raise motivation to participate in lifelong learning, because the individual only needs to complete modules in areas where they do not possess the required competence within a given qualification. From an economic point of view it might make lifelong learning more affordable, insofar as the individual competence clarification opens access to qualification on a partial basis over an extended period.

Policy response 9: Better manage the qualifications system

Improving management performance of qualifications systems might arise through use of mechanisms that introduce clear structures (frameworks), monitor the way the system is operating, and communicate clearly about how the system works. Involving stakeholders in these processes will also help with co-ordination. However better tools for co-ordination are a crucial part of the management process, as is the deployment of an effective quality assurance process.

Other mechanisms to link qualifications and help co-ordination are credit transfer systems and arrangements for making sure qualifications are optimally portable. Supporting the drive for better management will be mechanisms such as development of effective needs analysis methods and making sure information to users about the system is accurate and useful.

In Ireland, a process of reform and redevelopment of the qualifications system is under way. This process is based on legislation (the 1999 Qualifications [Education and Training] Act) and involves a combination of structural reorganisation and the introduction of a national framework of qualifications.

Three new statutory organisations were established in 2001, a National Qualifications Authority and two Awards Councils. They have been set the task of developing and implementing a National Framework of Qualifications based on standards of knowledge, skill and competence. A blueprint for the Framework was published in March 2003 and is becoming operational over a short transitional period.

The establishment of the new bodies, and the other provisions in the legislation, have already had significant effects throughout the structures and organisations that make up the qualifications system in Ireland. Arising out of a concerted process of consultation driven by the new Qualifications Authority, there has been widespread discussion on issues concerning all aspects of awards and qualifications, which has contributed greatly to the design of the new system of qualifications. The Authority is the single, independent policy-making and development engine driving the reform process. The introduction of the new Awards Councils has removed much of the complexity that characterised the previous system. Several awards systems previously located in various vocational education and training organisations have been gathered together under the remit of the new "Further Education and Training Awards Council", which is now the only statutory body awarding vocational education and training qualifications in Ireland. The new Council awards qualifications for a wide range of higher education institutions.

The National Framework is a structure of levels allowing qualifications to be compared easily. The Framework is defined as:

"The single, nationally and internationally accepted entity, through which all learning achievements may be measured and related to each other in a coherent way and which defines the relationship between all education and training awards."

Following the launch of the Framework in October 2003, implementation has proceeded quickly. New "framework" qualifications have been in use throughout higher education and training since the autumn of 2004 and the introduction of a new system of awards for further education and training (including vocational) was expected in mid-2005. In the meantime, work is proceeding on referencing hundreds of existing and former qualifications that will now be replaced by new awards, to the levels in the Framework.

The Framework is a structure of ten levels that accommodate awards gained in schools, the workplace, the community, training centres, colleges and universities, from the most basic to the most advanced levels of learning. All learning can thus be recognised, including that achieved through experience in the workplace or other non-formal settings. Details of the Framework and its operation can be found at *www.nfq.ie*.

For each level in the Framework, standards of knowledge, skill and competence have been set out that define the outcomes to be achieved by learners seeking awards. This introduces new meaning to an award, that it recognises learning outcomes – what a person with an award knows, can do and understands – rather than time spent on a programme.

In addition to the development of the Framework itself, the Qualifications Authority was mandated to introduce policies and procedures to promote learner mobility and improve opportunities for learners to gain access to qualifications. The resulting strategy sets out to bring about changes in relation to:

- Credit systems and recognition of prior learning.
- Transfer and progression routes.
- Entry arrangements.
- Information provision for learners.

The Framework's design takes into account the need to facilitate the mobility strategy. Further details of the strategy can be found in the paper "Policies, Actions and Procedures for Access, Transfer and Progression for Learners", available at *www.nqai.ie*.

5.3. Power and versatility of the mechanism

As noted above, mechanisms are placed into two categories according to whether they play a strong or supporting role. It is therefore possible to review the ways mechanisms support each policy response using Table 5.1 and to rank each mechanism according to the number of policy responses it is capable of supporting. Table 5.2 shows the outcome of this ranking process. Mechanisms that have a strong role to play in many policy responses are likely to be important. However, again, the boundary between strong and weak is arbitrary; and it is necessary to investigate carefully what the ranking is telling us.

Table 5.2. **Ranking the influence of mechanisms**

Mechanism	Number of policy responses where the mechanism has a strong role	Number of policy responses where the mechanism has a supporting role	Ranking
1. Communicating returns to learning for qualifications	1	2	19
2. Recognising skills for employability	2	0	16 =
3. Establishing qualifications frameworks	4	4	4
4. Increasing learner choice in qualifications	2	0	16 =
5. Clarifying learning pathways	4	1	8
6. Providing credit transfer	7	1	1
7. Increasing flexibility in learning programmes leading to qualifications	3	3	10 =
8. Creating new routes to qualifications	4	3	5
9. Lowering cost of qualifications	3	1	12 =
10. Recognising non-formal and informal learning	5	1	3
11. Monitoring the qualifications system	2	6	14
12. Optimising stakeholder involvement in the qualifications system	5	3	2
13. Improving needs analysis methods so that qualifications are up to date	3	1	12 =
14. Improving qualification use in recruitment	1	1	20
15. Ensuring qualifications are portable	3	3	10 =
16. Investing in pedagogical innovation	1	4	18
17. Expressing qualifications as learning outcomes	3	4	9
18. Maximising co-ordination in the qualifications system	4	2	6 =
19. Optimising quality assurance	4	2	6 =
20. Improving information and guidance about qualifications system	2	4	15

What does the ranking tell us?

First, it is important to appreciate that policy responses are derived from the country evidence provided. They exist in countries as mature policies or as a clear policy intention. The mechanisms are not directly derived from country evidence in the same way. They are based on a wider evidence base concerned with the ways they might change the behaviour of the main stakeholders. It is quite possible that some mechanisms are not used in some countries.

A useful exercise is to consider the meaning of a top rank for a mechanism. It might mean any or all of the following:

- It is the most useful way of improving lifelong learning through qualifications systems because it supports more policy responses than the other mechanisms.

- It is the most cost-effective action since it supports many policy responses.

- Where policy responses are ill-defined, perhaps because of the absence of reliable diagnosis of issues, the mechanism represents a safe option for optimising lifelong learning.

- It serves more purposes than the lower ranked ones because the purposes the latter serve are more specific.

The high-ranking mechanisms will have some properties that are worthy of further exploration. There are five mechanisms that support many policy responses: these are *providing credit transfer, optimising stakeholder involvement in the qualifications system, recognising non-formal and informal learning, establishing qualifications frameworks* and *creating new routes to qualifications*. Each of these five mechanisms supports almost all the policy responses and most support the policy responses strongly. The origins of these mechanisms are elaborated in Chapter 4 and their supportive function is described above. It might be useful to consider the possible source of their power in a little more detail.

Providing credit transfer

Allowing a person to have some of their learning achievement for one qualification be recognised for another seems a relatively simple process. However, there are preconditions for that transfer that call on many parts of the qualifications system. First, the achievement to be transferred must be defined and communicated. This means the curriculum and learning outcomes must be made explicit for each qualification. Second, the reliability and validity of the assessment of the learner and the quality of the qualification process must command respect. Third, the institution that provides the recognition of achievement and the receiving institution must be in some kind of systemic relationship where operations are compatible.

Thus providing credit transfer touches on a range of important characteristics of qualifications systems and, if a transfer process is designed and established, it acts as a useful reforming tool and a generator of coherence in the system. Providing credit transfer requires all partners in the qualifications system to review processes and reform those that are incompatible with the goal of allowing a learner's achievement recognised in one place to be recognised in another. The result is that the qualifications system becomes more systemic in function and many of the policy responses are strengthened. The more obvious examples are that the more systemic approach makes the qualifications system more transparent and makes qualifications progressive, but could also lead to greater efficiency in delivering learning for qualifications.

Optimising stakeholder involvement in the qualifications system

In the final analysis, stakeholders own the qualifications system. As providers and consumers of learning, their views on the ways of improving the system are obviously important. If policy responses aimed at improving the qualifications system are to be effective, the stakeholders need to be engaged as fully as possible. This engagement can take two forms – first as managers and operators of the qualifications system: it can be improved by creating an infrastructure of advisory and management boards that handle different aspects. Second, stakeholders can be engaged by providing a feedback loop from monitoring and evaluation activities to the core management of the system. Stakeholders are also a conduit for monitoring the qualifications system and communicating how the system works in practice; they can act to bring about transparency and coherence. Involving stakeholders can therefore create the conditions for further development in qualifications systems. It is not surprising this has a potential as a mechanism.

Recognising non-formal and informal learning

Recognition systems that generate information about learning achievements that have been acquired in a range of settings and that contribute to formal qualifications act as a means of opening access to these qualifications for many people. Having some learning recognised may encourage people to undertake further learning, possibly for an additional qualification. The volume of informal and non-formal learning is huge and therefore the potential to create routes into learning for qualification for individuals is also huge. These systems may also be effective "early warning" devices for specific learner needs and employer needs that are arising in life and work. They may also create a need for innovation in terms of assessment methodology. If the formal system is conducive to development, then the information arising from the recognition of non-formal and informal learning may be a rich source of developmental ideas. That recognition also brings in a range of new stakeholders who have been outside the formal systems (*e.g.* small enterprises, specific social groups). These stakeholders can create the conditions for involving more people in learning for qualification.

Establishing qualifications frameworks

Qualifications frameworks make explicit the relationship between qualifications. They aim to increase transparency and to show potential progression routes; they can become the basis of credit transfer systems. They are overarching tools that can be used to engage all stakeholders in developing and co-ordinating the qualifications system. Often they are used as tools for regulation and quality assurance. At the same time a qualifications framework can open opportunities to potential learners, because it makes progression routes clear and can offer the opportunity to rationalise qualifications by reducing the overlap between them. In all of these ways, frameworks create an environment where the whole qualifications system can be reviewed. This means that the management of the qualifications framework can be used as a tool to enhance many policy responses.

Creating new routes to qualifications

The creation of new routes to qualifications, including more flexible and multi-entry pathways, requires careful analysis of need beforehand and stakeholder discussions about the most appropriate form for these new routes. Their development would help clarify relationships between qualifications. Because they do not involve the creation of a new qualification, this is a relatively simple way of developing an environment more conducive to lifelong learning. Often the new route to qualification will draw on other mechanisms, such as the recognition of non-formal and informal learning; in focusing attention on these, it will be effective in promoting lifelong learning.

The value of supporting mechanisms

Some "strong role" mechanisms often appear as having a supporting role as well. This is unsurprising because a strong mechanism would also expected to have a supportive role in some instances. Some mechanisms that are significant in the "supporting role" do not feature in the "strong" category (*monitoring the qualifications system, investing in pedagogical innovation* and *improving information and guidance about qualifications systems*). Why should that be so? These three mechanisms deserve some attention from the policy-making point of view.

The rationale for the *monitoring of the qualifications system* has to do with providing bottom-up information to decision makers. In systems that have often been criticised as being too supply driven, it is not a surprise that listening to demand is a mechanism that can have a strong supportive role without being a key engine. To a large extent, *improving information and guidance about qualifications systems* enters the same category but the other way round: there is clear evidence that informing potential learners and/or learners seeking a qualification may have a supportive role (OECD, 2003, 2004 and 2005a). The rationale is twofold. First, individuals who are not aware of the possibility they have to undertake learning activities for a qualification must be informed about the potential benefits of *a*) learning; and *b*) learning for a qualification. Second, for the individuals already convinced about the value of learning and learning for a qualification, appropriate information and guidance would lead to better choice of qualification because these individuals need to be guided through a system that is almost always complex. Finally, *investing in pedagogical innovation* is also typically a mechanism that must have a supporting role. In the field of adult learning for instance, it is clear that lack of pedagogical innovation has been a strong deterrent to participation. Adults cannot be taught in the same way as young people. It may not be classified as a powerful mechanism but again, it is a good complement to strong mechanisms by acting on individuals' motivation to learn and to learn for a qualification.

In addition to identifying top-ranked mechanisms that should probably be considered top priority, Table 5.2 also identifies mechanisms that, if implemented with the strongest ones, "oil" the system and make it run smoothly. Some mechanisms are therefore engines while others act as lubricant. Interestingly, these mechanisms that have a supporting but not decisive role are very close to the needs of the individuals, namely: listening to them, adapting the pedagogy to their abilities and expectations, and informing and guiding them through their own qualifications system. This is highly relevant for policy making because these considerations have an impact in terms of costs. Whereas *providing credit transfer*, *recognising non-formal and informal learning* or *establishing qualifications frameworks* might be expensive, there are reasons to believe that *monitoring the qualifications system*, *investing in pedagogical innovation* or *improving information and guidance about qualifications systems* might be less costly and still provide support for policy responses.

The implications of these conclusions are discussed further in Chapter 6, and are the focus of a new OECD study on recognition of non-formal and informal learning and credit transfer (OECD, 2005b).

5.4. Change mechanisms

There is evidence that some countries attach special significance to particular mechanisms because their deployment can have deep or wide-ranging effects on other mechanisms, and therefore systems. One mechanism might, for example, enable another or multiply its effect. On the basis of this analysis, it is possible to identify three mechanisms called *change mechanisms*:

- Communicating returns to learning for qualifications.
- Establishing qualifications frameworks.
- Investing in pedagogical innovation.

This analysis has been carried out on a theoretical basis with no reference to Table 5.1.

In interpreting how these three mechanisms are used, it becomes clear that in contrast to the "lubricant" mechanisms discussed above, they generally do not affect learners directly, and provide few direct benefits for learners. Their effect is seen in the system dimension, and their main characteristic is that they are agents of change. We can contrast the benefits for learners arising out of the introduction of a credit system with the less immediate results of the introduction of a qualifications framework. However, from a system perspective, it is clear that a qualifications framework can facilitate the development of credit systems, for example by providing an environment in which credit arrangements can apply on a wider scale than is otherwise possible (nationally or even internationally).

These "change mechanisms" are seen to have particular effects in their interaction with other mechanisms, where they can operate as "enablers", "multipliers" or "triggers".

Investment in pedagogical innovation can provide the environment that enables reforms to increase flexibility in learning programmes. Communicating the returns to learning for qualifications can directly focus attention on employability, and provide the trigger for improvement in the use of qualifications in recruitment processes. The establishment of qualifications frameworks is identified as a multiplier, enhancing and co-ordinating the effects of many other actions such as the development of learning pathways, the introduction of credit systems, and the provision of new routes to qualifications. Table 5.3 arranges the set of mechanisms to illustrate the key "change mechanisms" and the other mechanisms with which they primarily interact; obviously, multiple interactions are possible.

Table 5.3. **Change mechanisms and their interaction with other mechanisms**

Change mechanism	Establishing qualifications frameworks	Communicating returns to learning for qualification	Investing in pedagogical innovation
Mechanisms with which "change mechanisms" primarily interact	Clarifying learning pathways. Providing credit transfer. Creating routes to qualifications. Recognising non-formal and informal learning. Monitoring the qualifications system. Optimising stakeholder involvement in the qualifications system. Ensuring qualifications are portable. Improving co-ordination in the qualifications system. Optimising quality assurance.	Recognising skills for employability. Increasing learner choice in qualifications. Optimising stakeholder involvement in the qualifications system. Improving qualification use in recruitment. Improving information and guidance about qualifications systems.	Increasing flexibility in learning programmes leading to qualifications. Lowering cost of qualifications. Improving needs analysis methods so that qualifications are up to date. Expressing qualifications as learning outcomes.

The use of mechanisms as change agents is illustrated with particular clarity in the establishment of qualifications frameworks. In the countries where this mechanism has been deployed as part of a policy response, it is often explicitly identified as a means of initiating wider system change or of deepening the effect of such change (Coles, 2005). The Irish country background report heralds the introduction of a national framework of qualifications as the overture to a thorough reform of the qualifications system. This process is outlined in an appendix to the report of Thematic Group 1 of this study, which addresses the effect of qualifications frameworks as "drivers of change".

At the time of preparing this book, it is known that several European countries are actively considering the development of national or systemic frameworks of qualifications. International framework development is also under way. The European Heads of State have asked for a European Qualifications Framework to be in place by the end of 2006.

References

Coles M. (2005), *International and National Developments in the Use of Qualifications Frameworks*, ETF (European Training Foundation), Turin.

OECD (2003), *Beyond Rhetoric: Adult Learning Policies and Practices*, OECD, Paris.

OECD (2004), *Career Guidance and Public Policy – Bridging the Gap*, OECD, Paris.

OECD (2005a), *Promoting Adult Learning*, OECD, Paris.

OECD (2005b), *Recognition of Non-formal and Informal Learning and Credit Accumulation and Transfer*, Discussion Paper, document prepared for the expert meeting held in Paris, 16-17 June.

ISBN 978-92-64-01367-4
Qualifications Systems
Bridges to Lifelong Learning
© OECD 2007

Chapter 6

Using Mechanisms to Review Policy Responses

This chapter draws on all the evidence and analysis presented in earlier chapters to discuss three tools that policy makers can use to develop qualifications systems to deliver more and better lifelong learning. The emphasis is on concrete actions and practical advice. The first tool is the use of mechanisms to review present and future policy on qualifications systems, to test their robustness and see if the benefits they promised have been delivered. Some mechanisms are more powerful than others in that they appear to have greater potential influence on policy responses to lifelong learning than others. The practical application of these special mechanisms is the second tool. The third is based on an analysis of the complexity of interactions between mechanisms and of how mechanisms can be used to support one another (and therefore the policy response) and avoid counterproductive interactions.

In Section 6.1 the potential of qualification systems to influence lifelong learning positively is reviewed and the three tools are outlined. In Section 6.2 the ways mechanisms interact with one another is discussed and, in Section 6.3, two examples of problems are used to illustrate how mechanisms can be set in a hypothetical country context. Section 6.4 offers some concluding thoughts on the outcomes of the study and possible next steps.

6.1. A positive influence on lifelong learning

Policy making for lifelong learning in the arena of qualifications systems is difficult, underdeveloped and possibly undervalued. This chapter suggests that it is useful to review the role of qualifications systems in promoting lifelong learning and discusses some of the practical issues for policy makers.

Lifelong learning is one item on the political agenda that has positive consequences in almost all domains of life in a country. It is crucially important in terms of the well-being of a population. It is used as a way of achieving global benefits such as economic advantage, but also wider benefits such as good health. Lifelong learning has certainly a role to play in many of the main issues than cut across most OECD member countries: ageing of populations, skills shortages, human capital development, productivity, competitiveness, immigration, democracy and citizenship. In recent years, policies for developing lifelong learning have ranged over many areas of social and economic activity that influence education and training systems; the latter have been changed significantly in many countries with renewed efforts to increase accessibility and participation in learning. Policies for raising basic skill levels and the creation of financial incentives for learning or providing learning are examples. Participation in this OECD study has led countries to examine qualifications systems as potential levers to enhance lifelong learning. As a result, many have made their qualifications system much more central to lifelong learning policy and the key question has shifted from "can qualifications systems influence lifelong learning?" to "how can we optimise the qualifications system so that it provides the greatest incentive to learn throughout life?". In this study information has been scrutinised from 23 countries regarding the latter question.

From the wide-ranging discussion of evidence generated by this study it is clear that there are indeed opportunities to use qualifications systems to develop lifelong learning. This chapter deals with three main tools that policymakers could use:

- Using the set of mechanisms as the basis for a review of policy responses.
- Ensuring that the powerful mechanisms are included in policy responses wherever possible.
- Paying attention to possible positive and negative interactions between the mechanisms.

The first tool is applied to existing policy responses to lifelong learning. The set of mechanisms can be used to discover if the original logic underpinning the creation of policy responses remains robust. For example, have the benefits they promised been delivered, or are they still expected? In most countries policy responses have not been evaluated for impact, and there is a belief that some of them are still to deliver the desired outcomes several years after their deployment. That belief is emerging from a close look at the qualitative data collated and analysed in this study. It is clear that the main statistical sources of impact of qualifications systems on lifelong learning are not able to yield the feedback policy makers require; limited quantitative evidence is reported in Chapter 3, and it does not point to a clear positive correlation between learning for qualifications and improving lifelong learning, except perhaps for those with low qualifications.

Systematic review of current policy responses is therefore a good starting point. It is possible to use the mechanisms for building new policy responses, keeping in mind that each mechanism is defined as *a means of influencing the behaviour of main stakeholders* and can therefore enhance policy responses. During the spring of 2001, the Swedish government presented goals and strategies for the development of adult learning based on the needs of the individual in a bill that sets out a strategy for support from the state and the municipalities. This approach clearly has to do with the four mechanisms that put the learner at the centre of the learning process: communicating returns to learning for a qualification, increasing learner choice in qualification, investing in pedagogical innovation and improving information and guidance. Another example comes from Mexico, where attention has been paid to diversifying assessment processes through the use of three initiatives: setting up systems to recognise non-formal and informal learning; increasing the use of outcome-based assessment methods; and providing credit transfer. These mechanisms are also identified in many other countries.

The second tool involves analysing policy responses to ensure they incorporate the powerful mechanisms identified in this book as decisive in making qualifications systems more responsive to the lifelong learning agenda. This tool involves the use of a specific set of mechanisms that appear to have greater influence on policy responses to lifelong learning than others, either in their wide applicability to policy responses or in their potential as "agents of change". As the Swiss background report indicates, the political structure and cultural diversity in Switzerland has required that special attention be paid to consensus building through *optimising stakeholder involvement in the qualifications system*. Recently, the importance of this mechanism to support specific reforms has been made clear. The practical application of these special mechanisms in policy responses to lifelong learning is also examined in this chapter.

A third tool for policy makers arising from the study is the opportunity that mechanisms offer to appreciate the interaction between different reforms within a country. In Ireland for example, rhetoric developed around the newly implemented qualifications framework, which clearly states that a qualifications framework is a way of making other mechanisms more efficient. The country context matters a great deal when considering the usefulness of mechanisms and will make the deployment (or otherwise) of mechanisms unique in each case. An issue that arises immediately is the complexity of interactions between mechanisms, how they can be used to support one another (and therefore the policy response) and how counterproductive interactions can be avoided. This issue is also examined through examples later in the chapter.

6.2. Mechanisms in strategic combination

Some if not all the mechanisms presented in this book connect with one another, at least to some extent. Policy makers need to take account of these possible interactions and assess the consequences of using combinations. It is not possible here to provide a comprehensive review of the strategic use of mechanisms in combination, however the chapter does draw attention to possible effects of interactions, both strategic and counterproductive. These interactions may positively amplify the expected effects of mechanisms or create undue competition among stakeholders whose behaviour they trigger.

The five highly ranked strong mechanisms identified in Chapter 4 are, in order of descending importance: *providing credit transfer, optimising stakeholder involvement in the qualifications system, recognising non-formal and informal learning, establishing a qualifications framework* and *creating new routes*. The five require special attention in terms of interactions as the case is made that they are powerful because they are strong elements of many policy responses. It is also possible to analyse the set of mechanisms in terms of their potential as "multipliers" or "enablers"; on this basis a second set of change mechanisms emerge which have been identified in Section 5.3. A third group of mechanisms has been identified as important because they play a supportive role in many policy responses, possibly because they act at the level of the individual. All three categories of powerful mechanisms are summarised in Table 6.1.

Table 6.1. **Powerful mechanisms**

Five highly ranked strong mechanisms	Three change mechanisms	Five highly ranked supporting mechanisms
Providing credit transfer	Establishing qualifications framework	Monitoring the qualifications system
Optimising stakeholder involvement in the qualifications system	Communicating returns to learning for qualifications	Establishing qualifications frameworks
Recognising non-formal and informal learning	Investing in pedagogical innovation	Investing in pedagogical innovation
Establishing a qualifications framework		Expressing qualifications as learning outcomes
Creating new routes to qualifications		Improving information and guidance about qualifications system

Reviewing Table 6.1 suggests that *establishing qualifications frameworks* is particularly significant as it is highly ranked as a strong mechanism against others, has the potential for system change and is a significant supporting mechanism. Especially noteworthy is the fact that *establishing a qualifications framework* is a change mechanism that enables the four other highly ranked strong mechanisms. Few countries have a qualifications framework but many are considering the potential, especially in Europe. The benefits of introducing a qualifications framework have been discussed in Chapters 4 and 5 and a summary listing is included in Annex A. For all these strengths, there may be some good reasons not to introduce a qualifications framework. These could include reasons of devolved governance, perceptions of a challenge to the primacy of demand-led driving forces, and cost.

6.3. Examples of policy review – addressing two problems

From a policy-making point of view, there are two main approaches to using qualifications systems (and mechanisms) to develop lifelong learning. The first is to work on motivation of learners and the intermediaries that work with learners, and the second is to reduce barriers to learning for qualification. There is research suggesting that motivation of key stakeholders may not be the most important aspect of delivering lifelong learning (Coffield, 2001). The removal of structural and social barriers (*e.g.* gender, employment status) is considered to be more important. While it clearly is important, there is evidence in the context of lifelong learning regardless of qualification that motivation of learners and intermediaries may not be present even if all the possible barriers are lifted. Therefore, motivation itself cannot be only a second-order condition. However, even if it is accepted as a primary factor, there is little research evidence about the link between motivation to learn and learning. That lack of evidence may be a reason for the high level of interest from countries in this OECD study.

Motivation needs to be understood in this wider context, for three reasons. First, if national qualifications systems are to impact on lifelong learning, all stakeholders involved in designing and shaping them should be convinced about the possible linkages between the two and be motivated to work purposely toward an improvement in the direction of a better promotion of lifelong learning. Second, the motivation of individuals – the main stakeholder group – is one of the necessary conditions for those individuals to undertake lifelong learning activities (OECD, 2003 and 2005). Third, observing the mechanisms listed in Chapter 4, it is obvious that motivation is the key concept underlying many of them, as it is through analysis of motivation in Chapter 3 that they were identified.

Addressing the issue of motivation involves all the other issues that the reader came across in the previous chapters: lower cost, better coherence, greater transparency, maximum responsiveness, some stability, a high degree of trust, etc. When motivation is added, all these factors create the conditions for the full involvement of the main stakeholder groups: individuals, employers, providers of learning and providers of qualifications. This requires analysis to be performed locally, nationally and internationally when evidence appears. Here the aim is to identify 1) the stakeholders that must be motivated (not all of them need motivation at any point because they may already be highly motivated or because it is not relevant in a particular context or at a particular time); and 2) the best way to motivate them, given the analysis to date.

Policy makers confront problems, and the approach in this section is to use the diagnosis of two specific problems to bring together different kinds of evidence – about how mechanisms work and about the ways stakeholder groups can be motivated. The problems will inevitably be hypothetical since no single country context is a usefully general model for contexts in other countries.

Even if there is clear evidence of a problem area – for example, there is no culture of learning for a qualification, or the performance of the labour market is not very high – analysis of the problem can be difficult. The difficulties may arise from the point of view of almost any given stakeholder. In the first example for instance, individuals seem to be the prime cause of this lack of "qualifications culture". However, further thinking immediately leads to the providers that may not have created an effective culture of learning for a qualification, perhaps by not communicating enough about its potential benefits. It is also probably the case that employers do not reward qualification(s) highly enough and therefore they also contribute to the problem. Interestingly, in some countries, the problem may arise because individuals value learning for its own sake. As a consequence, the possible outcomes of learning are not well known and certainly not fully utilised.

Precisely because the matter is complex and because most of the stakeholders are involved in every analysis that can be made, the mechanisms proposed in this book can be used in combination to target the appropriate stakeholders, according to where motivation is deficient. This has to be so because the motivation of stakeholders depends on many factors and the stakeholders described in this book are very different one from another. To be efficient, the mechanisms have to be utilised according to the diagnosis being produced; that is the main thesis underpinning this section. The use of motivation in this way is based on mechanisms because the latter are designed from analysis of motivation.

However, in this chapter, the effect of motivating more than one group is important whereas each mechanism may act on only one.

Qualifications systems are "heavy" bodies, with high inertia, and it is rather costly to change them – they are usually extremely complex and the product of decades of evolution. Change is costly time-wise because of the many stakeholders involved and the time it may take to build a consensus. It is costly also in terms of financial resources because it is rarely possible to change just one part of the system in isolation. In short, national qualifications systems are slow-moving and even when it is clear that the main stakeholders have an interest in making it move.

Two broad problems are now discussed: lack of performance of the labour market, and lack of perception of the value of qualification(s).

Problem 1: Weak link between education and the labour market

If labour market performance is an issue and if the policy response to the lifelong learning agenda is to try to motivate stakeholders through *linking education and work* (Policy Response 3), then ten mechanisms can be used in a strong role and six in a supporting role. They are described in Table 5.1 and repeated here (Table 6.2). These affect all three stakeholders groups and to analyse all the interactions would be very complicated. The country context will also affect the analysis. This section nevertheless identifies some of the interactions as examples.

The policy response *link education and work* can affect most of the stakeholder groups in a positive way. Individuals in particular will feel they should seek a qualification because, with this link made explicit, it is likely that the return to investing in additional learning and/or getting a qualification will be higher. For example, individuals will have the incentive to undertake learning activities but they could also claim a qualification through recognition of prior learning. However, typically, too narrow a focus on employability may revive the usual gap of understanding and the lack of consensus between the education side and the labour market side: the former usually privileges rapid job placement whereas the latter is more interested in skills and competencies being acquired and documented. There are situations where an individual needs rapid placement into a job; for example, when their subsistence is too meagre or where a family is to be fed. Taking time to study for a qualification is not a priority. There are also situations where individuals would be

Table 6.2. **Link education and work as a policy response (extract from Table 5.1)**

Policy response	Mechanisms with a strong role	Mechanisms with a supporting role
Link education and work through qualifications	Recognising skills for employability.	Creating new routes to qualifications.
	Establishing qualifications frameworks.	Monitoring the qualifications system.
	Clarifying learning pathways.	Investing in pedagogical innovation.
	Providing credit transfer.	Expressing qualifications as learning outcomes.
	Increasing flexibility in learning programmes leading to qualifications.	Maximising co-ordination in the qualifications system.
	Recognising non-formal and informal learning.	Improving information and guidance about qualifications system
	Optimising stakeholder involvement in the qualifications system.	
	Improving needs analysis methods so that qualifications are up to date.	
	Improving qualification use in recruitment.	
	Ensuring qualifications are portable	

better off completing a cycle of qualification before (re-)entering the labour market; this is the case when individuals need a qualification to progress further in the system. There is evidence in many countries that, when economic growth is good and employers are in need of additional labour, individuals undertaking learning activities – either in the initial education and training system or in the adult learning system – are recruited even before the completion of their qualification. This book does not aim at deciding which way is best, but it is clear that there are competing purposes, and careful evaluation of the pros and cons is needed when a job is in competition with learning for a qualification.

Using other mechanisms such as *investing in pedagogical innovation* or *improving information and guidance about qualifications system* will certainly have a positive effect on individuals (OECD, 2004). However, they may have an impact on cost and a deterrent effect on either or both of the other stakeholder groups: employers and providers. Several other mechanisms will create positive incentives for some stakeholders but may create additional complexity for others. This is the case with mechanisms such as *creating new routes to qualifications*. Another clear example of the complexity of policy making in this field is the mechanism *recognise skills for employability*. It will clearly encourage individuals to seek a qualification but it may scare employers away if they feel there is a risk of poaching, *i.e.* employees leaving for a better labour market position after acquiring qualifications. Poaching effects are also to be expected with mechanisms such as *ensuring qualifications are portable*.

In summary, there is no such thing as a set of mechanisms operating in strategic combination that provide only positive impacts on the main stakeholders and the national qualifications and lifelong learning systems. Many more examples of possible positive and negative influences between mechanisms. Here, the intention is to raise awareness regarding the complexity of using the mechanisms together. Having said that, there are simpler examples where the range of possibilities is narrow and therefore where the appropriate use of mechanisms is easier to determine. This is the case with the second example.

Problem 2: Lack of perception of the value of qualification(s)

If a lack of perception of the value of qualification(s) is a problem, there are many possible policy responses. If the policy response to the country lifelong learning agenda is to try to motivate stakeholders through facilitating open access to qualifications (Policy Response 4), then five mechanisms with a strong role can be used. They are described in Table 5.1 and repeated here (Table 6.3). As in the previous example, the problem can be

Table 6.3. **Facilitate open access to qualification as a policy response (extract from Table 5.1)**

Policy response	Mechanisms with a strong role	Mechanisms with a supporting role
Facilitate open access to qualification	Providing credit transfer. Creating new routes to qualifications. Lowering cost of qualifications. Recognising non-formal and informal learning. Improving information and guidance about qualifications system	Establishing qualifications frameworks. Increasing flexibility in learning programmes leading to qualifications. Monitoring the qualifications system. Optimising stakeholder involvement in the qualifications system. Expressing qualifications as learning outcomes. Maximising co-ordination in the qualifications system

treated by motivating individuals or employers. Some of the former may not realise all the benefits they could have from being qualified. Some of the latter may not see any interest in matching their recruitment policy with a particular set of qualifications.

Many of the mechanisms listed in Table 6.3 and seen as having a strong role are likely to have an impact on the motivation of individuals. These mechanisms are interesting for policy makers because often individuals are not interested in a qualification. They often believe they will have to learn again if they engage in a qualification process. This belief that there is a learning component in the process is a strong deterrent for many individuals, especially if they think they will have to learn in a formal setting, such as a classroom (an unattractive prospect), and especially for low-skilled people who are the ones most commonly denying their (re-)skilling needs (OECD, 2003, 2005).

However, many of these mechanisms are disconnected from any additional formal learning. *Providing credit transfer* or *recognising non-formal and informal learning* does not necessarily require additional learning in formal settings. *Expressing qualifications as learning outcomes* supports the process of awarding a qualification without reference to additional formal learning. As a consequence, if the lack of motivation stems from a lack of interest in learning in formal settings, using any of these mechanisms and communicating potential outcomes would provide a clear incentive for individuals to learn which, in time, may be recognised in a qualification.

Interestingly, this communication issue again raises the question of the typical gap between education and employment. The gap is also still embedded in the policy response *facilitating open access to qualification*. There is indeed some evidence that *improving information and guidance about qualifications systems* is a mechanism with a strong role in motivating individuals because, as seen above, individuals must know that there are other ways than traditional learning in a classroom setting to achieve a qualification. In addition, explaining the potential benefits of a qualification may provide individuals with incentive: there is evidence that poor awareness of the direct and indirect effects of a qualification is a clear factor in people disregarding it.

If individuals become aware of the return on investing in a qualification, they are more willing to undertake a qualification process. However, there is clearly a difference between information about qualification(s) programmes and guidance on progression in work. In the former case, information and guidance officers would clearly focus on lifelong learning issues, such as obtaining a qualification or progressing through the qualifications system. In the latter case, guidance officers would instead stress job placement issues and job progression. As an example, this latent issue has become particularly important with the growing use of one-stop centres to provide a wide range of services in a single place. The initial idea is quite tempting: minimising cost and time spent for potential learners by providing all sorts of related services in one single institution. Information and guidance are very relevant here because there is evidence of some conflicts between education officers and employment officers. Again, this book does not aim to provide a clear-cut answer to whether lifelong learning goals have priority over job placement or the other way around, especially considering that they have many purposes in common. However, the potential competition should be underlined.

6.4. The way forward

Many studies have been carried out on both national qualifications systems and lifelong learning. However, very few of them explicitly link the two; the intersection is under-researched and therefore still relatively poorly understood. This book and the publications associated with it – especially the country background reports and the Thematic Groups' reports[1] – are therefore important for improving understanding of the potential role of national qualifications systems in promoting lifelong learning. The dissemination of this book could for instance improve communication among experts, users and practitioners by providing a common language and useful concepts based on discussion and significant international consensus. Beyond the conceptual component, the many examples reported throughout this book could help shape the future thinking and, ultimately, policy responses.

The book identifies the development of frameworks at national level as a significant feature emerging in the qualifications landscape. Frameworks have a strong potential for system change and reform, and can be a key factor in the implementation of other mechanisms such as credit transfer systems and the recognition of non-formal and informal learning. In those countries where the framework mechanism has been deployed as part of a policy response, it is explicitly identified as a means of initiating wider system change or of deepening the effect of such change. Although only a few countries have a qualifications framework in place, many are considering the potential of this mechanism, especially in Europe. A further development, very recently, is the emerging concept of transnational qualifications frameworks, or "meta-frameworks" which are effectively ways to relate national frameworks to each other: in the European Union, rapid progress is being made towards the development of a European Qualifications Framework, and within Europe generally the Framework for Qualifications of the European Higher Education Area has now been established (EC, 2005).

Much work remains to be done to grasp fully the consequences of the findings contained in this book in terms of policy responses. The most useful way to use the book would be for countries to reflect on their priorities and their possible policy responses to the lifelong learning agenda. Not all countries would like to see the same issues addressed (in the field of education and training or regarding the labour market), nor do they all have the same target groups for their policies. There are some common high-priority target groups across countries, such as low skilled individuals, small and medium enterprises and low-quality providers of qualifications – but there are many more that need to be defined locally. The possible outcomes, in terms of socio-economic benefits for the main stakeholders, very much depend on adequately setting this policy framework. Despite the glaring lack of theoretical support to underpin the empirical findings provided in this book, some recent work has been helpful in providing a background to help policymakers (Grubb, 2004; ETF, 2004).

It may be useful to consult with countries that did not participate in this study, to review whether all these policy responses to lifelong learning have been fully considered. The value of international activities relies greatly on the capacity to exchange and share. If not used comprehensively everywhere, all the responses are used to some extent somewhere. If generalisation may not always be appropriate, awareness of other countries' policy responses to specific issues in specific circumstances often offers added value. To that extent, the policy response review using mechanisms suggested earlier in this chapter is a step toward improving policy learning from one country to another. These reviews would provide an excellent opportunity to carry out a cost evaluation. Any type of comparative exercise would bring added value in the search for diagnoses of common problems related to lifelong learning.

All the participants in the OECD study are well aware of the many other ways lifelong learning can be promoted that do not include the use of national qualifications systems. However this book points to a widely shared belief among those closest to the qualifications systems in a large range of countries that appropriate qualifications reform can be instrumental in influencing lifelong learning. Although the firm evidence has yet to emerge that they are correct, what is significant is the very similar range of tools that they are using to relate qualifications systems to lifelong learning issues. This book has helped to identify some of these potentially useful tools for policy makers, and has proposed 20 mechanisms that provide a means by which qualifications systems can promote better lifelong learning. The ways these mechanisms are deployed depends on the specific problems, the country context and the prevailing social and cultural conditions. Because these external conditions are so significant – and as is often the case – this book probably raises more questions than it answers. Nevertheless, an agenda seems to be set for the further development of qualifications systems targeted at lifelong learning. One of the most important agenda items for future action is the development of better quantitative data.

Recognition of non-formal and informal learning and credit transfer (in the context of a qualifications framework) are two themes that have emerged from this study as particularly important, and the OECD plans to investigate them further in a follow-up study. While some countries have made significant progress in these fields, recognition of non-formal and informal learning and credit transfer are fairly new on the policy agenda of many countries, and institutional arrangements are fragmented at the international level. To help develop useful information for policy makers, there is a need to gather extensive evidence. What are the actual arrangements for developing these fields? How are such arrangements linked to the qualifications systems? Who governs the arrangements? Who finances them? What are the drivers behind such developments? The new study aims to examine the key issues, on which the lack of data is conspicuous: the different institutional arrangements; technical organisation; the cost of different arrangements and the means for the public and private sectors to finance the systems; the characteristics of users and the relevance to the labour markets; and the impact of current trends such as internationalisation and the new information and communication technologies. The study aims to research the answers to questions that are critical in promoting lifelong learning: under what conditions can experiential knowledge, skills and wider competencies best be codified and credit transfer best be arranged? Under what conditions would such codification and credit transfer potentially bring "negative" effects? The outcome will serve a wide range of stakeholders – government policy makers, institutional decision makers, the industry leaders, and learners.

Note

1. The full reports can be downloaded from *www.oecd.org/edu/lifelonglearning/nqs*.

References

EC (European Commission) (2005), *Framework for Qualifications of the European Higher Education Area*, Bologna Working Group on Qualifications Frameworks, Brussels.

Coffield, F. (2001), *The Necessity of Informal Learning*, The Policy Press, Bristol.

ETF (European Training Foundation) (2004), *Policy Learning*, Annual Report, Turin.

Grubb, N. (2004), *The Education Gospel: The Economic Power of Schooling*, Harvard University Press, Cambridge (Massachusetts) and London.

OECD (2003), *Beyond Rhetoric: Adult Learning Policies and Practices*, OECD, Paris.

OECD (2004), *Career Guidance and Public Policy – Bridging the Gap*, OECD, Paris.

OECD (2005), *Promoting Adult Learning*, OECD, Paris.

ISBN 978-92-64-01367-4
Qualifications Systems
Bridges to Lifelong Learning
© OECD 2007

Suggested Further Reading

Acemoglu, D. and J.-S. Pischke (1999a), "Beyond Becker: Training in Imperfect Labour Markets" *The Economic Journal,* 109 (1), S. F112-F142.

Acemoglu, D. and J.-S. Pischke (1999b), "The Structure of Wages and Investment in General Training", *Journal of Political Economy,* 107 (3), S. 539-572.

Altonji, J.G. (1993), "The Demand for and Return to Education When Education Outcomes Are Uncertain", *Journal of Labor Economics,* 11 (1), pp. 48-83.

Altonji, J.G. and J.R. Spletzer (1991), "Worker Characteristics, Job Characteristics, and the Receipt of On-the-Job-Training", *Industrial and Labor Relations Review,* 45 (1), pp. 58-79.

Bainbridge, S. and J. Murray (2000), *An Age of Learning: Vocational Training Policy at European Level,* CEDEFOP, Office for Official Publications of the European Communities, Luxembourg.

Becker, G.S. (1993), *Human Capital: A Theoretical and Empirical Analysis with Special Reference to Education,* University of Chicago Press (3rd Edition), Chicago, London.

Becker, G.S. (1996), *Accounting for Tastes,* Harvard University Press, Cambridge, London.

Ben-Porath, Y. (1967), "The Production of Human Capital and the Life Cycle of Earnings", *Journal of Political Economy,* 75, pp. 352-378.

Bjørnåvold, J. (2000), *Making Learning Visible,* CEDEFOP, Office for Official Publications of the European Communities, Luxembourg.

Bjørnåvold, J. (2001), "Assessment and Recognition of Non-Formal Learning in Europe", KRIVET Conference Paper, 5 December.

Brown, B.L. (2003), *International Models of Career-Technical Educations,* ERIC Clearinghouse on Adult Career and Vocational Education, *www.ericacve.org/pubs.asp.*

Budge, D. (2000), *Motivating Students for Lifelong Learning,* Centre for Educational Research and Innovation, OECD, Paris.

Coles, M. (2004), Evaluating The Impact of Reforms of Vocational Education and Training in Europe: Examples of Practice, *3rd Research Review of VET* (Vol. 3), CEDEFOP, Thessaloniki.

Davey, J. and A. Jamieson (2003), "Against the Odds: Pathways of Early School Leavers into University Education: Evidence from England and New Zealand", *International Journal of Lifelong Learning,* 22, 3, pp. 266-280.

De Rick, K., K. Valckenborgh and H. Baert (2003), "Towards a Conceptualisation of 'Learning Climate'", Conference Paper for the 7tn European Workshop, Implementing the Learning Society in an Enlarging and Integrating Europe, Stirling, Scotland.

Descy, P. and M. Tessaring (2001), *Training and Learning for Competence,* CEDEFOP, Office for Official Publications of the European Communities, Luxembourg.

EC (European Commission) (2000), "Staff Working Paper: A Memorandum on Lifelong Learning", Conference Paper, Biarritz, France, 5 December 2000.

EC (2001), "European Forum on Transparency of Vocational Qualifications: Preliminary Results of Survey", draft paper.

EC (2001), *European Innovation Scoreboard 2001,* Brussels.

EC (2001), *National Actions to Implement Lifelong Learning in Europe,* CEDEFOP, Eurydice, Brussels.

EC (2002), *European Report on Quality Indicators of Lifelong Learning,* Directorate-General for Education and Culture, Brussels.

Edwards, R., P. Raggatt, R. Harrison, A. McCollum and J. Calder (1998), "Recent Thinking in Lifelong Learning – A Review of the Literature", Department for Education and Employment, Sheffield, England.

Esser, H. (1991), *Die Rationalität des Alltagshandeln: Eine Rekonstruktion der Handlungstheorie von Alfred Schütz*, in Zeitschrift für Soziologie 20 (6), pp. 430-445.

Field, J. (1998), *The Silent Explosion – Living in a Learning Society*, Adult Learning Australia Inc.

Gealy, N. (2001), *On Linkages between Qualifications Frameworks*, Joint Forum, London.

Hillage, J. and J. Aston (2001), *Attracting New Learners: A Literature Review*, Institute for Employment Research/Learning and Skills Development Agency, London.

Hogarth, R.M. and M.W. Reder, eds. (1987), *Rational Choice: The Contrast between Economics and Psychology*, University of Chicago Press, Chicago, London.

Kapteyn, A., T. Wansbeek and J. Buyze (1979), "Maximizing or Satisficing?" *The Review of Economics and Statistics*, No. 61, pp. 549-563.

Keating, J. (2002), "The Role of Qualifications Systems in Supporting Lifelong Learning", paper prepared for the OECD activity National Qualifications Systems in Promoting Lifelong Learning, Paris.

Kirchgässner, G. (1991), *Homo oeconomicus: Das ökonomische Modell individuellen Verhaltens und seine Anwendung in den Wirtschafts- und Sozialwissenschaften*, Mohr, Tübingen.

Leeuwen, M. (1999), "The Costs and Benefits of Lifelong Learning", paper presented to the European Conference on Educational Research, 22 September, Lahti, Finland.

Lindenberg, S. (1990), "Homo Socio-oeconomicus: The Emergence of a General Model of Man in the Social Sciences", *Journal of Institutional and Theoretical Economics* (Zeitschrift für die gesamte Staatswissenschaft) 146 (4), pp. 727-748.

Lindenberg, S. and B.S. Frey (1993), "Alternatives, Frames and Relative Prices: A Broader View of Rational Choice Theory", *Acta Sociologica*, 36 (3), pp. 191-205.

McDonnell, L. and N. Grubb (1991), *Education and Training for Work: The Policy Instruments and the Institutions*, R-4026-NCRVE/UCB, RAND, Santa Monica.

Mincer, J. (1974), *Schooling, Experience and Earnings*, National Bureau of Economic Research, New York.

NQAI (National Qualifications Authority of Ireland) (2001), *Towards a National Framework of Qualifications*, Dublin.

NQAI (2002), *Frameworks of Qualifications: A Review of Developments Outside the State*, Dublin.

OECD (2000), *Education at a Glance*, OECD, Paris.

OECD (2003), *Education at a Glance*, OECD, Paris.

OECD (2004), *Ageing and Employment Policies*, OECD, Paris, *www.oecd.org/els/employment/olderworkers*.

OECD (2004), *Lifelong Learning*, Policy brief, Paris.

OECD (2004), *The Development and Use of "Qualifications Frameworks" as a Means of Reforming and Managing Qualifications Systems*, E. Mernagh, A. Murphy and T. Simota (eds.), Final Report of the Thematic Group 1 of the OECD activity on "The Role of National Qualifications Systems in Promoting Lifelong Learning", Paris, *www.oecd.org/edu/lifelonglearning/nqs*.

OECD (2004), *Standards and Quality Assurance in Qualifications with Special Reference to the Recognition of Non-formal and Informal Learning*, J. Doyle (ed.), Final Report of the Thematic Group 2 of the OECD activity on "The Role of National Qualifications Systems in Promoting Lifelong Learning", Paris, *www.oecd.org/edu/lifelonglearning/nqs*.

OECD (2004), *Co-operation of Different Institutions and Stakeholders of the Qualifications Systems*, G. Hanf and J. Reuling (eds.), Final Report of the Thematic Group 3 of the OECD activity on "The Role of National Qualifications Systems in Promoting Lifelong Learning", Paris, *www.oecd.org/edu/lifelonglearning/nqs*.

OECD (2004), *Career Guidance and Public Policy – Bridging the Gap*, OECD, Paris.

OECD (2007), *Qualifications and Lifelong Learning*, Policy Brief, OECD, Paris.

OECD and Statistics Canada (2000), *Literacy in the Information Age – Final Report of the International Adult Literacy Survey*, Paris, *www.nald.ca/nls/ials/introduc.htm*.

Orazem, P.F. and J.P. Mattila (1991), "Human Capital, Uncertain Wage Distributions and Occupational and Educational Choices", *International Economic Review*, 32 (1), pp. 103-122.

Planas, J. (1998), *Agora 2: The Role of the Company in Lifelong Learning*, CEDEFOP, Thessaloniki.

QCA (Qualifications and Curriculum Authority) (2001), *Evaluation of the Feasibility and Potential Impact of the Introduction of a Credit-based Qualifications Framework*, London.

QCA (2002), *Evaluation of the National Qualifications Framework*, London.

Schultz, T.W. (1961), "Investment in Human Capital", *American Economic Review,* 51 (1), pp. 1-17.

Sellin, B. (2002), "Scenarios and Strategies for Vocational Education and Lifelong Learning in Europe", summary of findings and conclusions of the joint CEDEFOP/ETF project (1998-2002), Office for Official Publications of the European Communities, Luxembourg.

Simon, H.A. (1955), "A Behavioral Model of Rational Choice", *Quarterly Journal of Economics,* 69, pp. 99-118.

Stigler, G.J. and G.S. Becker (1977), "De Gustibus Non Est Disputandum", *American Economic Review,* 67 (2), pp. 76-90.

Tissot P. (2003), "80 Terms to Better Understand European Vocational Education and Training Policy", CEDEFOP, Luxembourg.

Verhar, K. and R. Duvekot (2001), "To Value Informal Training as a Contribution to European Lifelong Learning Policy", Universidad Computense Madrid conference, 30 July 2001.

Westerhuis, A. (2001), *European Structures Of Qualification Levels*, CEDEFOP, OOPEC, Luxembourg.

Young, M. (2001), *Contrasting Approaches to the Role of Qualifications in the Promotion of Lifelong Learning*, commissioned paper for the OECD study on "The Role of National Qualifications Systems in Promoting Lifelong Learning", Paris.

ISBN 978-92-64-01367-4
Qualifications Systems
Bridges to Lifelong Learning
© OECD 2007

ANNEX A

Summary Reports of the Three Thematic Groups

These are summaries* of three larger reports contributed to the OECD study on "The Role of National Qualifications Systems in Promoting Lifelong Learning". The study is designed to investigate how different national qualifications systems influence the patterns and quality of lifelong learning within countries, and what actions within qualifications systems countries can take to promote lifelong learning. It examines countries' experiences in designing and managing systems, and attempts to identify the impact of different approaches and innovations.

While the study is being implemented primarily through the preparation and synthesis of country background reports, it also includes a thematically focused inquiry into certain key aspects of the agenda. Three Thematic Groups were established to explore and develop key themes that have emerged within the study:

1. The development and use of "qualifications frameworks" as a means of reforming and managing qualifications systems.

2. Recognition of non-formal and informal learning.

3. Involvement of stakeholders in qualifications systems.

* The full reports can be found on *www.oecd.org/edu/lifelonglearning/nqs*.

THEMATIC GROUP 1

The Development and Use of Qualifications Frameworks as a Means of Reforming and Managing Qualifications Systems

Co-ordination:
Ms. Anna Murphy, Ms. Tina Simota and Mr. Edwin Mernagh

This report assembles the products and outcomes of the work of Thematic Group 1 on the development and use of qualifications frameworks as a means of reforming and managing qualifications systems. It does not set out to synthesise the detailed work of the group; rather, it provides a compendium of main outputs, which separately and together can contribute to the wider OECD study as a whole.

The Group formed after the November 2002 plenary meeting of national representatives in Paris. Ireland, with Greece, took the lead role in establishing the Group, beginning a process of document exchange by email that was continued throughout its work. This process was further enhanced by the initiation of a Smartgroups.com website. In this way, a small initial core group of participants gradually expanded (to 11 countries in all, see Annex B) and a group agenda began to form. Group participants represented countries with extensive, well-established frameworks as well as countries that have recently introduced them or are actively considering them. It also included participants from CEDEFOP (the European Union's agency for the promotion of vocational education and training) and from the International Labour Organization. This agenda provided the basis for a first meeting of the Group in Dublin in May 2003. A second meeting took place in Athens in September 2003.

Products

The Group developed a range of products that might assist any country in developing a general concept of qualifications frameworks, in gaining an overview of current practices in various countries, and in reaching an understanding of how frameworks can benefit qualifications systems' further development. These products comprise the following:

1. Definitions of qualifications frameworks and qualifications systems

These definitions were developed in order to clarify the distinction between qualifications frameworks and qualifications systems, and to contribute to a common understanding on the meaning of the terms below.

Qualifications system

Qualifications systems include all aspects of a country's activity that result in the recognition of learning. These systems include the means of developing and operating national or regional policy on qualifications, institutional arrangements, quality assurance processes, assessment and awarding processes, skills recognition and other mechanisms that link education and training to the labour market and civil society. Qualifications systems may be more or less integrated and coherent. One feature of a qualifications system may be an explicit framework of qualifications.

Qualifications framework

A qualifications framework is an instrument for the development and classification of qualifications according to a set of criteria for levels of learning achieved. This set of criteria may be implicit in the qualifications descriptors themselves, or made explicit in the form of a set of level descriptors. The scope of frameworks may take in all learning achievement and pathways or may be confined to a particular sector, for example initial education, adult education and training or an occupational area. Some frameworks may have more design elements and a tighter structure than others; some may have a legal basis whereas others represent a consensus of views of social partners. All qualifications frameworks, however, establish a basis for improving the quality, accessibility, linkages and public or labour market recognition of qualifications within a country and internationally.

2. Features of qualifications framework models

A range of common features of qualifications frameworks was identified from case studies developed by Group members to examine and compare frameworks in different countries. As a model of how a framework has been introduced into a qualifications system, the example of Ireland is presented.

Common features of frameworks are set out as follows:

Purpose

The studies indicate that countries introduce qualifications frameworks in order to:

- Better match qualifications with knowledge, skills and competencies and to better relate qualifications to occupational (and broader labour market) needs, present and future. It is clear that in some countries there is a tension between the objectives of facilitating lifelong learning and the labour market needs, at least in the short term.

- Bring coherence to subsystems of qualifications, e.g. higher education, adult learning, school awards, and in particular vocational education and training qualifications, by creating an overarching framework for them.

- Support lifelong learning (by opening up access, targeting investments and recognising non-formal and informal learning).

- Facilitate the involvement of political actors and stakeholders, especially in vocational education and training.

Drivers of change

In general, government ministries with responsibility for education and labour appear to be the main drivers of change. In many cases, significant reforms of vocational education and training are under way and qualifications frameworks are being considered or introduced in this context. In addition, particular groups play key roles, depending on the national situation. In some countries, autonomous communities (for example Spain) and partners in social dialogue (for example Germany, Spain, and Greece) are significant. The involvement of social partners in developing the framework and qualifications is highlighted in the Czech Republic case study as being important to making qualifications more relevant. In Ireland's case, the engagement of statutory agencies is considered to be very important.

The need for underpinning legislation is underlined in most of the case studies. This allows certainty about the framework and may be used to allocate clear responsibility for the framework to a particular body or bodies.

A number of cases refer to the need to take account of and link with social partnership agreements, and to national employment strategies (for example Germany, Greece, Spain). This may also be an important consideration in many other countries, the EU countries in particular.

Members of the Group felt that the case studies may not have identified certain underlying key drivers of change that steer developments in many countries – for example, the internationalisation and globalisation of learning and the development of wider regional (European or transnational) labour markets.

Quick overview of the benefits of qualifications frameworks

From the case studies, a list of main benefits, expected by countries from the introduction of frameworks, was identified. Frameworks can:

- Contribute to a coherent, transparent and more integrated qualifications system.
- Increase and target access to qualifications for certain disadvantaged groups.
- Open up progression routes (to both higher and broader skills).
- Introduce flexibility for learners, providers and users.
- Promote recognition and validation of all qualifications (including non-formal/informal learning).
- Promote vocational education and training and adult learning (in its own right and through opening access to higher education).
- Make qualifications more relevant to societal and labour market needs.
- Promote investment and participation in skill development in the workplace.

Among them, two main benefits were highlighted. First, they can be a tool for communications about qualifications systems, acting as a common reference point for all kinds of qualifications and promoting a culture of lifelong learning. Second, they can be used as a regulatory tool, in which case they create certainty about the value of qualifications, set out key requirements of qualifications (e.g. standards) and provide quality assurance mechanisms for qualifications.

The international dimension of frameworks was highlighted in a number of case studies. They have the potential to support mutual recognition and the transparency of qualifications across different jurisdictions.

Conditions for the introduction of frameworks

The Group identified a number of general conditions deemed to be significant in the successful development and implementation of frameworks:

- The importance of a legislative basis for a qualifications framework is underlined in a number of case studies. However, it was also noted that a voluntary "buy-in" and the commitment of stakeholders are important to successful framework implementation.
- The case studies point to the general need for all those engaged in education and training and in labour market policy to work together.
- National frameworks of qualifications need to be communicated to the population in general if they are to be successful.
- It seems from the case studies that it takes some considerable time to develop, maintain and successfully introduce frameworks of qualifications.

3. The benefits of qualifications frameworks in detail

A paper was developed setting out the benefits of qualifications frameworks. Benefits are identified on two levels: general, and more specifically relevant to the development of lifelong learning.

General benefits of qualifications frameworks

Qualifications frameworks can bring benefits in four areas:

- **Benefits for qualifications systems and provision**
  - ❖ To reduce complexity and enable coherence, transparency and integration despite increasing regionalisation, decentralisation and individualisation of provision (notably in relation to post-compulsory and continuing provision of education and training).
  - ❖ To open access and enable progression to further qualifications, independent of whether they are initial, higher or VET/LLL qualifications.
  - ❖ To enable learners and trainers/teachers to be guided and to facilitate them in identifying appropriate learning pathways.
  - ❖ To set targets, taking into account societal, labour market, companies and citizens' or learners' needs, attitudes and preferences.
  - ❖ To provide support for quality assurance and the development of standards, for systems of credit accumulation and transfer, and to enhance transferability, comparability and compatibility of qualifications.
- **Benefits to career development, guidance and employment placement, and information and orientation, including occupational mobility**
  - ❖ To enable coping with accelerated change of needs and adaptation of learners, providers and enterprises within a sustainable framework.
  - ❖ To communicate reference points for qualifications and increase their social acceptance and recognition on the labour market and in education and training.

❖ To enable mapping of provision and qualifications in relation to skills supply, demand and occupational challenges.

● **Benefits to the international and transnational dimension of qualifications**

❖ To contribute to increasing mobility, co-operation and exchange as well as intercultural understanding and mutual recognition.

❖ To enable a more in-depth co-operation and the development of mutual trust between providers, teachers and trainers from different countries and world regions.

❖ To promote recognition, transparency and (credit) transfer of outcomes of (modules) of training, delivered by different countries.

❖ To enable the development of a common language in the discourse on qualifications (*e.g.* the concept of "meta-frameworks").

● **Benefits to regulation, legislation and institutional arrangements**

❖ A regulatory framework would allow for the building of mutual trust, reliability and sustainability of quality of provision within national qualifications systems.

❖ Frameworks can establish reference points for standards for and between sectors.

❖ Frameworks can include regulatory elements for, and facilitate, quality assurance.

❖ Frameworks can provide for stability of qualifications while at the same time allowing for flexibility and adaptation.

❖ Frameworks can allow for decentralising, and for increasing the autonomy of providers of education/training.

❖ Frameworks can provide the basis for establishing minimum requirements for standards of qualifications and skills as well as their accreditation.

● **Benefits of qualifications frameworks to lifelong learning**

❖ To promote a culture of lifelong learning to a wider set of learners in the context of demographic developments and trends in most OECD countries, *e.g.* ageing of the working population and skill supply/mismatch problems.

❖ To ease the transferability and transportability of skills and competencies from one area to another.

❖ To enable non-standard forms of access, including accreditation of prior learning and recognition of non-formal and informal learning.

❖ To enable a further improvement of basic skills, *e.g.* language and social-communicative skills and basic ICT skills for different target groups of adult learners with different backgrounds of education attainment level and work experience.

❖ To support the development and improvement of guidance materials, which could be more easily developed, produced and disseminated if they referred to largely accepted frameworks.

❖ In the context of qualifications frameworks, establishing equivalences between qualifications provided by different segments of education, learning can be more easily focused on both individual and company learning needs.

❖ Frameworks can reduce amounts of time spent by learners relearning to reach outcomes already achieved in other contexts.

❖ Frameworks provide clarity and simplicity – to policy makers, stakeholders and companies preparing new measures and reforms – about skills and qualifications needed.

4. Scenarios for future development

This was a scoping exercise, in which members of the Group have sketched out scenarios for the future development of qualifications frameworks in their countries.

5. The international dimension of the debate on qualification frameworks

In the work of Thematic Group 1, a number of increasingly important elements and points were identified about the international dimension of framework development. This section summarises contributions from papers and meetings. Sources referred to in this debate include studies implemented and published by CEDEFOP and the National Qualifications Authority of Ireland on European developments linked to qualifications frameworks and their comparison, and also a study by Keating (2001).

The section concludes by noting that the increasing use of international (worldwide or regional) frameworks could assist:

● In facilitating the increasing international mobility of labour, students and trainees.

● In finding co-operating partners for training providers, not only at bilateral but also at multilateral and international levels.

● In identifying more effectively issues for sustainable co-operation and exchange.

● In promoting understanding of the context in which education and training is delivered and to enable comparison and discussion despite geographic and linguistic distance or difficulties.

● In contributing to mutual recognition or transparency of qualifications and skills.

THEMATIC GROUP 2

Standards and Quality Assurance in Qualifications with Special Reference to the Recognition of Non-formal and Informal Learning

Co-ordination:
Ms. Jo Doyle

In exploring its topic, Thematic Group 2 quickly identified that the focus should be on:

● The recognition of non-formal and informal learning.

● Reference to standards and quality assurance systems, but be only in the context of how they support or hinder the recognition of non-formal and informal learning.

1. Development of the report

The work of Thematic Group 2 took place between April 2003 and October 2004. Two meetings were held in July and November 2003. Further work was carried out through electronic exchange of information.

2. Definitions

The group immediately came to the issue of commonly accepted definitions. The range of definitions used by participant countries[1] to capture the concept of recognising learning that takes place outside formal educational settings and is not normally recognised was the first item to be agreed. There was some commonality of definitions used, particularly among European Union countries. Credit here needs to be given to the work on the recognition of non-formal and informal learning carried out by the European Centre for the Development of Vocational Training (CEDEFOP). The descriptions that were arrived at by Thematic Group 2 encompassed elements of existing definitions and are also broad enough to allow countries not familiar with the CEDEFOP definitions to locate their own practices within them.[2]

3. Policy opportunities and challenges

Opportunities

The recognition and certification of competencies obtained outside formal education provide numerous opportunities on a policy level. These opportunities may relate to a country's objectives in areas such as skilled employment, education, equity and immigration. The countries that participated in Thematic Group 2 viewed these opportunities within the context of lifelong and life-wide learning.

The key opportunities afforded by having a system of recognition of non-formal and informal learning are outlined below.

The ability to contribute to the quality, quantity and distribution of lifelong learning by:

- Facilitating a tailored approach to learning where the learner, not the system, is the focus.
- Optimising existing training paths and more efficient training expenditure as a positive outcome for recognition of non-formal learning.
- Promoting individuals' self-knowledge, self-esteem and self-concept, thus increasing the likelihood that they will engage in learning.
- Reducing the study time required to gain a recognised formal qualification.
- Increasing participation (especially for members of disadvantaged groups within societies) in formal education and qualifications.

Harnessing the human resource potential of citizens: improving access to and mobility within the labour market by:

- Enhancing the appreciation of skills gained in the workplace.
- Providing opportunities to have personal capital formally recognised and thus improving employment and career prospects and access to further learning opportunities.
- Assisting employers in overcoming skill shortages, meeting industry standards and gaining competitive advantages.

Overcoming social, cultural and economic inequity by:

- Improving the access of members of disadvantaged groups to further education and employment.

Challenges

While recognition of non-formal and informal learning provides a number of policy opportunities linked to high-level goals such as building a country's skill base and achieving equity, challenges also arise from the systems employed. Thematic Group 2 identified a number of policy challenges, summarised below.

Achieving acceptance in the labour market

If qualifications gained partly, or fully through the recognition of non-formal and informal learning are not accepted in the labour market, the value of a recognition system to the individual and to society is diminished.

Maintaining consistency across the system

This is a risk particularly in decentralised systems, where there are many local or industry-specific variations in the way recognition of non-formal and informal learning is implemented. It is therefore important that recognition systems are built on commonly agreed principles and those measures and methods are structured and integrated as much as possible into existing quality assurance and assessment systems, in order to avoid the system losing legitimacy.

Managing expectations

Recognition systems could be set up to fail if the expectations of individuals and society in relation to better job prospects and entry or credit towards formal education are not met.

Ensuring recognition is not ghettoised

If validation is available only to specific groups, such as immigrants, indigenous populations or those with no formal education, that may result in segregation rather than integration if these groups are forced to use the system to have their informal knowledge confirmed.

Maintaining engagement with formal learning

Recognition systems, if widely used, could lead to a changing pay structure, which could in turn result in a lowering of value placed on formal education. In this situation, a lower participation rate in formal education would be an unintended negative consequence of the recognition system.

4. Current practices

Many countries in the world are investigating or developing ways to raise awareness of the fact that people learn always and everywhere, and formal education is only one of many learning pathways available. While formal education has formed the backbone of what are becoming known as knowledge societies, the importance of harnessing the full range of available skills and knowledge is increasingly appreciated. Evidence suggests that countries see advantages for individuals, communities, enterprises and the economy in recognising this informal and non-formal learning.

Each country implements its practices depending on the context, the system, and its own barriers. Therefore each country has its own challenges to deal with. Some countries overtly encourage or require processes for the recognition of non-formal and informal learning. Others have systems that allow or facilitate the recognition of that learning, but do not regulate it. In some cases a legislative base exists; in others, change has been influenced through high-level strategic policies linked to skilled employment or equity, or through initiatives developed by local communities.

The range of practices that take place in the countries that contributed to the work of Thematic Group 2 are summarised below. In many ways this summary does not do justice to the innovation, pragmatism or boldness of the various initiatives. Group members hope, however, that it gives readers a "taste" of the activities being undertaken.

Legislation and policy

Participant countries use a variety of legislative or policy levers to influence the provision of recognition systems. In some countries individuals have a legal right to be examined without having completed formal courses. In others, qualifications frameworks have an embedded principle of recognising all forms of learning so that it is part of everyday practice rather than an exception.

Linking to the formal system

For most countries that participated in Thematic Group 2, the links between the recognition of non-formal/informal learning and the formal qualifications systems are access, entry and credit towards the formal qualification. There were a number of examples of specific initiatives to recognise non-formal and informal learning for the purpose of meeting entry requirements for formal education programmes.

Local initiatives

Some countries have systems for recognition of non-formal and informal learning that developed from local communities, organisations or industries rather than from a nationwide or government-led approach. These initiatives occur when groups with specific interests identify a need and develop a process to address that need – local solutions to local problems. Within the participant countries there were examples of specific industries establishing processes for recognising learning that occurred in the workplace in order to raise the overall skill level of their workforce. Other examples included community organisations establishing learning centres for disadvantaged groups, where a range of flexible packages is developed according to the individual's needs. These packages might include formal, non-formal or informal learning and the opportunity to gain qualifications.

Social partnerships

Many countries have recognised the importance of having strong social partnership models that facilitate recognition of non-formal and informal learning. Examples from within the participant countries included engaging with professional advisory groups that set standards, devolved systems where social partners such as employers' organisations and trade unions are included in decision making and in implementation of policy, and systems based on networks of recognition centres located in and accountable to local communities.

Target groups

While the participants in Thematic Group 2 considered that access to systems for the recognition of non-formal and informal learning is important for all sectors of society, they noted that some groups, due to their needs, interests and relative level of disadvantage, may gain more from having their non-formal and informal learning recognised than the less disadvantaged. Participant countries provided a number of examples of how the recognition of non-formal and informal learning may be targeted for disadvantaged groups.

Demand for recognition systems

Thematic Group 2 found that there was a limited amount of data on the uptake of recognition systems. In some cases this was because the system does not require the method of learning to be recorded. In other cases, relatively new recognition systems have not been in operation long enough to produce such data. It is anticipated that as systems develop, rich sources of data will become available.

5. Barriers to the recognition of non-formal and informal learning

All participating countries were able to identify barriers to the recognition of non-formal and informal learning. Given the diversity of systems involved, the commonalities among the barriers are perhaps surprising. The issues raised can be categorised according to whether they relate to the supply of learning and assessment opportunities (the system), or the demand for such opportunities (the individual).

Barriers relating to the system included:

- Inconsistency in the development and implementation of standards.
- Costs in terms of time and money in relation to benefits.
- Restricted access resulting from inadequate or badly targeted promotional activities.
- Lack of parity of esteem with the formal education system.
- Funding systems often do not provide incentives, particularly for educational institutions, to implement systems for recognising non-formal and informal learning.

Barriers relating to the individual were:

- Inability to recognise the potential value of knowledge and skills gained through non-formal and informal learning.
- Fear of failure due to negative formal educational experiences.
- Low perception of potential benefits.
- Difficulty in accessing recognition systems due to financial cost or the time involved.

6. Addressing the barriers – developing principles for recognition systems

A number of suggestions can be made about improvements to policy or practice that go some way toward breaking down the barriers discussed in this summary. The following general principles were accepted by Thematic Group 2 as a way of guiding the development of recognition systems.

- Recognition systems are a mechanism for individuals to have all of their skills, knowledge and competencies identified and valued (some countries express this as a "right" of the individual).
- Participation in recognition systems must be voluntary.
- Recognition systems must be flexible enough to meet the needs of diverse individuals and contexts.
- Standards and procedures must be transparent, reliable, objective, relevant and impartial.
- High-quality guidance and counselling should be part of the system.
- The system should ensure equity of access to recognition procedures.
- Parity of esteem with the formal system is desirable.

- Mechanisms to enhance awareness and access should be part of the system.

- Recognition systems should be part of a holistic approach to lifelong learning and therefore be linked to other services such as quality assurance and career guidance.

- Mechanisms for measuring the effectiveness of the system in reaching its stated objectives should be included in the design.

7. Recommendations

Through sharing information about the practices of recognition of non-formal and informal learning, the participants of Thematic Group 2 identified some common themes and issues that a country wishing to establish or enhance systems may need to consider. It is recommended that while developing or reviewing such systems, countries give consideration to the following factors.

Purpose of the system

It is important that the purposes of a system are clearly identified. It is difficult to design a system if the desired end-result is unknown.

Context

The educational, political and social context in which the system will operate must be considered. This context may affect what is possible and will dictate the areas that resources must be directed to. For that reason, this report does not suggest one model. Each country must develop its own model, learning from the practice of other countries and considering the benefits and constraints of their own context.

Establishing national standards

In implementing a recognition system, countries often face the dilemma of balancing the need for consistency with the desire of local communities to develop their own solutions. The development of national goals, principles and standards within which local communities and/ or individual providers of recognition services is recommended in addressing this issue.

Assuring quality

It is essential that quality assurance be built into any system for the recognition of non-formal and informal learning. This can be achieved in many ways, including the setting of national standards and guidelines, self-assessment by providers of recognition services, and monitoring for consistency and transparency. The goals of quality assurance may vary from maintaining a minimum benchmark to promotion of continual improvement.

Targeting user groups

Countries need to consider carefully the issue of targeting services to certain disadvantaged groups. While this can be the most effective use of resources, it runs the risk of encouraging people to view the recognition of non-formal and informal learning as only relevant for disadvantaged groups. This, in turn, can lead to the devaluing of non-formal and informal learning.

Enhancing awareness and access

Recognition systems will only be successful if individuals are aware of them, consider them to be of value, and are able to access them without unnecessary restriction. This means that consideration needs to be given to appropriate mechanisms for raising awareness of recognition systems and their potential value to individuals and to society. Consideration also needs to be given to the minimisation of barriers to participation, such as cost and time.

Removing disincentives in the system

The Group recommends examining current systems to identify disincentives that may exist. Funding systems for formal education are often the source of such disincentives, particularly where funding hinges on the number of enrolments rather than the credits or qualifications gained. This can mean that there is little incentive for formal education institutions to recognise non-formal or informal learning.

Notes

1. Thematic Group 2 included two countries that do not belong to the European Union. The participation of Mexico and New Zealand in this thematic group added to the diversity of input.

2. For a summary of the definitions arrived at by Thematic Group 2, refer to the full report of the Thematic Group on *www.oecd.org/edu/lifelonglearning/nqs*.

THEMATIC GROUP 3

Co-operation between Different Institutions and Stakeholders of the Qualifications Systems

Coordination:
Mr. Georg Hanf and Mr. Jochen Reuling

Acceptance and credibility of qualifications and qualifications frameworks greatly depend on the involvement of social institutions and stakeholders. Therefore Thematic Group 3 – Belgium (Flanders), the Czech Republic, England, Germany (co-ordinator), the Netherlands, and Switzerland – was looking at the various roles of partners in the development of occupational standards and vocational qualifications, and at new forms of co-operation between them (see Dunon and Cabus, 2003; Hövels, 2003; Kopicová, 2003; Oates, 2003; Reuling and Hanf, 2003; and Zulauf with Gentinetta, 2003).

1. Describing the content of work – an essential but problematic aspect of vocational qualifications

Thematic Group 3 has elaborated a framework for analysing the role of partners in the processes that is used to move from analysis of the content of work through to the production of a final qualifications specification. It is understood that the scope of the final qualifications specification varies in different national settings. The development of qualifications is not a simple reductionist process dependent on, and explained purely in terms of, simple empirical analysis of occupational competence. While that analysis remains at the heart of vocational qualifications, the final form of qualifications can only be explained as being a product of complex social processes of mediation by participating partners.

The working group suggests that an adequate theoretical basis for analysis has to include 1) recognition of the value-laden and theory-laden nature of processes generally used for analysis and thus the existence of explicit or implicit bias; 2) recognition of social processes of mediation in the production of qualifications, which introduces further specific orientations/bias in the final content.

The significance of bias deriving from the choice of observational/analytic method is highlighted by the differing descriptions of the content of similar work, which can be derived from different methodologies: work flow analysis, Delphi, critical incident analysis, analytic work, and functional analysis.

Observation of work for the purpose of qualifications design is thus not a simple matter. Nor is observation the sole process involved in the development of the qualification's final version that will operate in learning settings and selection processes. There are four mediating processes associated with the content of qualifications:

- Direct observation of work, or analysis of practitioners' descriptions of work (indirect observation).
- Development of agreed/consensus descriptions that will be included in the final qualification.
- Interpretation by the training providers, assessors, etc. implementing the qualification.
- Interpretation by those using the qualification in selection.

2. Development of qualifications – a complex socio-political process

Even in processes where consensus is readily obtained over the function and content of a specific vocational qualification, the participation of different groups with different perspectives and aims entails processes of mediation. Understanding this complex mediation is essential to understanding why a qualification takes a particular form in a particular (national) setting. This is illuminated by the following questions:

- Who decides who should be involved?
- What is their relative power?
- What are their aims/aspirations/intentions in participating in the development of the qualification?
- How well equipped are they to participate in the development process?
- What access do they have to the content of work in order to make judgements/assertions?
- What forms of support are available to specific groups with respect to participation (funding, etc.)?
- How tight are the structural arrangements – what are the rules within which the discussion takes place?

From the questions given above it can be seen that the development of qualifications is not merely a practical process but political (the relative power of different groups) and value-laden. Proceeding through arrangements that are more strongly structured (formalised) in some national contexts than others, the development process can readily manifest difficult tensions.

The description of processes outlined above (observations/empirical information/ consensus descriptions) requires far more sophisticated critique, which includes at least the following:

- An understanding of implicit/explicit models of competence.
- An understanding of power relations.
- An understanding of the existence of multiple functions.

3. The notion of "representation" in qualifications systems

There are many questions to be addressed – questions of power relations, of (unequal) partnerships, of voices (loud/powerful, weak/unheard), of models of competence, of value-laden language, of mediated empirical evidence from the processes of work, of implicit and explicit attempts to stimulate economic and social processes – of all things that are crucial to understanding the (actual and possible) role of qualifications and related mechanisms.

While diverse, these aspects can be brought together through the notion of "representation". This is a powerful concept for synthesising consideration of the operation and purposes of qualifications. It includes mediation of observation by theory; description of reality through language; and the informal and formal representation that occurs through consultation. By using the notion of "representation", the extent to which groups' interests, meanings and understandings are represented in the development processes also becomes clear. Alongside this, use of the concept allows theory and practice in representative apparatus (democratic representative arrangements) to be brought to bear. That in turn allows the administrative arrangements in place to support representation to be subjected to due critique.

Even more than a basis for effective review and critique, this could be the means of developing far more legitimate, accountable and inclusive practical arrangements for the development and refinement of qualifications.

4. Ongoing changes in qualifications system regimes

In recent years numerous initiatives to change qualification system regimes have been seen in all countries that have participated in Thematic Group 3. Central to the analysis in this report, "qualifications system regimes" is taken to include: the specific partners who develop and maintain occupational qualifications, the forms of co-operation in which such work takes place, the levels on which it takes place, and the instruments used to carry it out. Some of the initiatives examined in our analysis have already been implemented, and relevant experience has been obtained regarding their effects. Some of these initiatives are still in progress however, and it is thus not yet possible to determine whether they will truly achieve their intended aims.

For this study, the Thematic Group 3 participants selected relevant initiatives in their own countries and described them in working papers. In the following sections these papers are used as a basis for analysing the participation structures and co-operation forms applied by the partners involved in regulating qualifications. Before doing this, however, we briefly present the drivers, goals and focuses of the various initiatives.

5. Drivers, goals and focuses of initiatives for change

The selected initiatives for changing the qualification system regimes were prompted especially by quantitative and/or qualitative problems in the relevant national labour markets. In some cases, the problems had already arisen. In others they were expected to arise in the near future, given the growing requirements to which the countries' workforces were being subjected. Only in the case of Belgium (Flemish Community) did the changes in the regime relate directly to the aim of promoting lifelong learning and the development of competences. At the same time, the changes carried out in other countries could have the function of promoting lifelong learning. This becomes apparent on closer inspection of the goals and focuses of the various initiatives.

These initiatives are aimed at changing individual components of qualifications systems.[1] In all cases except Switzerland, measures have been taken to change control of the system. In Switzerland, a new law on professional education has been prepared and adopted. Its aims include changing access to qualifications and progression for individuals, and changing accreditation and awarding processes, in order to enhance flexibility for future developments and thereby make it possible to meet the demand for modern skills.

In Belgium (Flemish Community), the administrative structure of ministries responsible for vocational training – and co-operation between such ministries – has been reorganised via implementation of arrangements between government, social partners and key agencies. This is formalised as the Education, Training and Work Project, intended to permit development of a comprehensive, coherent qualifications framework. The effort will also include revising the descriptors present in qualifications and in accreditation and awarding processes.

The central aims of the Czech initiative include integrating social partners in the development of qualifications. The aim here is to enhance the scope of application of the vocational training system and to open the way to tighter regulation of the continuing training system.

The initiatives described by Dutch and German representatives are located at the sectoral level. In the Netherlands, an attempt has been made to promote cross-sectoral development of qualifications – in order, *inter alia*, to expand the scope of application of innovative learning programmes.

In Germany, initiatives to change qualification system regimes are aimed at continuing training in the information technologies sector. A mixture of public and private control has been introduced in the development of qualifications, and accreditation and awarding processes have been changed with the aim of linking informal learning, work experience and the traditional methods of upgrading training.

In all of the qualifications systems considered here, control lies with the government. In some cases, responsibilities are distributed among several different ministries or among different state institutions on different levels (such as the federal government and the cantonal authorities in Switzerland or the federal government and the *Länder* in Germany). In addition, important players such as the social partners and representatives of the education sectors are involved in consultation and decision-making processes.

6. What is the relative power of partners in qualifications systems?

The systems in question involve a range of different partners, with the aim of making appropriate decisions that will be acceptable to all parties. This is best expressed as "mediated consensus". In principle, existing power structures can be changed through inclusion of new partners. The nature of the initiatives in the various countries suggests, however, that the powers of new partners are likely to remain rather limited. The reasons for this include:

- Additional partners are included only for the duration of change processes (Switzerland).
- Participation of social partners is on a voluntary basis and is not legally enshrined (Czech Republic).
- Participation extends primarily to consultation processes, and not to decision-making processes (Switzerland, Belgium [Flemish Community]).
- New partners are competent only for limited functions, such as accreditation and awarding of qualifications (Germany).

The cross-sectoral initiatives in the Netherlands, which aim to establish networks between various sectoral organisations, tend to strengthen the position of the partner who receives ownership of, and operates, the newly developed qualifications.

In line with this, the study of Thematic Group 3 has produced evidence that qualifications become a focus of various partners' aims to incorporate their own interests, through influence on the design and regulation of those qualifications.

7. Conclusions

As the sample cases from the various countries show, the past few years have seen a number of relevant changes in the countries' qualification-systems regimes. New partners have been included in the governance of qualifications, and many different forms of co-operation have been applied or tested. In closing, we will briefly discuss the potential significance of these changes – which have come about primarily as a result of problems in the countries' labour markets – in the promotion of lifelong learning.

The study shows the different structural forms that have emerged in the transformation of arrangements – and reinforces the notion that the promotion of lifelong learning must include strengthening the links between the various different qualification and training areas. This process, in turn, includes strengthening the links between general education, vocational training and higher education, and intensifying co-operation between education and employment, with the aim of integrating formal, non-formal and informal learning. Overall, this process entails extensive participation and co-operation among relevant partners. Analysis of the various sample cases has revealed that in some instances new partners have been included in qualification-systems regimes and that this has changed participation structures and forms of co-operation. The state or other responsible parties have sought to maintain their existing influence in the face of such changes, by selecting the partners and thus deciding on the "admission" of interests. What is more, discussion and decision making have often been confined to carefully and narrowly selected subjects at the expense of other, potentially relevant issues. For example, in some cases new arrangements have been out in place in particular sectors with no challenge to sector demarcations. It is essential to recognise the persistence of existing power relations, even within reformed structural arrangements. Under these conditions, no comprehensive co-operation between old and new partners has ensued, and traditional power structures have remained largely in place. This tends to preserve the influence of established interests and block access to the options that would be available for all participants under arrangements with more comprehensive co-operation and integration.

Still, it should be remembered that more comprehensive co-operation between various partners would not be without its own problems. The extent to which new partners' decision-making processes could be integrated in such consultation and decision-making systems is unclear. What is more, a polarisation of interests could emerge from newly integrated systems, with the result that the systems would block decisions or permit agreements only at the level of the "lowest common denominator". Such risks grow as the spectrum of involved partners, interests and issues becomes more comprehensive. Whether the "strategy of limited co-operation" seen in the case studies enables links between training sectors to be strengthened to an extent conducive to promotion of lifelong learning is a question that needs continued empirical monitoring.

We would suggest that if qualifications are to promote lifelong learning, their development must not stop at sectoral and occupational boundaries. Such demarcations must thus become more permeable, or at least must be changed, in keeping with the requirements of process-oriented labour organisations and the development of overarching competence profiles – in other words, in line with the transformation of work processes themselves. As the case studies show, it is usual for social partners and education sector representatives, or organisations engaged by these partners, to develop qualifications or be involved in relevant development steps. With such arrangements, the state frees itself of a number of weighty management problems and decision-making responsibilities. It no longer has to take the various relevant interests into account; it can leave this task up to the participating partners. Still, as the example of the Netherlands indicates, sectoral organisations do not always find it easy to co-operate inter-sectorally. Industrial relations within individual sectors – manifested, for example, in various labour market regulations – can tend to make existing demarcation lines inflexible. At the same time, the example of the Netherlands also shows how network-oriented co-operation, across sectoral boundaries, can make such demarcations more permeable, thereby permitting development of more innovative competence profiles that are more relevant to the labour market.

Finally, lifelong learning can also be promoted via recognition of a wide range of forms of learning used to acquire qualifications. The relevant spectrum includes organised, virtual, and workplace learning, including informal and non-formal learning (see Colardyn and Bjørnåvold, 2005). The key to this approach is that comparable qualifications earned in different ways must be considered to have the same value. The case studies show how different countries are seeking solutions in this area, on different levels. In Switzerland, a legal framework has been created that includes all relevant political and societal groups. In Belgium (Flemish Community), an inter-ministerial organisation has been created, through administrative reorganisation, in order to strengthen coherence between qualifications earned via formal, non-formal or informal learning. In Germany, a new decision-making body, consisting of experts from the "practical" sector, has been created to control the development of workplace-oriented qualifications, including their certification and awarding. This body, like the qualifications it has developed, remains a part of the traditional qualifications system, however. A common feature of all these approaches is that they seek to promote mutual confidence in the value of different avenues to qualifications, by promoting co-operation between strong partners and co-ordinating different interests in defined, planned ways. This finding emerges powerfully from the study: policy makers are recognising the need to adapt qualifications systems to new forms of industrial organisation but are not switching to fully "flexibilised" and "individualised" arrangements. Tripartite and wider forms of organised co-operation are not being abandoned but are being refined and transformed. Co-operation, consensus and collaboration remain prominent in the management and operation of systems; they retain a crucial role in mediation of sectoral and competing interests.

Note

1. Behringer and Coles (2003) differentiate the following components of qualifications systems: scope of application, control accreditation processes for qualifications, the framework within the qualifications system, descriptors present in qualifications, access to qualifications and progressions for individuals, and stability of the qualifications system.

References

Behringer, F. and M. Coles (2003), *The Role of National Qualifications Systems in Promoting Lifelong Learning: Towards an Understanding of the Mechanisms that Link Qualifications and Lifelong Learning*, OECD Education Working Papers, No. 3, Paris.

Colardyn, D. and J. Bjørnåvold (2005), "The Learning Continuity: European Inventory on Validating Non-Formal and Informal Learning", *National Policies And Practices in Validating Non-Formal and Informal Learning*, CEDEFOP Panorama series 117, Office for Official Publications of the European Communities, Luxembourg.

Dunon, R. and R. Cabus (2003), *Towards Future Oriented Forms of Co-Operation between Training Institutions and the Labour Market*, Department of Educational Development, Ministry of Education, Flemish Community, Brussels.

Hövels, B. (2003), *Sector Institutions for Defining National Qualifications and the Challenge of Cross-Sector Competence-Areas*, Knowledge Centre for Vocational Training and Labour Market (KBA), Nijmegen.

Keating, J. (2001), "Qualifications Frameworks: Why have they been established and what are their purposes?", paper prepared for the OECD activity on "The Role of National Qualifications Systems in Promoting Lifelong Learning", unpublished.

Kopicová, M. (2003), *Involvement and Co-operation of Relevant Stakeholders in the Development of the Qualifications System – Example of the Czech Republic*, National Training Fund, Prague.

Oates, T. (2003), *The Roles of Partners in the Development of Occupational Standards and Vocational Qualifications*, Qualifications and Curriculum Authority, London.

Reuling, J. and G. Hanf (2003), *New Forms of Co-Operation between Institutions and Stakeholders in Continuing IT Training to Promote Lifelong Learning*, Federal Institute for Vocational Training (BIBB), Bonn.

Zulauf, M. (in co-operation with P. Gentinetta) (2003), *The Process of Preparation for the New Federal Law on Professional Education: How the Stakeholders Co-operated in the Modernisation of the Federal Certificate of Competence*, Federal Office for Professional Education and Technology (OPET), Bern.

ANNEX B

Education and Training Systems:
How They Relate to Qualifications

Australia

Australia introduced the Australian Qualifications Framework (AQF) in 1995. It is inclusive of all national qualifications (15 in 2005) in the three sectors of education and training: schools (final two years), vocational education and training, and higher education. The AQF has built upon the previous, long-established system of national tertiary course award levels in Australia, and was introduced with the main aim of supporting major reforms towards industry-based vocational education and training in the last decade. The Australian Qualifications Framework is seen as a powerful tool for:

- Better transition pathways for all young people through the addition of two lower-level vocational education and training qualifications to the system. These can be achieved in a range of learning settings – including upper secondary school education, which has now been further broadened with the introduction of school-based apprenticeships with an AQF qualification outcome.

- Strengthened linkages (including credit transfer) between qualifications in all three sectors. This includes articulated programmes between school education, vocational education and training and higher education; scope for delivery of qualifications in sectors other than the sector that sets the standards, in order to optimise student choice within the constraints of local infrastructure; and institutional partnerships at the sectoral interface, in particular diploma to degree.

- Innovatory training packages based on national industry competence standards. The qualifications specified in the training packages are all accredited against the AQF requirements for the vocational education and training certificates and diplomas, and so are fully integrated into the national system of qualifications in post-compulsory education and training.

- Expanded education, training and employment opportunities through Recognition of Prior Learning (RPL), where explicit and detailed AQF requirements underpin reliable assessments of an individual's informal learning as an alternative pathway towards achievement of an AQF qualification.

- Improved capacity to respond to 21st century technology advances through a new short-cycle sub-degree qualification in higher education, combining a multidisciplinary academic knowledge base with generic employment-related skills.

- New industry-based learning pathways through the addition of postgraduate qualifications focusing on competence in a workplace environment that are more readily accessible by a wider range of the adult population.

● Enhanced comparability of Australian qualifications with qualifications in other countries – based on significant commonalities in rigour of standards and accreditation and delivery and assessment requirements under the AQF – supporting transnational recognition and global mobility.

Table B.1 and Figure B.1 provide a description of the Australian Qualifications Framework.

Table B.1. **Australian Qualifications Framework – Table of qualifications 2005**
By sector of accreditation

Schools Sector Accreditation	Vocational and Technical Education (VTE) Sector Accreditation	Higher Education Sector Accreditation
		Doctoral Degree
		Masters Degree
	Vocational Graduate Diploma	Graduate Diploma
	Vocational Graduate Certificate	Graduate Certificate
		Bachelor Degree
	Advanced Diploma	Associate Degree, Advanced Diploma
	Diploma	Diploma
Senior Secondary Certificate of Education	Certificate IV	
	Certificate III	
	Certificate II	
	Certificate I	

Source: Australian Qualifications Framework Advisory Board.

Figure B.1. **Australian Qualifications Framework – Cross-sectoral linkages**

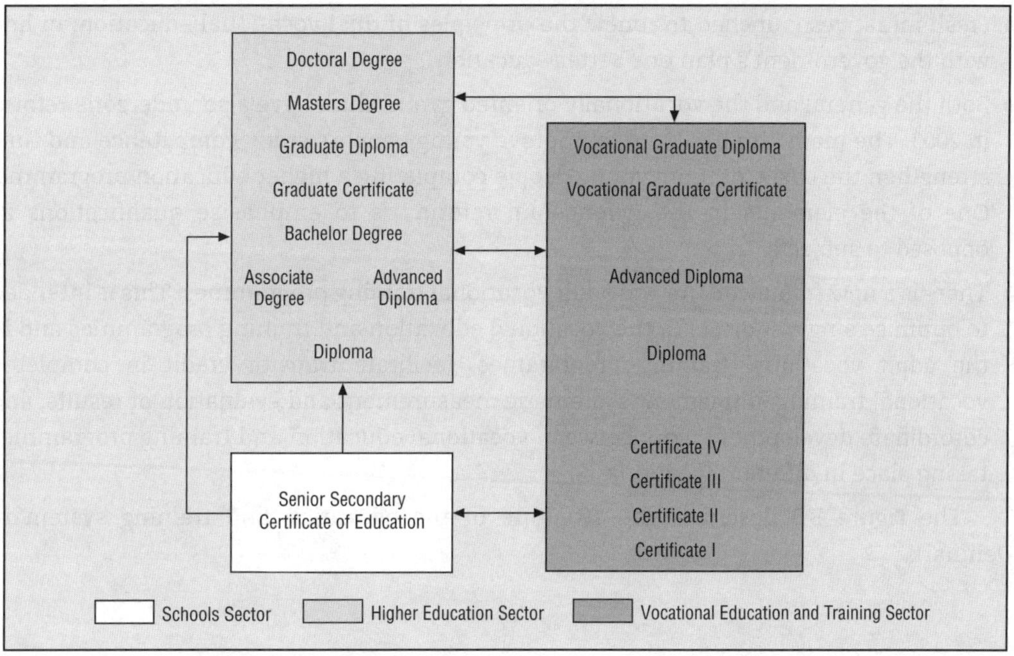

Source: Australian Qualifications Framework Advisory Board.

Belgium (French-speaking)

Recent reforms of the qualifications system in French-speaking Belgium include:

- The creation, following up on a co-operation agreement among the non-federal French-speaking entities, of a transversal framework for the validation of vocational competencies. The main objective of this framework is to allow citizens aged 18 and above to have competencies acquired in the workplace during vocational training or by their experience recognised. These competencies will be formally recognised through Competencies awards (*Titres de compétences*) given by the French Community of Belgium (*Communauté française de Belgique*), the Walloon Region (*Région wallonne*) and the French Community Commission (*Commission communautaire française – Cocof*).

- Reinforced collaboration among the sector of education, the sector of vocational training and the branches. This has allowed for a better match between the objectives of the education sector as a whole and the more specific needs of the firm.

- The progressive evolution towards teaching practice based on the acquisition of competencies.

Figure B2 describes the structure of the education and training system in French-speaking Belgium.

Denmark

Recent reforms of the national qualifications system in Denmark include:

- New IT-based information and advice for all learners on qualification systems and programmes offered by social partners.

- Fresh initiatives launched to renew the principles of dual vocational education, in line with the government's plan on "Better Education".

- Both the general and the vocationally oriented gymnasium have also undergone reform in 2003. The main aim has been to improve young people's study competence and thus strengthen the basis for more young people completing a higher education programme. One of the elements in the gymnasium reforms is to emphasise qualifications as opposed to subjects.

- There is a new framework for the adult vocational training programmes. This is intended to optimise single subjects in the vocational education and training programmes and in the adult vocational training programmes, facilitate transfer credit in completed vocational training, implement systematic measurement and evaluation of results, and co-ordinate development work between vocational education and training programmes taking place in different locations.

The Figure B.3 describes the structure of the education and training system in Denmark.

Figure B.2. **Education and training system in French-speaking Belgium**

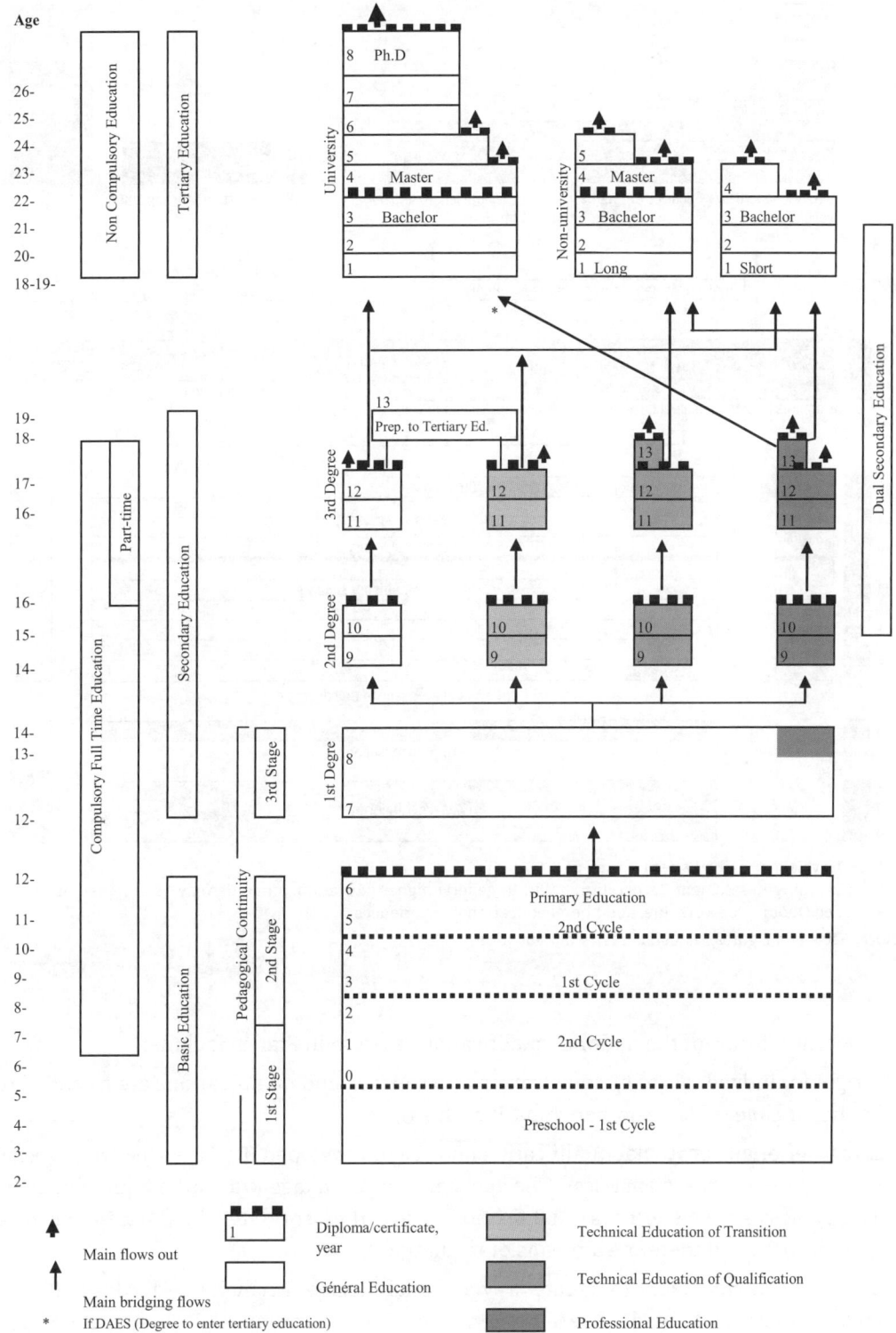

Source : Ministry of French Community, Directorate for International Relations, Brussels, 2004.

Source: Ministry of French Community, Directorate for International Relations, Brussels, 2004.

Figure B.3. **Education and training system in Denmark**

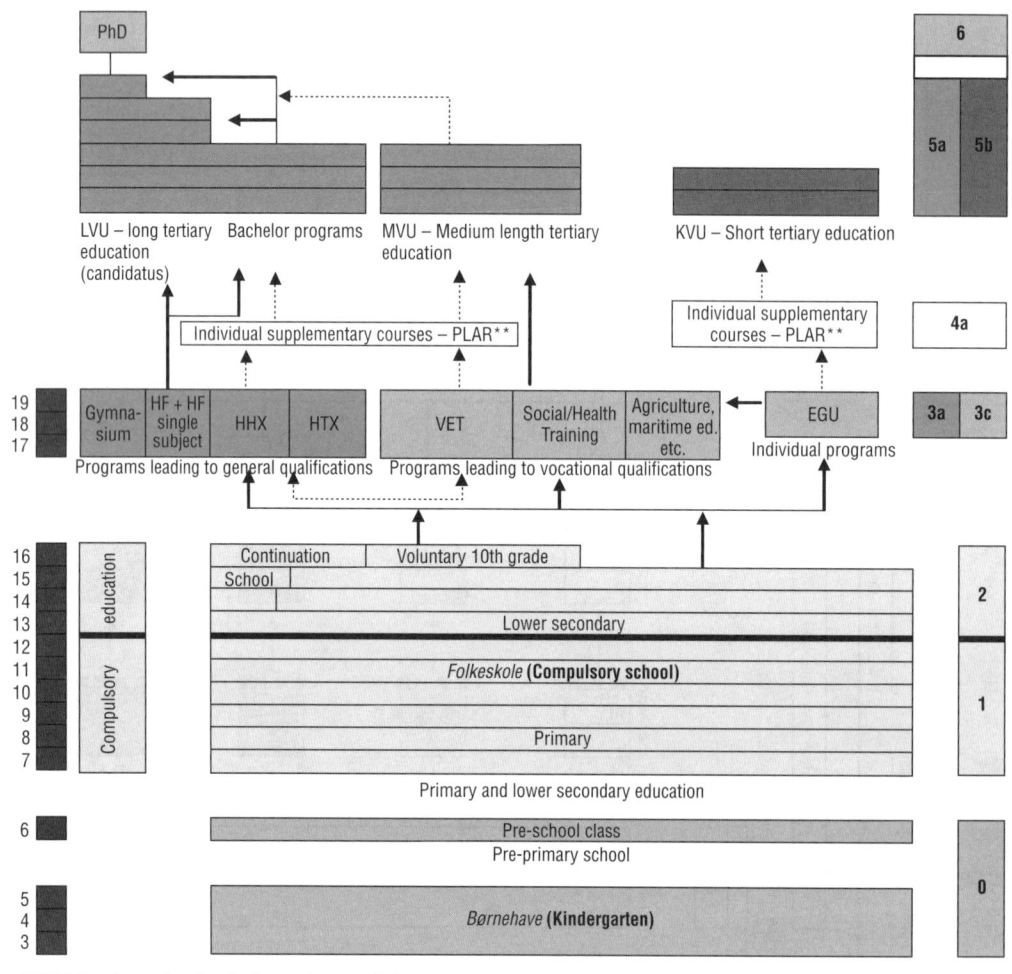

* ISCED levels maintained after reforms of 2003.
** Prior Learning Assessment Recognition – Within general higher education, students may be accepted under the so-called Quota II for work, life, and liberal educational experiences.
Source: Facts and Figures, Danish Ministry of Education, 2002.

France

Recent reforms of the national qualifications system in France include:

- A right for individuals to lifelong learning now exists, and qualifications are intended to be the tangible evidence or benchmark of this right.

- A register of all vocational qualifications has been developed (RNCP – *Répertoire national des certifications professionnelles*). The register shows linkage with other qualifications. The process of registering a qualification is a compulsory step in the creation of a qualification, and therefore a means of regulation.

- Steps are being taken to create a vocational degree in higher education (*licence professionnelle*), intended to strengthen the links between higher education and vocational training/preparation.

Figure B.4 describes the structure of the education and training system in France.

Figure B.4. **Education and training system in France**

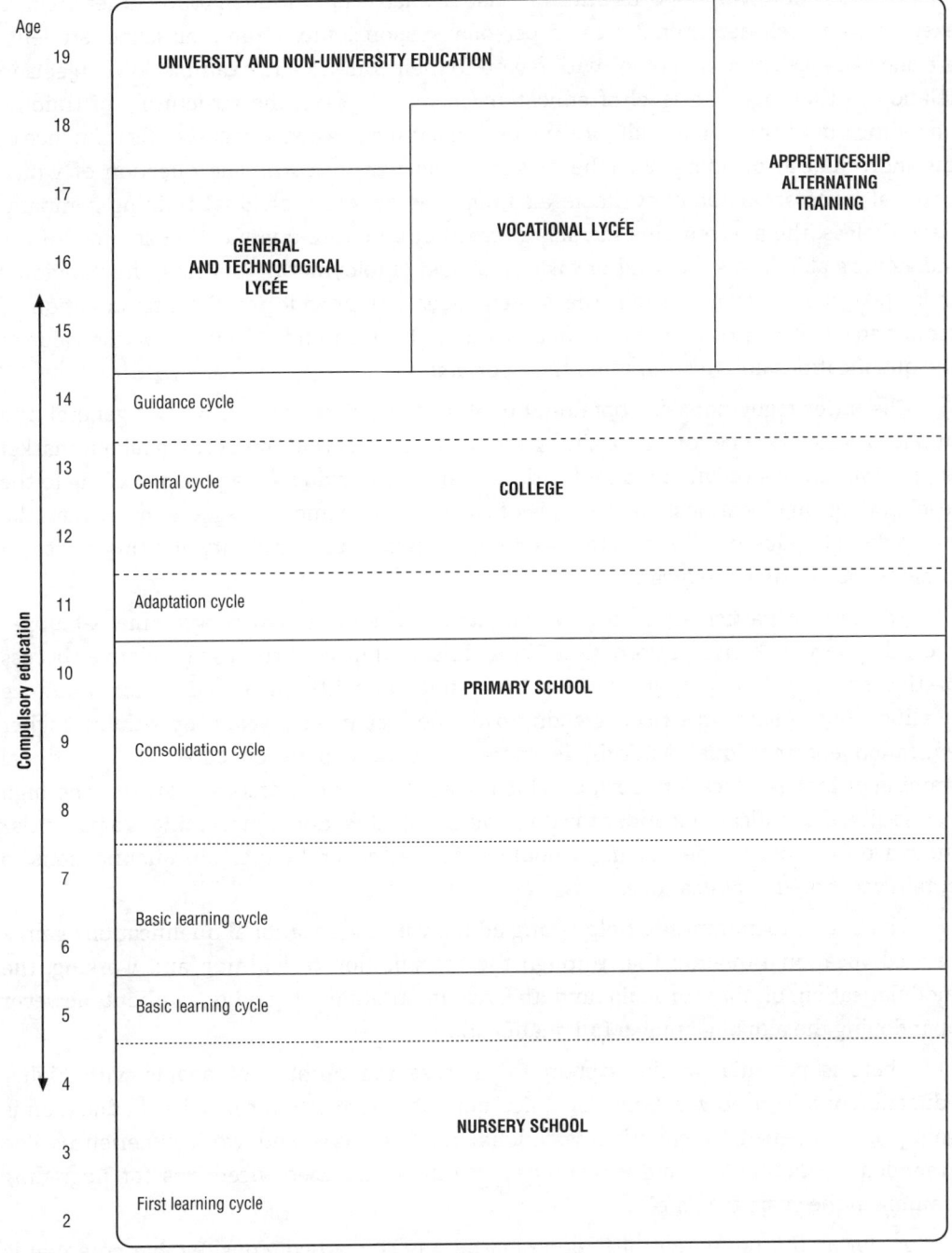

Source: Ministry of National Education, Higher Education and Research, France.

Germany

In order to encourage lifelong learning, recent initiatives to reform the German qualifications system have focused particularly on the close relationship between initial and continuing vocational education and training and/or academic education.

The qualifications acquired at the end of upper secondary education prepare the individual for access to institutions of higher education and/or transition into the employment system. The majority of the learning programmes cover a period of several years and are targeted towards adolescent learners and the achievement of the entire qualification. However, opportunities are also available for various groups of learners to exercise more self-determination and personal responsibility. Grammar school students are allowed an element of choice with regard to their courses and examination subjects in relation to their age and level of education. In recent years, the structuring of training under the dual system in mandatory and optional units has also increased the influence of the individual in deciding what he or she would like to learn. The question of which optional units are actually available also depends on the individual training company. Nevertheless, the aim remains the achievement of an entire qualification as proof of the individual's ability to study and/or take up skilled employment. As a rule, the individual must take a final examination; the system does not provide for the accumulation of employable skills to form an entire qualification. This is intended to preserve the value of the qualifications and to strengthen their portability.

The strict regulations for obtaining qualifications during the phase of general and initial vocational education and training are due to the fact that the German labour market is predominantly a vocational qualifications market. Individuals are paid according to the level of their qualifications, on the basis of collective agreements negotiated between the two sides of industry. The strictness expresses public responsibility for this phase of general and vocational education.

The rate of participation in and completion of educational programmes at upper secondary level is high by international comparison, thus confirming the relative success of this strategy. The proportion of school students with higher education entrance qualifications (*Abitur*) has risen steadily over the last twenty years. By gaining higher education entrance qualifications, learners can choose between access to vocational training or higher education, both of which open the way to attractive careers. The high portability of qualifications under the dual system of education and training is a particular incentive for those people leaving school with lower general education qualifications to obtain vocational qualifications.

There are programmes to help young adults without vocational qualifications gain a belated vocational qualification through the combination of learning and working, the modularisation of the curricula and the documentation of credits, without however abandoning the aim of gaining a full qualification.

There is potential in the system to increase the number of people with higher education or advanced vocational qualifications. The access to tertiary-level education is going to be opened by crediting vocational qualifications and work experience. The amended Upgrading Training Assistance Act offers increased incentives for upgrading training in the years to come.

As far as the promotion of lifelong learning is concerned, considerable potential is seen in the introduction of additional qualifications, which began several years ago. These may take the form of independent, supplementary qualifications or units that count towards advanced vocational qualifications. There are also great expectations for new qualifications frameworks, the certification of informally acquired competencies, and the introduction of a credit transfer system. These initiatives should open up new prospects for closer links between initial and continuing vocational education and training. Learners will be offered a number of opportunities.

There will be possibilities for a relatively smooth transfer between vocational training and continuing training for competent trainees interested in acquiring demanding vocational qualifications, particularly for those with *Abitur*. Apart from numerous dual courses of study with integrated initial vocational qualifications, the introduction of qualification frameworks, which is already taking place in the IT sector and is planned for further sectors, should help individuals obtain qualifications right up to the tertiary sector.

The question of access to continuing vocational education and training is particularly relevant for learners without formal vocational qualifications. For this group, flexibility of provision and the possibility of acquiring qualification units are just as important as the recognition of what they have learned informally. This applies not only to adolescents with poor starting chances and to young adults with low qualifications, but also to lateral entrants who are thus able to acquire a qualification in the field of continuing vocational training.

These initiatives, which are now also anchored in the new Vocational Training Act (as of 23 March 2005), are aimed at making the qualifications system as a whole more coherent, by restructuring training and continuing training, by introducing different forms of learning (both formal and informal), and by creating flexible learning paths from initial vocational training to continuing training and/or higher education. This means that learners enjoy framework conditions that allow more personal responsibility and self-determination when acquiring qualifications and developing competencies.

Outside the formal qualifications system several initiatives have been launched creating infrastructures and tools for the promotion of lifelong learning. The federal programme "Learning Regions – Support for Networks" involves the relevant stakeholders and institutions at local, regional and national level (such as continuing vocational training institutions, schools, universities, enterprises, associations, social partners, local communities and labour administration) and creates new infrastructures for lifelong learning. EUR 118 million have been made available for the period 2001-07 (51 million of which are ESF money). This bottom-up approach of the Learning Regions considerably promotes further development of the qualifications system in accordance with practical needs. The Learning Regions provide a framework for the joint development of proposals for new study courses by institutions such as the chambers of crafts, universities, and universities of applied sciences. Furthermore, the Learning Regions are testing concepts for the recognition of non-formal and informal learning and contribute to increasing the responsiveness to the needs of enterprises, in particular SMEs.

With the project "Quality Certification in Continuing Education" of the Bund-Länder Commission for Educational Planning and Research Promotion (BLK), the Federal Ministry of Education and Research (BMBF) has set in motion the nationwide establishment of the LQW 2 quality development and certification procedure in the field of continuing education. Apart from an internal quality development process, LQW 2 guarantees that certified institutions also meet externally reviewed minimum requirements.

With the BLK's project "Lifelong Learning Passport with Certification of Informal Learning", the BMBF has introduced the test phase of a widely usable "Continuing Education Passport" with an integrated advisory concept. The *ProfilPASS* attaches particular importance to the documentation and recognition of informal and non-formal skills. It will be compatible with other relevant instruments to validate skills and qualifications, both in Germany and at European level.

Figure B.5 describes the structure of the education and training system in Germany.

Figure B.5. **Education and training system in the Federal Republic of Germany**

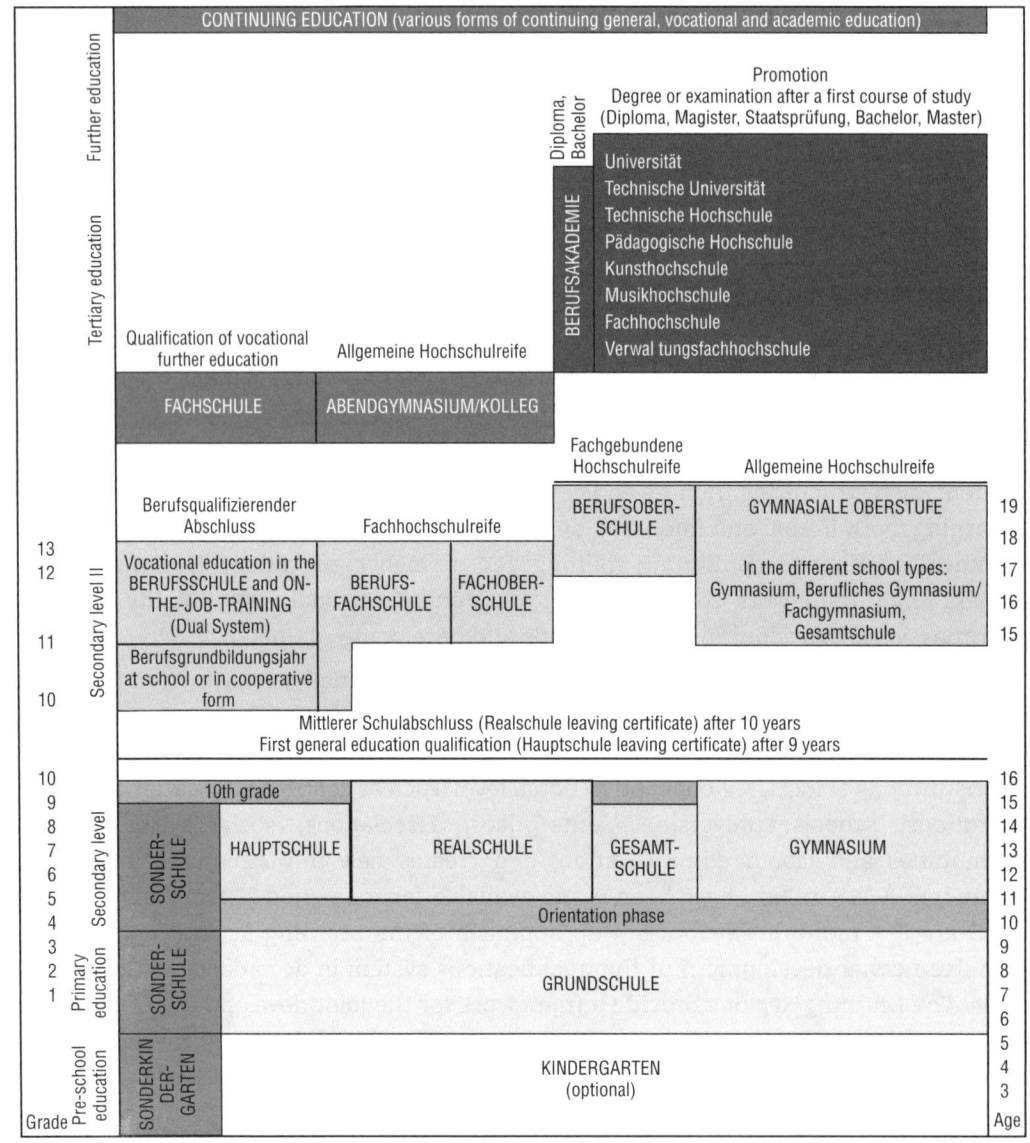

Source: Secretariat of the Standing Conference of the Ministers of Education and Cultural Affairs of the Länder in the Federal Republic of Germany.

Greece

Recent major reforms of the national qualifications system in Greece include:

- The upper-secondary cycle of education has been reformed with the establishment of Technical Vocational Schools (TEE) to provide technical and vocational knowledge and skills as well as an occupational awareness to facilitate young people's entry into the labour market. The day TEE are for young people 15+ who do not work, while the evening TEE are for working people up to the age of 50.

- The establishment of the Open University providing open access to higher education for all citizens.

- The introduction of the National System for Linking Vocational Education and Training with Employment (ESSEKA), which sets out the regulating framework for the implementation of an integrated and coordinated policy for human resources development and maximization of employment. This entails the linkage between Initial and Continuing VET systems (2003).

- The Cooperation Memorandum between the Ministry of Education and the Ministry of Employment for the planning and implementation of an integrated strategy for Life Long Learning in Greece (2005). This strategy is based on the following Actions:

  ❖ Monitoring labour market trends for the identification of labour market needs.

  ❖ Development of job profiles and their accreditation.

  ❖ Development of training programmes to be based on accredited job profiles.

  ❖ Accreditation of Centres, Trainers and Training Programmes.

  ❖ Accreditation of knowledge, skills and competencies.

- The Law on the Systematization of Life Long Learning (2005), which sets the legislative framework for:

  ❖ the accreditation of job profiles to be executed by EKEPIS, the National Accreditation Centre for Continuing Vocational Training;

  ❖ the accreditation of VET Programmes and the awarding of the respective Certificates to be executed by:

    – OEEK, the Organisation for Initial Vocational Education and Training, the authority body for initial VET; and

    – EKEPIS, the National Accreditation Centre for Continuing Vocational Training, the authority body for continuing vocational training.

  ❖ the accreditation of knowledge, skills and competencies and the awarding of the respective Certificates to be executed by OEEK and EKEPIS respectively;

  ❖ the establishment of LLL Institutes (IDBE) at Higher Education institutes.

It is to note that the participation and involvement of the Social Partners is engaged for in all stages of the planning and implementation of the integrated strategy for LLL in Greece.

Providers of adult Education within the context of LLL are mainly:

- Second Chance Schools, providing adults who have not completed the nine-year compulsory education with the opportunity of reintegrating into the formal education system and opening access opportunities into the initial and continuing VET.

- Adult Education Centres, providing adult VET for key competences.

- Local Authorities Centres, providing adult VET tailored to local needs.

- Institutes for Life Long Education, operating within the institutes of Higher Education for higher education graduates.

- The National Centre for Public Administration and Local Government, for public sector employees.

Providers of adult Training within the context of LLL are mainly:

- The Vocational Training Institutes (IEK) accredited by OEEK, which provide basic vocational knowledge, skills and competencies at post-secondary level to equip learners with qualifications for employment.

- The Vocational Training Centres (KEK) accredited by EKEPIS, which provide complementary, updated and/or upgraded knowledge, skills and competencies for the learners' integration and/or reintegration into the labour market, employment security, professional advancement and personal development.

Figure B.6 describes the structure of the education and training system in Greece.

Figure B.6. **Education and training system in Greece**

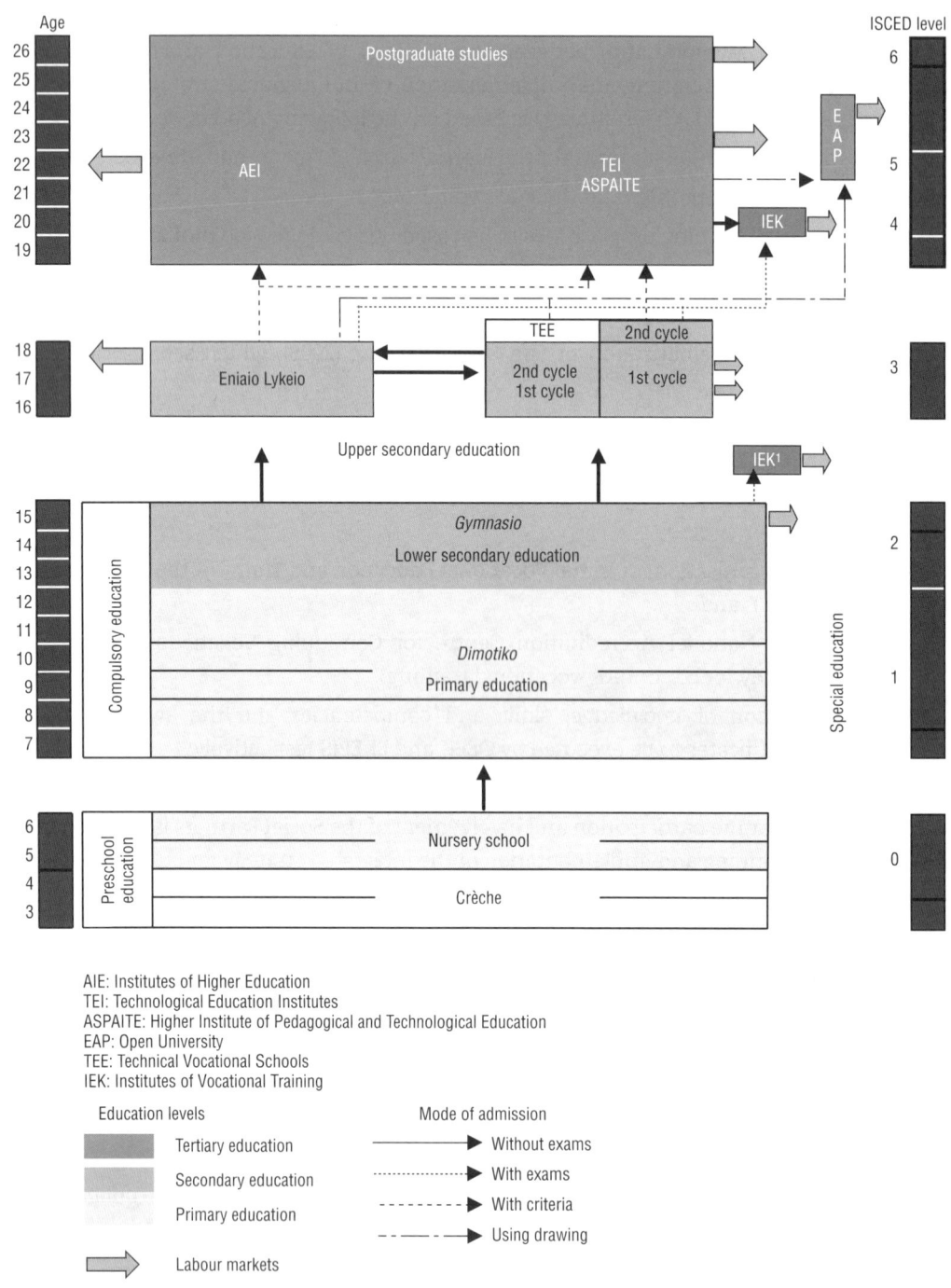

AIE: Institutes of Higher Education
TEI: Technological Education Institutes
ASPAITE: Higher Institute of Pedagogical and Technological Education
EAP: Open University
TEE: Technical Vocational Schools
IEK: Institutes of Vocational Training

Education levels

Tertiary education
Secondary education
Primary education

Labour markets

Mode of admission

———▶ Without exams
·············▶ With exams
– – – – – ▶ With criteria
— – — – ▶ Using drawing

1. Post-Gymnasium initial training in specialities placed in post-secondary IEK.

Source: CEDEFOP, Panorama series 59, 2003.

Ireland

Recent reforms of the national qualifications system in Ireland include:

● The development of a national framework of qualifications that is inclusive of all qualifications and will lead to credit transfer systems.

- The development of the Applied Leaving Certificate, recognising achievement across a whole programme rather than simply individual subject attainment. It is focused on vocational preparation, and a range of modes of assessment is used.

- The development of the Accumulation of Credits and Certification of Subjects (ACCS) scheme, initiated in 1989. The scheme allows learners to follow programmes for individual subjects and accumulate the credits gained towards an award. Its objective is to facilitate greater participation by learners on a part-time basis and promote adult learning.

- The development of a new model of standards-based apprenticeship.

- The development and implementation of the Higher Education Links Scheme, a process designed to facilitate transitions from further education awards to programmes leading to higher education awards.

- The Higher Education Links Scheme, a response to increasing participation in programmes leading to Level 2 NCVA awards in post-secondary education. Essentially, higher education places are made available through links between particular higher education programmes and one or more NCVA Level 2 Certificate awards in related areas of study.

Another major reform of the qualifications system in Ireland has been under way since 2001. The central element in the reform is the development of a National Framework of Qualifications, a structure of levels allowing qualifications to be compared easily. Following the launch of the Framework in October 2003, implementation has proceeded quickly. New Framework qualifications have been in use throughout higher education and training since the autumn of 2004, and the introduction of a new system of awards for further education and training (including vocational education and training) is expected in mid-2005.

The Framework is a structure of ten levels. Standards of knowledge, skill and competence have been set out for each level, defining the outcomes to be achieved by learners seeking to gain awards. This introduces new meaning to an award, that it recognises learning outcomes –

Figure B.7. **The Irish Qualifications Framework**

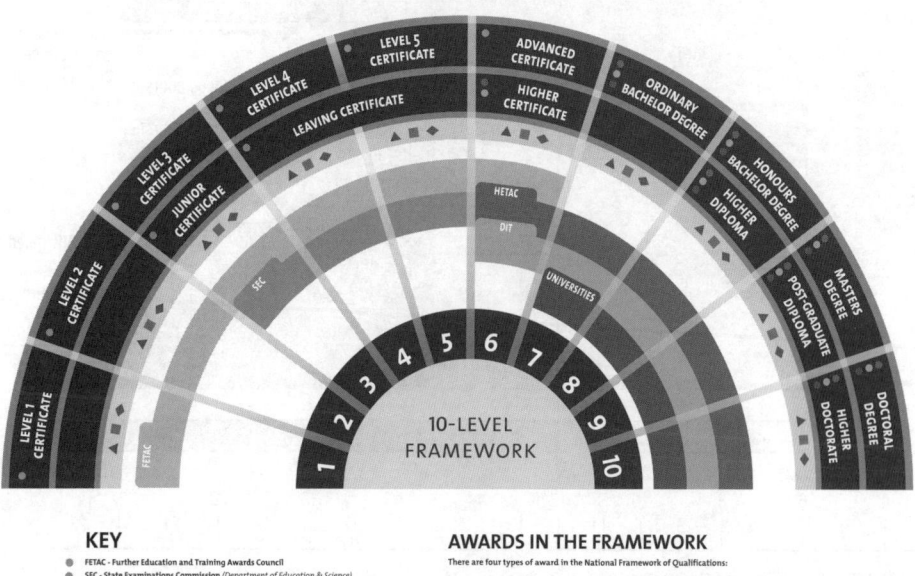

Source: National Qualifications Authority of Ireland.
(See figure in colour at *www.nfq.ie/nfq/en/frame_action/documents/NQAIFANENGLISH.pdf*.)

what a person with an award knows, can do and understands – rather than time spent on a programme.

The ten levels accommodate awards gained in schools, the workplace, the community, training centres, colleges and universities, from the most basic to the most advanced levels of learning. All learning can thus be recognised, including that achieved through experience in the workplace or other non-formal settings.

A key feature of the Irish reform is that responsibility for awarding qualifications now rests with a small number of awarding bodies. A particular innovation is that all vocational education and training qualifications in Ireland are now awarded by one body, the Further Education and Training Awards Council.

Figure B.7 describes the Irish qualifications framework.

Japan

Recent reforms of the national qualifications system in Japan include the creation of a new vocational ability evaluation system through a combination of private and public bodies. The trade skill tests lead to the title of Certified Skill Worker.

Figure B.8 describes the structure of the education and training system in Japan.

Figure B.8. **Education and training system in Japan**

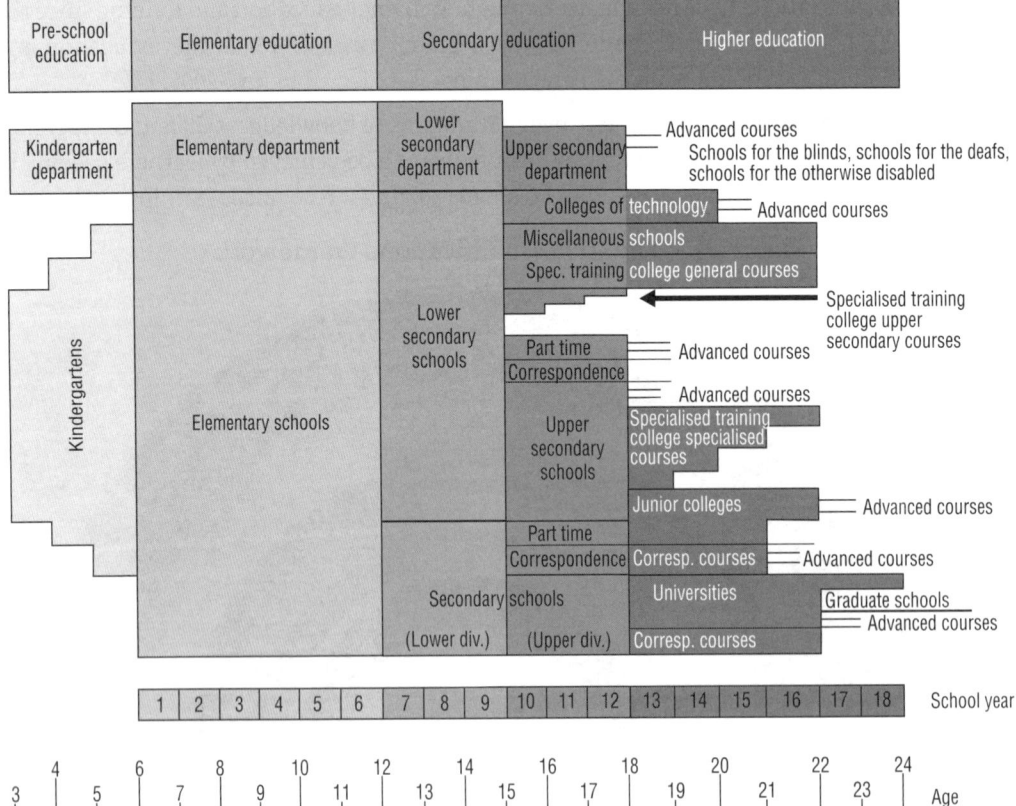

Source: MEXT (Ministry of Education, Culture, Sports, Science and Technology), Japan.

Korea

Recent reforms of the national qualifications system in Korea include:

- A programme based on the Workers' Vocational Training Promotion Act: the purpose of the Act is to stimulate the development and improvement of peoples' vocational capabilities throughout their working life, and to encourage the participation of the private sector in developing career capabilities and to provide better- quality public or national vocational training.

- The Lifelong Learning and Lifelong Education Act meets demand for equal recognition of individual achievements through lifelong learning with those from regular education and provides credits towards obtaining of degrees or credits.

- The Educational Reform Proposal of 1996 and Reform Proposals on Regulations of the Qualifications System of 1999 (two major reform efforts).

Figure B.9 describes the structure of the education and training system in Korea.

Figure B.9. **Education and training system in Korea**

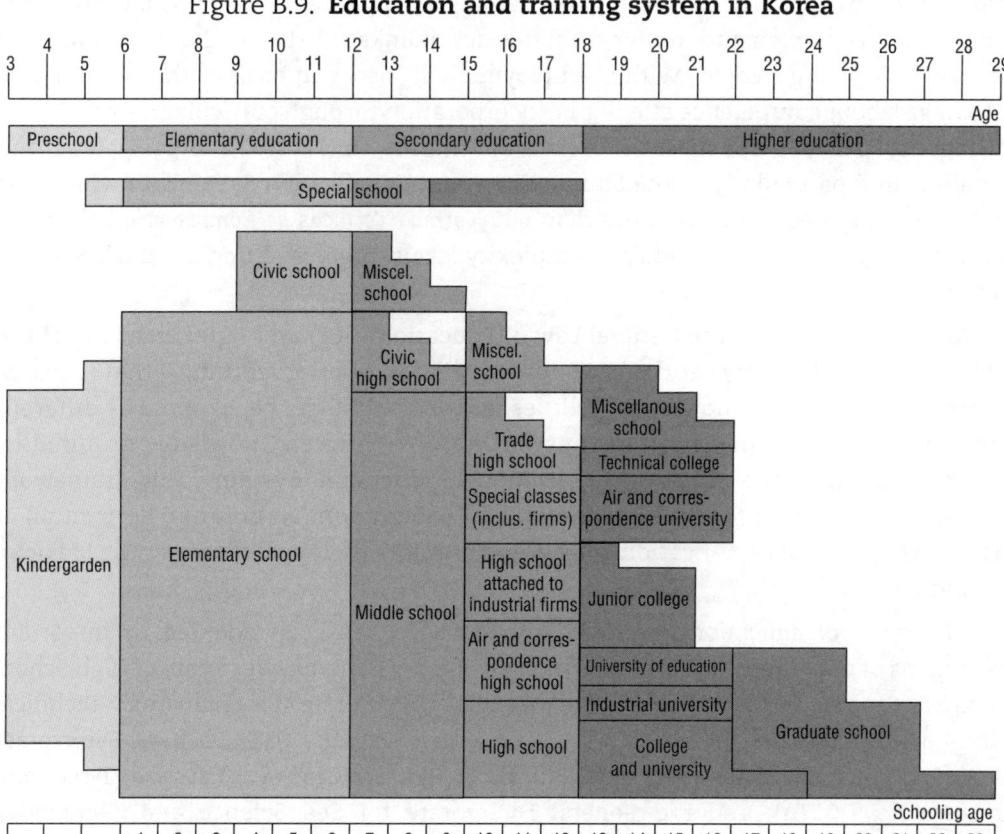

Source: Ministry of Education and Human Resources Development, Korea.

Mexico: The National System of Education – routes and qualifications

The National System of Education contains three education routes: *a)* academic, *b)* vocational and *c)* occupational. In general the first two operate in the formal context of the Mexican educational system, which comprises three consecutive stages of academic education: basic education (preschool, two years; primary, six years; and lower secondary, three years), upper secondary education (high school and technical professional, generally three years), and tertiary education (bachelor's degrees, normally four or five years; and graduate studies, between two and five years). Vocational education and training begins at lower and upper secondary levels and continues with higher education studies. Occupational learning includes job training, both in formal (training centres) and non-formal and informal environments (workplaces). Academic and vocational education qualifications are based on the accreditation of study subjects corresponding to each degree or study year. Qualifications for jobs are focused on prior learning recognition – formal, non-formal and informal – of people older than 15 and on the basis of Technical Standards of Labour Competence (*Normas Técnicas de Competencia Laboral, NTCL*), within the Project for the Modernisation of Technical Education and Training (*Proyecto para la Modernización de la Educación Técnica y la Capacitación, PMETyC*).

Some of the main reforms to the qualifications system

In relation to educational quality problems and challenges, the National Programme of Education (2001-06) highlights the importance of the abilities and skills required by employment, particularly concerning job training at upper secondary level. It also pays attention to the problems stemming from the lack of linkage between the curriculum and the needs of young people. Within employment it also emphasises the necessity to encourage labour competence standards' incorporation through curricular reform. These educational policy guidelines have had an impact in PMETyC´s organisation and operation, and particularly in the Standardised and Certification Systems to which it is linked. These systems involve more than 600 *Normas Técnicas de Competencia Laboral*, in 12 main employment areas and five complexity levels, organised under a qualifications matrix.

Articles 45 and 64 of the General Law of Education (GLE) and Agreement 286 of the Public Education Ministry set the basis for recognition of prior learning – that is to say, for the accreditation of knowledge, abilities and skills that can be acquired by different routes and education models, and thus for the link between knowledge acquired by labour experience and through the National Education System. This framework provides the principles for the construction and integration (vertical and horizontal) of a National System of Qualifications that could promote lifelong learning in the Mexican population.

The focus of education based on competencies has been adopted by important institutions of upper secondary education, for example: General Directorate of High School (*Dirección General del Bachillerato, DGB*), General Directorate for Industrial Technical Education (*Dirección General de Educación Tecnológica Industrial, DGETI*), General Directorate for Agriculture and Livestock Technical Education (*Dirección General de Educación Tecnológica Agropecuaria, DGETA*), and the General Directorate for Sea Science and Technology Education (*Dirección General de Educación en Ciencia y Tecnología del Mar, DGECyTM*), all belonging to the Sub-secretariat of Upper Secondary Education (*Subsecretaría de Educación Media*); and the National System for Vocational and Technical Education (*Colegio Nacional de Educación Profesional Técnica, CONALEP*). In this way several institutions have facilitated the implementation of important reforms to their corresponding models, to increase the flexibility, pertinence, equity and quality of their services.

Figure B.10 describes the structure of the education and training system in Mexico.

Figure B.10. **Education and training system in Mexico**

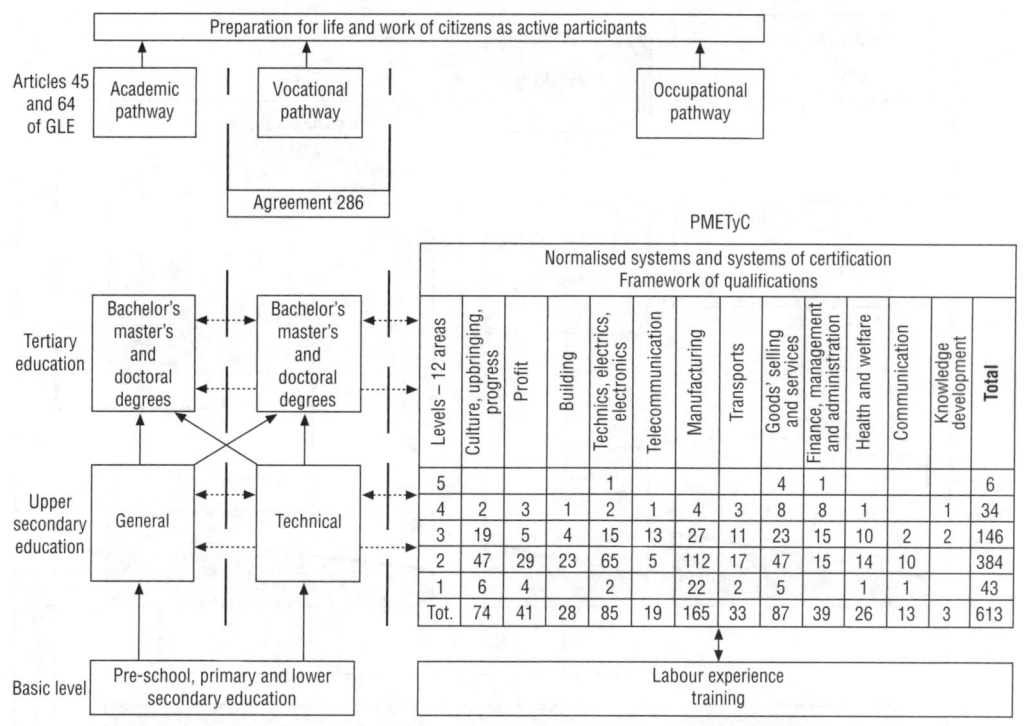

Levels – 12 areas	Culture, upbringing, progress	Profit	Building	Technics, electrics, electronics	Telecommunication	Manufacturing	Transports	Goods' selling and services	Finance, management and administration	Health and welfare	Communication	Knowledge development	Total
5				1				4	1				6
4	2	3	1	2	1	4	3	8	8	1		1	34
3	19	5	4	15	13	27	11	23	15	10	2	2	146
2	47	29	23	65	5	112	17	47	15	14	10		384
1	6	4		2		22	2	5		1	1		43
Tot.	74	41	28	85	19	165	33	87	39	26	13	3	613

Source: PMETyC (Project for the Modernisation of Technical Education and Training), Mexico.

The Netherlands

Recent reforms of the national qualifications system in the Netherlands include:

- A national action plan regarding lifelong learning, focusing on both promoting the employability of the employed, unemployed and teachers, and combating educational disadvantages and reorientating education and training towards lifelong learning.

- A co-ordinating agency for the regulation and control of qualifications.

- Development of broad competence-based qualifications, including cross-sector qualifications.

- Flexible dual trajectories combining learning and work.

- The accreditation of prior learning.

Figure B.11 describes the structure of the education and training system in the Netherlands.

Figure B.11. **Education and training system in the Netherlands**

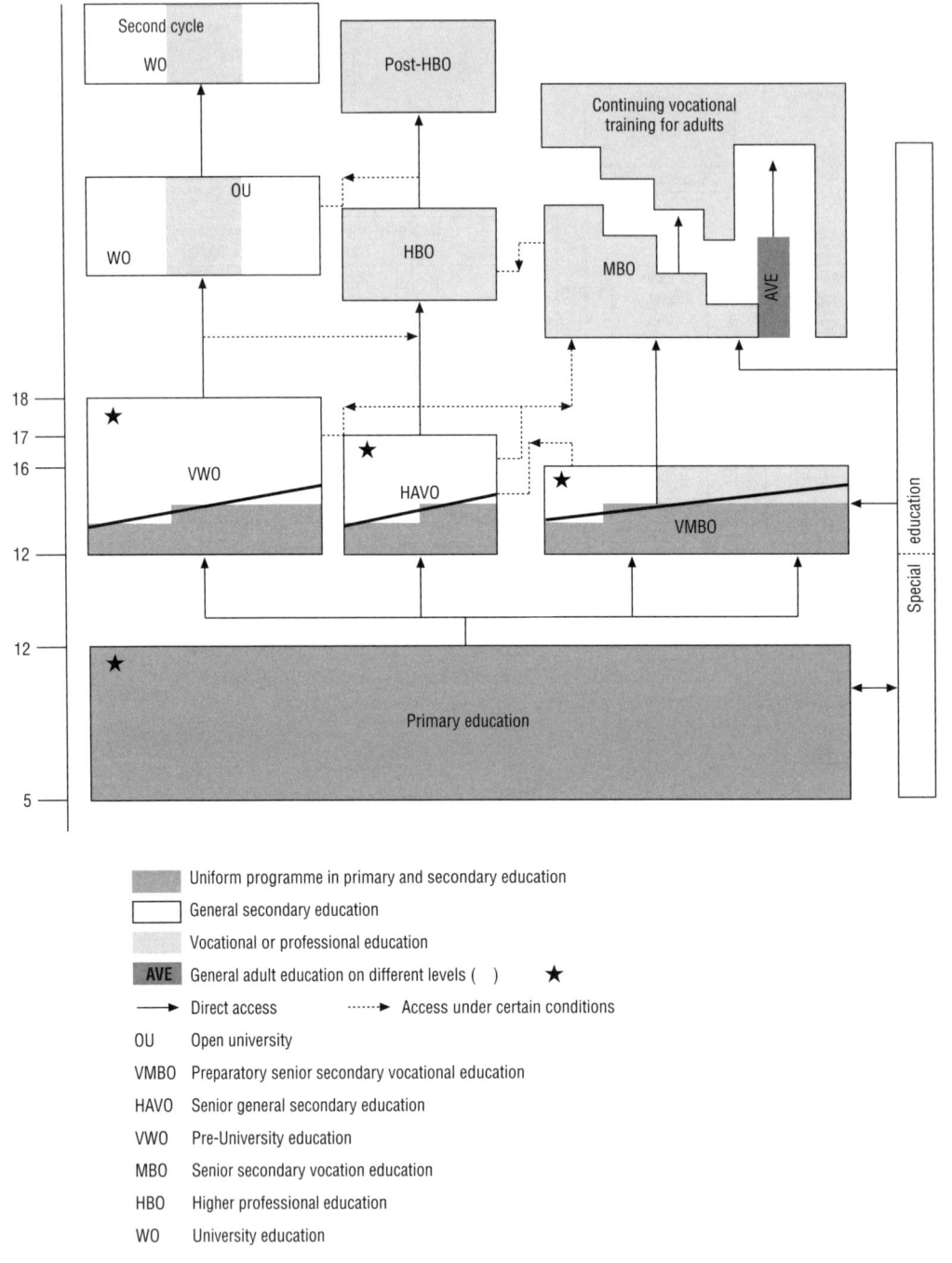

Source: CINOP (Dutch Institute for Innovation of Education and Training), 2004.

New Zealand

Reforms of the national qualifications system in New Zealand include:

- Development of the National Qualifications Framework.

- Development of unit standards.

- Development of the National Certificate of Educational Achievement (NCEA). The first stage was implemented in 2002, with level 2 implementation planned for 2003 followed by level 3 in 2004. The National Certificate of Educational Achievement will have full integration with the standards-based National Qualifications Framework, using "achievement standards" developed for the school curriculum and unit standards from the National Qualifications Framework. Achievement standards differ from unit standards in that there are three different levels of achievement (achieved, achieved with merit, and achieved with excellence), which in some cases are externally assessed.

- International benchmarking and mutual recognition agreements.

- The adult literacy strategy with the goals of increasing opportunities for adult literacy learning, developing capacity in the adult literacy teaching sector, and improving the quality of adult literacy programmes. The creation of a strategy for adult and community education (ACE).

Figure B.12. **Education and training system in New Zealand**

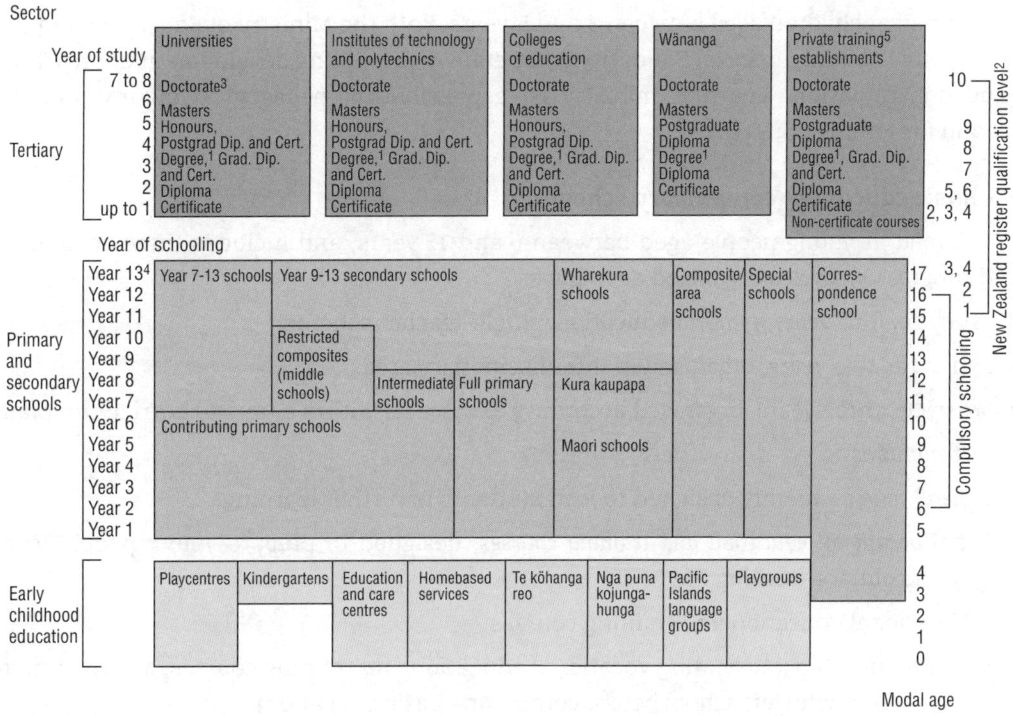

1. A small number of degrees are in excess of 3 years.
2. Certificates can be registered at any level, and diplomas can be registered at any level between 5 and 10.
3. Apart from the universities, currently only one of the institutes of technology also offers a doctorate.
4. The majority of students complete their schooling within 13 years but a small number continue to study in the school system for another year or two.
5. PTEs include a large range of institution types and sizes, many of which are focused on short-certificate or non-certificate level courses.

Source: Ministry of Education, New Zealand.

- The development and enhancement of policy for and funding and delivery of foundation education.

- Modern apprenticeships, credit recognition and credit transfer arrangements.

- A system that identifies and defines foundation skills critical to participation in society and the labour market, and acknowledges learner progress in these skill areas through the National Qualifications Framework. It is acknowledged that learners can acquire foundation skills without that learning being recognised by qualifications. Secondary education has been reformed to develop positive attitudes to lifelong learning.

- A common credit currency, a levels system, learning outcomes and subject classification system for all qualifications quality assured in New Zealand. This register provides a basis for credit recognition and transfer.

Figure B.12 describes the structure of the education and training system in New Zealand.

Portugal

The education and training system in Portugal is based on a series of principles aiming at facilitating and assuring the right to education and training, as well as ensuring equal opportunities of access to and success in lifelong learning, in close co-operation with three Ministries – Education, Science and Higher Education, and Labour and Social Solidarity.

1 – Preschool education (optional attendance)

Aimed at children aged between 3 and 5 years. Both the Ministry of Education and the Ministry of Labour and Social Solidarity co-operate in promoting development of preschool education provision. The first ministry is responsible for pedagogical quality and the second for families' support.

2 – Basic education (compulsory schooling)

Aimed at young people aged between 6 and 15 years, and includes three sequential and progressive cycles organised as follows:

- 1st cycle, four years, general education, single-teacher scheme.

- 2nd cycle, two years, organised in interdisciplinary areas.

- 3rd cycle, three years, organised according to subjects within a unified curriculum plan.

    It includes:

- *General courses*, mainly designed to lead students to further learning.

- *Initial vocational education and training courses*, designed to prepare young people (over 15 years old) for working life:

    ❖ Vocational education and training courses.

    ❖ Apprenticeship (alternating vocational education and training courses, aimed at first-job seekers who left school before completing basic education).

- *Recurrent basic education* (a second opportunity for those over 15 years of age who left school early).

Successful completion of basic education entitles a person to an academic diploma (lower secondary education) or double certification – academic and vocational qualification certification (level 1 or 2).

3 – Secondary education

Aimed at young people aged between 15 and 18 years who successfully complete basic education, to prepare them for further learning and/or qualify them for working life.

It includes:

- *General courses*, mainly designed to lead students to higher education (university or polytechnic).

- *Initial vocational education and training courses*, designed to prepare young people for working life:

  ❖ Technological courses.

  ❖ Vocational courses.

  ❖ Specialised artistic courses.

  ❖ Apprenticeship (alternating vocational education and training courses, aimed at first-job seekers who left school before completing upper secondary education)

  ❖ Vocational education and training courses.

- *Recurrent secondary education* (a second opportunity for early school leavers, over 18). The recurrent secondary education courses are flexible and organised in a system of capitalised blocks. They take into account learners' prior experience and skills in the design of personalised learning plans.

Successful completion of secondary education entitles the person to an academic diploma (upper secondary education), allowing access to higher education or double certification – academic and vocational qualification certification (level 3), qualifying them for working life and/or allowing access to higher education.

4 – Post-secondary education – technological specialisation courses

Aimed at those who have a secondary education course or a legally equivalent qualification , and at those who have a level 3 vocational qualification. These courses award a technological specialisation diploma (TSD) as well as a vocational qualification certificate (level 4) and/or allow access to higher education.

5 – Higher education

Higher education has a variable duration. It includes university education and the Polytechnic Higher Education, and awards a university degree (4 to 6 years) and a bachelor's degree (3 to 4 years) as well as the respective vocational qualifications (levels 4 and 5). At the present time, following the Declaration of Bologna, a number of recommendations were implemented, particularly those concerning the European Credit Transfer System (ECTS) – the change in academic degrees to grant them a higher comparability, facilitating therefore mutual recognition and the promotion of free mobility.

6 – Adult education and training

This includes:

- *Recurrent education* – second-chance learning to early school leavers: aimed at providing schooling to individuals who are no longer at an age to attend secondary education (older than 18). There should be a second chance to learn at every level. Second-chance learning is organised in accordance with a studies plan, adjusted to the targeted age group level. It awards certificates and diplomas equivalent to those granted by regular basic and secondary education: certificate of vocational initiation (level 1) and certificates of vocational qualification (levels 2 and 3).

● *Adult Education and Training Courses* (EFA): Aimed at adults (older than 18) without basic education or vocational qualification. These courses are based on a training model according to competencies units, through which previous formally or informally acquired competencies are recognised and where basic academic education is articulated with qualifying training. They award integrated certification (academic and vocational) through a certificate of adult education and training, equivalent in legal terms to one of the three levels of basic education and level 1 or 2 of vocational qualification.

● *The National System for Recognizing, Validating and Certifying Competencies* (RVCC System): Carried out on the basis of a National Key-Competencies Framework for Adult Education and Training points to the certification of an education level. This process is developed through the National Network of Recognition, Validation and Certification of Competencies Centres and awards a certificate equivalent in legal terms to one of the three levels of basic education.

● *Continuing vocational training*: This includes a range of actions-type for occupational qualification and further training of non-qualified or semi-qualified active population, and for the specialisation of qualified active population. It promotes training paths targeted at updating, recycling and professional improvement.

Recent reforms of the national qualifications system in Portugal include:

Development of vocational training using an alternation model. Two main areas of reform:

● Initial vocational education and training supply (which is now being implemented)

Review of the legal framework on the apprenticeship system:

❖ Development and implementation of vocational education and training courses aimed at young people over 15 at risk of dropping out, or those who left school before having completed 12 years of schooling, as well as at those who, having completed 12 years of schooling, wish to enter the labour market with a formally recognised vocational training level. These courses award double certification – school and vocational training (level 1, 2 or 3).

❖ Reform of vocational education and training as an alternative to the general upper secondary education. The reform adjusts the current and emerging vocational profiles and defines a modular curriculum matrix allowing for transferability of the various training pathways, thus introducing more choice into upper secondary programmes. In fact, initial vocational education and training awards double certification – school and vocational (level 3). The goal, for 2010, is a doubling of the number of vacancies for the vocational and technological education at upper secondary level, to be reached at an annual rate of increase of 10%.

❖ Strengthening the links between the education and training systems and the labour market.

❖ Promoting more involvement of the social partners in the process of vocational education and training.

❖ Development of vocational guidance services, making them more accessible. Communicating the opportunities offered to acquire qualifications can facilitate integration of young and adult people into the labour market.

● **Adult education and training provision**

❖ Development and implementation of the Adult Education and Training Plan since 2000/01, particularly targeting low-skilled working adults – employed and unemployed alike.

❖ Implementation of the National System for Recognising and Validating Knowledge, Skills and Competencies non-formally and informally acquired. The competencies recognition and validation process is grounded in a national "Key-Competencies Framework for Adult Education and Training", a reference for awards developed on the basis of clearly described learning outcomes.

❖ Implementation of the Adult Education and Training Courses, supervised jointly by the Ministry of Education and the Ministry of Labour and Social Solidarity. This kind of training awards double qualification: school and vocational training certificates. The courses offer modular, flexible, tailor-made pathways, articulating education and vocational training through organised programmes. They are based on an initial process of recognising and validating prior non-formal and informally acquired knowledge, skills and competencies according to the "Key-Competencies Framework for Adult Education and Training". The training programme is organised around the four key-competence areas proposed by the Framework: Language and Communication; Mathematics for Everyday Life; Information and Communication Technologies; Citizenship and Employability.

❖ Establishment of a minimum number of annual hours (20 training hours until 2006 and 35 training hours afterwards) of certified training on the responsibility of the employer, to take place internally or at external training institutions.

❖ With the regulation of the Labour Code, there are now rules about the training of minors admitted to work without having concluded compulsory education or without professional qualification.

❖ A reform of higher education that recognises the free mobility of people in Europe and the European dimension of the labour market as an important element for the restructuring of higher education.

❖ The creation of technological specialisation courses with a view to a new training entities supply alignment in higher education.

Figure B.13 describes the structure of the education and training system in Portugal.

Figure B.13. **Education and training system in Portugal**

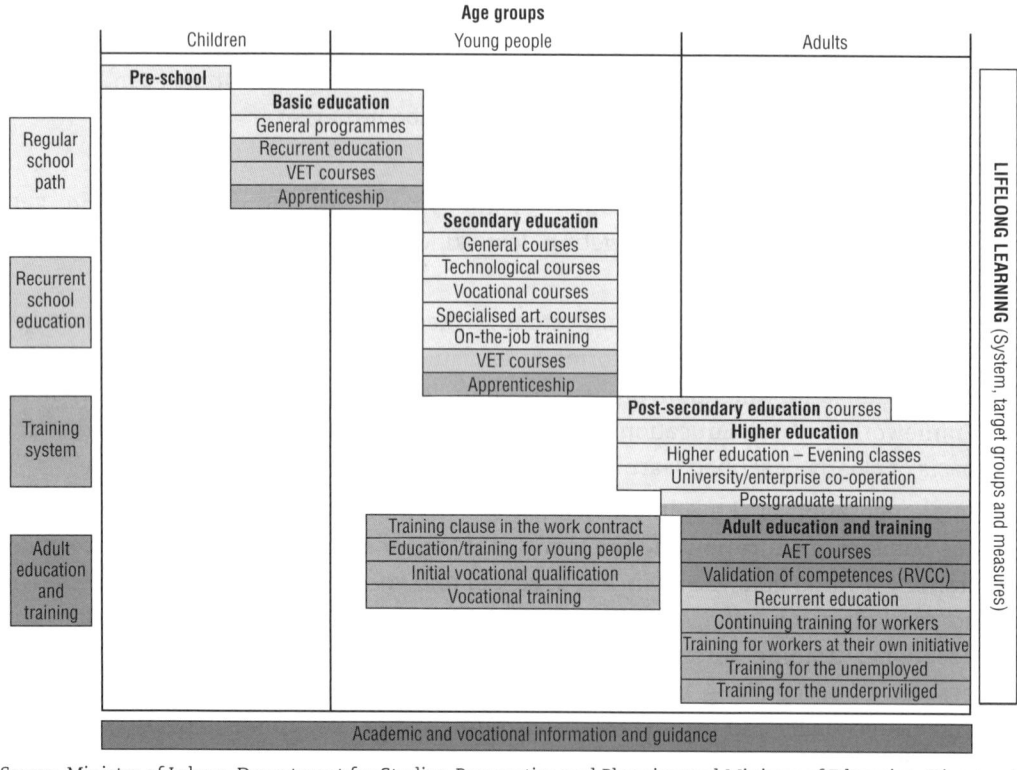

Source: Ministry of Labour, Department for Studies, Prospective and Planning and Ministry of Education, Directorate General for Vocational Education and Training, Lisbon, 2004.

Slovenia

Recent reforms of the national qualifications system in Slovenia include:

- A better choice of vocational programmes based on standards that open curricula (allowing local variation), "modularise" programmes, and integrate higher levels of knowledge. Modularisation of programmes reflects the need to increase adults' access to educational opportunities, especially in order to improve their formal qualification attainments.

- The transition from *nomenklatura*, a document that was a legal basis for vocational education and training programmes until 2002, to occupational standards as the basis for educational programmes or for modules that are parts of the educational programme and/or the system of assessment and accreditation of prior learning.

- Introduction of the certification system.

- Assessment and certification of non-formal and informal learning and experiences as a measure to support lifelong learning were introduced at the end of the 1990s. The assessment takes place against nationally agreed standards of knowledge and skill requirements for performing certain jobs in the labour market.

- Adoption of acts related to the national qualification system development.

- Introduction of new forms of education and training in the educational system in the upper secondary and post-secondary level, enabling easier vertical and horizontal transfer from one educational level to another.

- Reintroduction of the dual system of education and training into the educational system.

Figure B.14. **Education and training system in Slovenia**

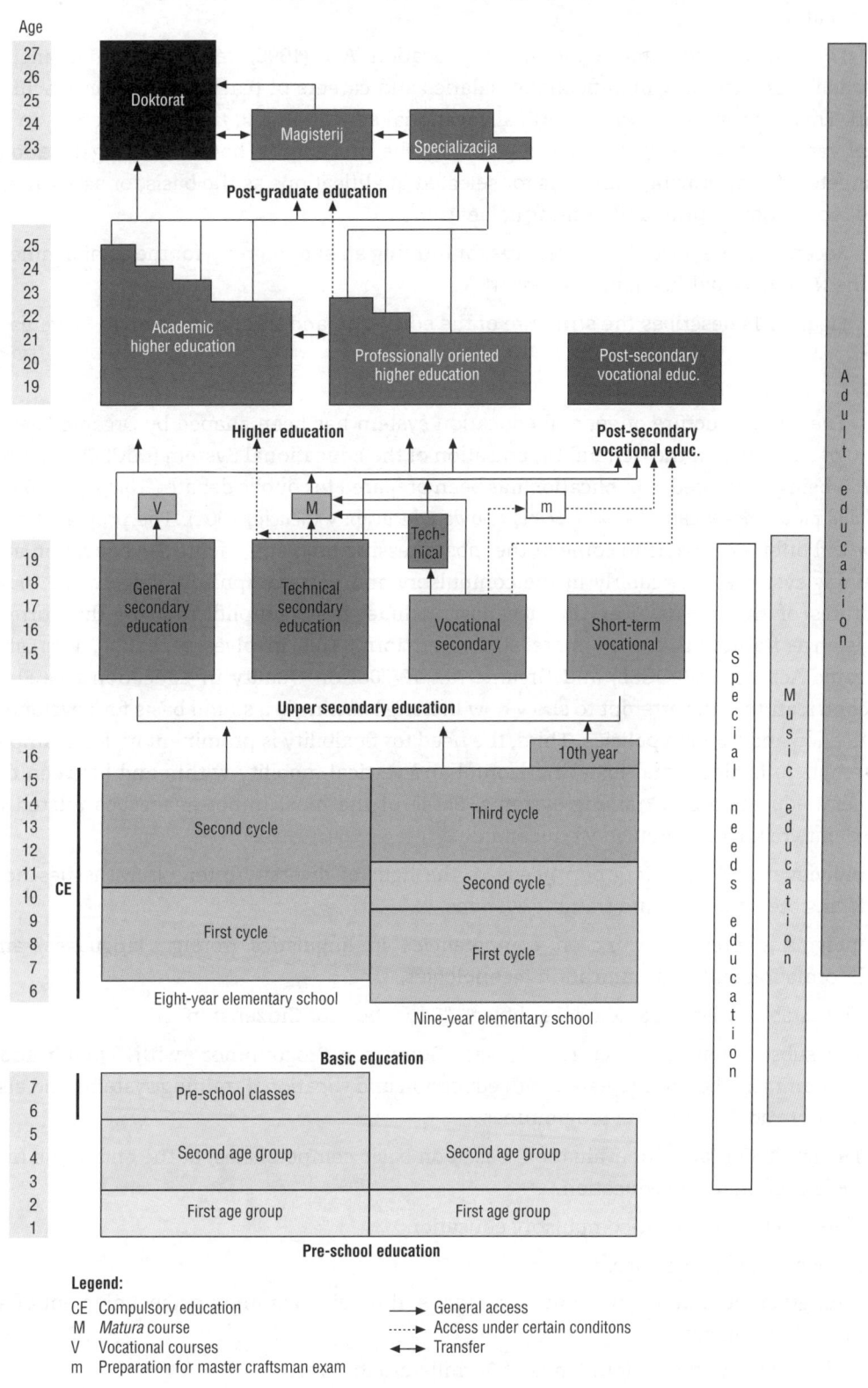

Source: Ministry of Education and Sport, Slovenia.

- Promotion of the greater involvement of the social partners in the process of vocational education.

The Organisation and Funding of Education Act (1996) regulates the financing mechanisms, including qualifications, salaries and careers of teaching and non-teaching staff. This Act covers the whole vertical vocational education and training structure. In its final version, it now regulates more generally the procedures, bodies and organisations competent for approving standards for selected qualifications as the basis for assessment and recognition of prior and non-formal learning.

Recently, there have been initiatives for forming an expert group for the establishment of the National Qualifications Framework.

Figure B.14 describes the structure of the education and training system in Slovenia.

Spain

The basic structure of general education system has been shaped by Organic Law 1/1990 of 3 October on the General Organisation of the Educational System (LOGSE). Another law is being developed; a publication has been prepared for public debate ("*Una educación de calidad para todos y entre todos*" – *Ministerio de Educación y Ciencia*, 2004). The proposed new law will offer a response to some of the most pressing problems facing the education and training systems, particularly in the compulsory and post-compulsory stages. The main features of the debate over the new law include, first, simplification of the current legislative framework into a more structured form: this involves repealing, *inter alia*, Organic Act 1/1990 (LOGSE) and Organic Act 10/2002 on Quality in Education (LOCE). A second feature is the attempt to show how lifelong learning is a sound basis for developing education and training policies. Third, the need for flexibility is prominent in, for example, attempts to facilitate and foster horizontal and vertical mobility within and between the general education and training systems. Some of the most important issues related to flexibility relate to compulsory education:

- Individual and specific group needs in the light of diversity/intercultural issues now facing the education and training systems.

- Integrating previous work on competencies in linguistics (foreign languages) and information and communication technologies.

- The establishment of a new core subject, "Education for Citizenship".

- The substitution of the current "Social Guarantee Programmes" with "Qualification Programmes", better integrated with education and vocational training systems and also linked to adult education programmes.

- The implementation of evaluation, based on basic competencies, at the end of the first cycle of compulsory education.

  And in terms of post-compulsory education:

- Students' need for choice.

- Strengthening training in scientific methods, through a common subject element of all kind of Bachillerato.

- Reducing the option of four kinds of Bachillerato to three.

Figure B.15. **Education and training system in Spain**

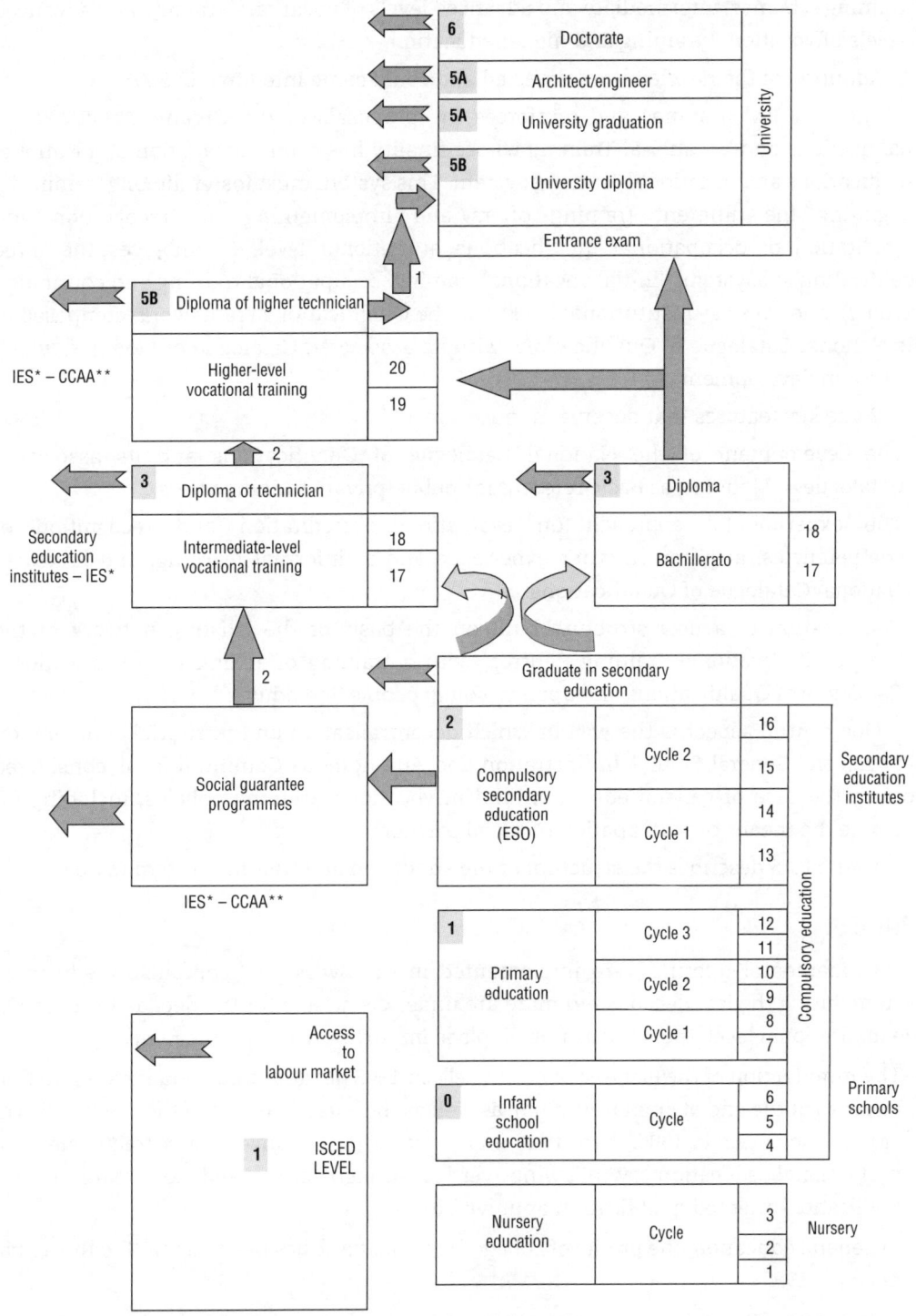

1. Direct access to university studies related to VET programme.
2. Entrance exam required.
* IES: Instituto de Education Secundaria (Secondary Education Institute).
** CCAA: Communidades Autónomes (Autonomous Communities).

Source: Ministry of Education and Science, Spain.

- Proposals concerning improving linkages among general education and vocational training schemes, intermediate and advanced levels of vocational training and advanced levels of vocational training and higher education.

Adoption of the new law was expected and could come into force in 2006.

The new law assumes and reinforces the proposals of the Organic Act 5/2002 on Qualifications and Vocational Training whose finality has been the creation of a National Qualifications and Vocational Training System. This system must foster lifelong training by integrating the different training offers and implementing the recognition and accreditation of occupational qualifications at national level. It embraces the three qualification subsystems (initial vocational training, occupational training and continuing training), and takes as institutional backbone the Qualifications Framework, composed of the National Catalogue of Qualifications with its associated Catalogue of Modules, which are now in development.

Some key features that deserve mention are:

- The development of the National Catalogue of Qualifications and its associated Catalogue of Modules, as basic referent for public/private training offers.

- The experimental approach on evaluation, accreditation and recognition of competencies, acquired in work experience and/or informal learning, and linked to National Catalogue of Qualifications.

- The creation of a new structure built on the basis of the existing network of the Integrated Vocational Training Centres, with a training offer linked to the National Catalogue of Qualifications and open to young people and adults.

One central aspect is the way in which decentralisation and territorial co-operation between the General State Administration and Autonomous Communities is considered both in the case of general education and in vocational training policies, including for example the means of participation of social partners.

Figure B.15 describes the structure of the education and training system in Spain.

Switzerland

Fundamental reforms were implemented in the Swiss post-compulsory education system during the last decade, and more are under discussion for the decade to come. On the institutional level, the reforms now in place improve vertical permeability:

- The introduction of the *maturité professionnelle* in 1993 (an additional qualification to that awarded at the end of apprenticeship), as well as the establishment of the universities of applied sciences in 1996, had two main goals: to enhance the attractiveness of professional education by allowing vertical transparency, and to create a new application-oriented qualification at university level.

- In general education, the profile of college-based *maturité* has been adapted to the actual needs in 1995.

- In the early 1990s, special measures were aimed at enhancing postgraduate programmes in universities, universities of applied sciences and higher professional education.

- In 2002, the *law on vocational education* was amended. One of the main goals was to dissociate qualifications from precise training programmes, in order to increase flexibility in the system. This reform is based on long experience in the sector of higher professional education ("professional exams" and "higher professional exams") as well as that in other sectors (federal exams for general *maturité* or professional *maturité*, professional qualification without apprenticeship). This kind of qualification has also come to be considered as an answer to the growing need for modularisation in education programmes.

- The university sector (universities and universities of applied sciences) is adopting the principles of the Bologna Declaration by restructuring study programmes (modularisation/ ECTS) and introducing new degrees (bachelor's, master's) through legislation.

Discussions on horizontal permeability (from general to professional education and *vice versa*) have also had tangible results.

Figure B.16 describes the structure of the education and training system in Switzerland.

Figure B.16. **Education and training system in Switzerland**

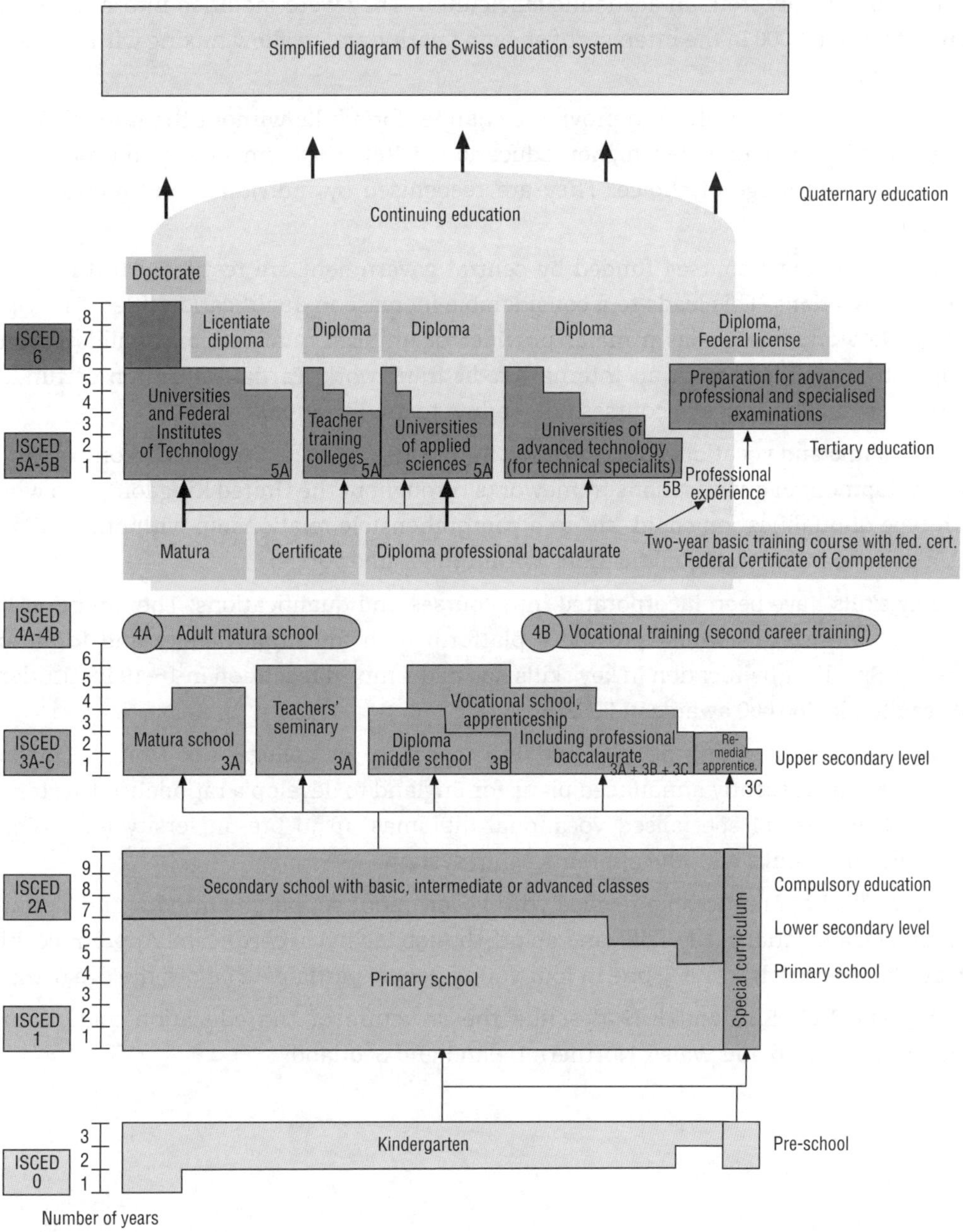

Source: EDK (Swiss Conference of Cantonal Ministers of Education).

United Kingdom

The National Vocational Qualifications system, introduced in late 1980s, involved features of modularisation, outcome standards drawn from work practice, core and options credit arrangements, and recognition of informal learning together with a centralised design framework. Uptake reached some 400 000 per year by the late 1990s, but National Vocational Qualifications do not – as originally envisaged – replace other forms of vocational qualification.

General National Vocational Qualifications (GNVQs), introduced from 1992, was an attempt to apply National Vocational Qualifications precepts to full-time learning of 16-to 19-year-olds. Though similar to existing BTEC awards, General National Vocational Qualifications carried greater official recognition and were used by school VIth forms wanting to diversify from an academic curriculum. They were modified into A level-style qualifications in 2000 in the interests of showing parity, and to allow mixing with academic qualifications.

"Access" courses evolved to provide a channel for adults without the normal A level entry qualifications to enter higher education. Often they embody credit principles, allowing a wide range of choice. They are recognised by individual, and groupings of, universities.

From 1992 most courses funded by central government are restricted to those that carry qualifications. This leads to a considerable increase in qualification titles. The Open College Network emerges as a major provider of unitised qualifications, validated on a co-operative basis and with an internal credit framework. Partial relaxation of funding restrictions in 2001 brings in courses not leading to qualifications.

Academic and vocational accreditation authorities merged. This was accompanied by the development of qualifications frameworks throughout the United Kingdom, into which each type of qualification could "fit" in a comprehensible relationship with others. There was a drive to rationalise qualifications within the frameworks.

Key skills have been incorporated into courses and qualifications. The intention has been that these skills would provide a platform both for employability and for future learning. Specific qualification in key skills has had a mixed reception in 16-19 institutions, but resulted in 260 000 awards in 2002/3.

In the case of young people studying in school or college, the United Kingdom government has recently announced plans for England to develop a rationalised system of a limited number of specialised vocational diplomas up to pre-university level. These would also have links with the apprenticeship system.

Since 1994 apprenticeship revived with government support, centred round National Vocation Qualifications, key skills and an off-the-job technical certificate. Apprenticeships are available at levels 2 and 3; one in four young people participate before the age of 22.

Figures B.17, B.18 and B.19 describe the structure of the education and training systems in England and Wales, Northern Ireland and Scotland.

Figure B.17. **Education and training system in England and Wales**

Phase of education	Type of institution			Year/grade key	Typical age
Higher and further education	Further education institutions (Such as further education colleges, tertiary colleges, specialist colleges, and adult education centres)	Higher education institutions (universities and other higher education institutions)			18+
Upper secondary education	GCE "A" levels, GCE "AS" level examinations and Advanced Vocational Certificates of Education (AVCEs) (taken at age 17/18) provide access to further and higher education and the world of work.				
	Further education institutions	School sixth forms or sixth form colleges			17-18
					16-17
	General Certificates of Secondary Education (GCSEs), General National Vocational Qualifications (GNVQs) and GCSEs in vocational subjects (Vocational GCSEs) (usually taken at age 16) provide access to post-compulsory general/academic and vocational studies and the world of work.				
Lower secondary education	Secondary schools			Key stage 4	Y 11 / **15-16**
					Y 10 / **14-15**
				Key stage 3	Y 9 / **13-14**
					Y 8 / **12-13**[2]
					Y 7 / **11-12**[2]
Primary education	Primary schools[1]			Key stage 2	Y 6 / **10-11**[2]
					Y 5 / **9-10**[2]
					Y 4 / **8-9**[2]
					Y 3 / **7-8**
				Key stage 1	Y 2 / **6-7**
					Y 1 / **5-6**
		Reception classes (R) in primary schools	Foundation stage[3]	R	4-5
Pre-school and nursery education	Pre-school setting which include pre-school groups, playgroups, day nurseries centres and nursery schools.				3-4
					0-3

Bold = compulsory education.

1. In some areas, there are separate schools for *key stage* 1 and *key stage* 2, known as infant and junior schools respectively.
2. In some areas of England, there are *middle schools*, which normally provide a four-year course for children aged between 8 and 12 years, or 9 and 13 years. In such cases, two-tier systems of primary and secondary schools exist alongside three-tier systems of first schools (for 5- to 8- or 9-year-olds), *middle schools* and secondary schools (for 12- or 13- to 16-/17-/18-year-olds).
3. Following a consultation in 2003, the National Assembly for Wales (NAfW) is planning to introduce a "foundation phase" of education for 3- to 7-year-olds. A pilot project for the foundation phase began in September 2004 and will be implemented gradually through a rolling programme running until 2008.

Source: NFER-Eurydice, April 2005.

Figure B.18. **Education and training system in Northern Ireland**

Phase of education	Type of institution			Year/grade key	Typical age
Higher and further education	Further education colleges	Higher education institutions (universities and other higher education institutions)			18+
Upper secondary education	GCE "A" levels, GCE "AS" level examinations and Advanced Vocational Certificates of Education (AVCEs) (taken at age 17/18) provide access to further and higher education and the world of work.				
	Further education institutions	School sixth forms or sixth form colleges			17-18
					16-17
	General Certificates of Secondary Education (GCSEs), General National Vocational Qualifications (GNVQs) and GCSEs in vocational subjects (Vocational GCSEs) (usually taken at age 16) provide access to post-compulsory general/academic and vocational studies and the world of work.				
Lower secondary education	Secondary schools			Key stage 4	Y 12	**15-16**
					Y 11	**14-15**
				Key stage 3	Y 10	**13-14**
					Y 9	**12-13**
					Y 8	**11-12**
Primary education	Primary schools			Key stage 2	Y 7	**10-11**
					Y 6	**9-10**
					Y 5	**8-9**
				Key stage 1	Y 4	**7-8**
					Y 3	**6-7**
					Y 2	**5-6**
					Y 1	**4-5**
Pre-school and nursery education	Pre-school setting which include pre-school groups, playgroups, day nurseries centres and nursery schools.			Foundation stage[1]		3-4
						0-3

Bold = Compulsory.

1. Following an extensive review of curriculum and assessment arrangements, a foundation stage covering the preschool year and years 1 and 2 of primary school (pupils aged three to six) has been proposed. Key stage 1 would then comprise years 3 and 4 and key stage 2 years 4, 5, and 6. Statutory changes are expected from September 2006.

Source: NFER-Eurydice, April 2005.

Figure B.19. **Education and training system in Scotland**

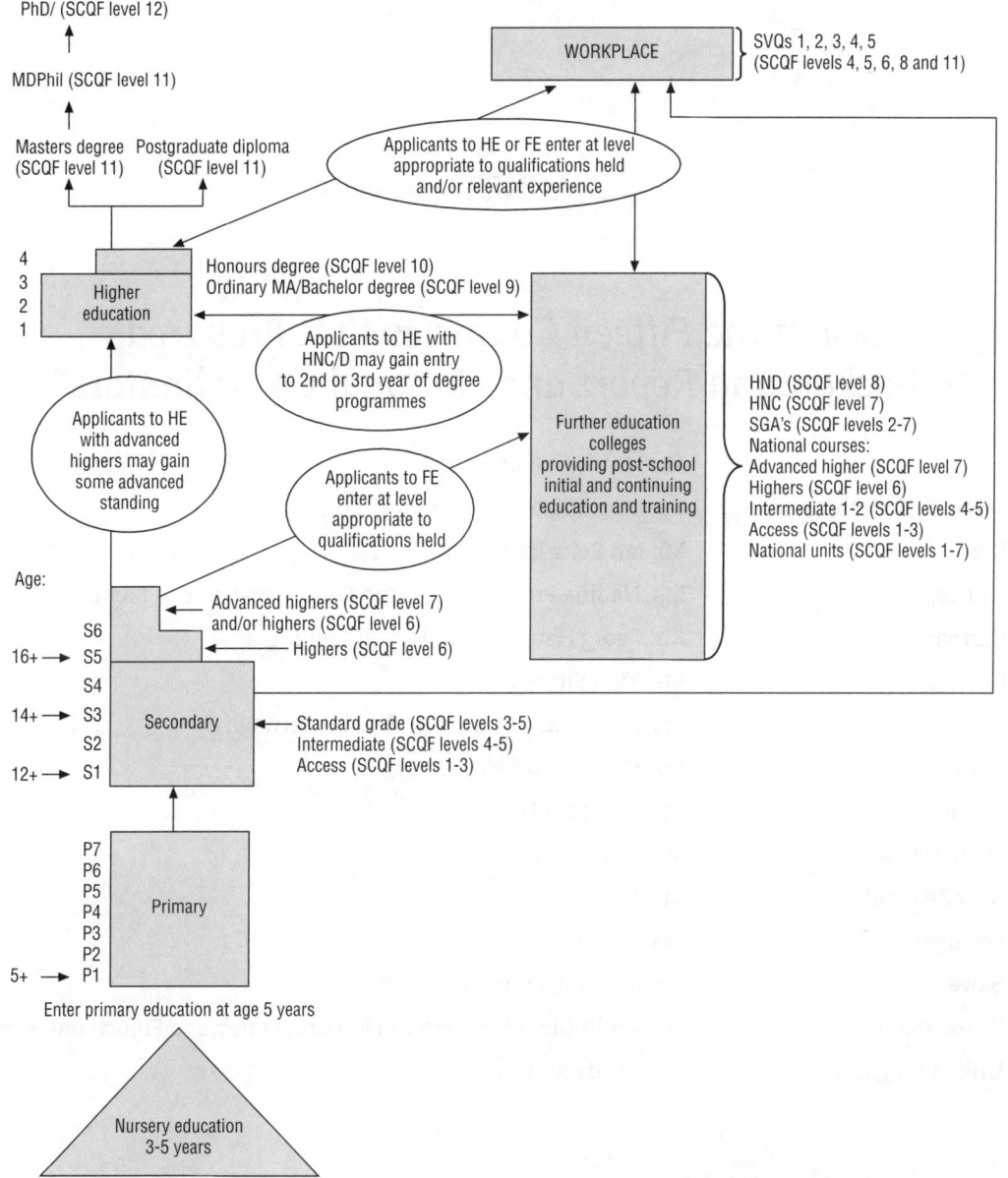

Note: The above diagram shows the main qualifications offered in Scotland's schools, colleges, universities and workplaces. Scottish qualifications are not generally tied to mode, place or time of study.

Source: www.refernet.org.uk.

ANNEX C

*List of the Fifteen Countries that Prepared a Background Report and National Co-ordinators**

Australia:	Mr. Matthew James
Belgium (French-speaking):	Mr. Dominique Barthélémy (in French)
Denmark:	Mr. Jan Reitz Jörgensen
France:	Ms. Nadine Prost (Background Report available in French only)
Germany:	Mr. Georg Hanf and Mr. Jochen Reuling
Greece:	Ms. Tina Simota
Ireland:	Ms. Anna Murphy and Mr. Edwin Mernagh
Japan:	Ms. Keiko Fujimori
Korea:	Ms. Dong-Im Lee
Netherlands:	Mr. Ben Hövels
New Zealand:	Ms. Jo Doyle
Portugal:	Ms. Cândida Soares
Slovenia:	Mr. Miroljub Ignjatovic
Switzerland:	Mr. Andri Gieré (Background Report available in French only)
United Kingdom:	Mr. Sandy Rodger

* The authors of the Country Background Reports are identified in most of the reports.

ANNEX D

Countries Participating in Thematic Groups and Co-ordination

Participants in Thematic Group 1 (8 countries)

Co-ordination

Ms. Anna Murphy, Ms. Tina Simota and Mr. Edwin Mernagh

Country delegates

Australia:

Ms. Judy Forsyth, Australian Qualifications Framework Advisory Board to MCEETYA

Czech Republic:

Mr. Miroslav Kadlec, National Institute of Technical and Vocational Education

Germany:

Mr. Georg Hanf, BIBB (Federal Institute for Vocational Training)

Greece:

Ms. Vasso Papadiamanti, EKEPIS (National Accreditation Centre)

Ms. Tina Simota, EKEPIS

Ireland:

Ms. Anna Murphy, NQAI (National Qualifications Authority of Ireland)

Mr. Edwin Mernagh, NQAI

Italy:

Ms. Gabriella Di Francesco, ISFOL

Spain:

Ms. Francisca Mª Arbizu Echávarri, INCUAL (National Institute for Qualifications)

Mr. José Luis García Molina, INCUAL

United Kingdom:

Ms. Mandy Hobart, QCA (Qualifications and Curriculum Authority)

International organisations

CEDEFOP:

Mr. Burkart Sellin

ILO:

    Ms. Akiko Sakamoto, Skills Development Department

OECD:

    Mr. Mike Coles, QCA (United Kingdom), Research consultant to the OECD
    Mr. Patrick Werquin, Head of project

Participants in Thematic Group 2 (12 countries)

Co-ordination

    Ms. Jo Doyle

Country delegates

Belgium (Flanders):

    Ms. Patrice Schoeters, VIZO
    Ms. Ria Van Herck, VIZO

Denmark:

    Ms. Annelise Hauch, Ministry of Education
    Ms. Vibe Aarkrog, the Danish University of Education
    Mr. Steen Høyrup, the Danish University of Education

Finland:

    Mr. Petri Haltia, University of Turku, Department of Education
    Mr. Kari Nyyssola, National Board of Education

France:

    Mr. Michel Aribaud, Ministry of Education

Ireland:

    Ms. Angela Lambkin, FETAC

Mexico:

    Mr. Miguel Ángel Tamayo Taype, Ministry of Education
    Ms. Maria Luisa de Anda y Ramos, Ministry of Education

Netherlands:

    Mr. Rigo Van Raai, Empowerment Centre EVC
    Ms. Betty Feenstra, Empowerment Centre EVC

New Zealand:

    Ms. Jo Doyle, New Zealand Qualifications Authority

Portugal:

    Ms. Cândida Soares, Ministry of Labour, Department for Studies, Forecasting and Planning

Slovenia:

    Mr. Miroljub Ignjatovic, Faculty of Social Sciences, Ljubljana

Sweden:

    Ms. Carina Lindén, Ministry of Education and Science

United Kingdom:
>   Mr. John Dick, SQA, Scotland
>   Mr. Sandy Rodger, Department for Education and Skills

International organisations

ILO:
>   Ms. Akiko Sakamoto, Skills Development Department

EUROPEAN COMMISSION:
>   Mr. Jens Bjørnåvold

OECD:
>   Mr. Mike Coles, QCA (United Kingdom), Research consultant to the OECD
>   Mr. Patrick Werquin, Head of project

Participants in Thematic Group 3 (6 countries)

Co-ordination

>   Mr. Georg Hanf and Mr. Jochen Reuling

Country delegates

Belgium (Flanders):
>   Ms. Rita Cabus, Service for Educational Development, Ministry of Education of the Flemish Community
>   Ms. Rita Dunon, Service for Educational Development, Ministry of Education of the Flemish Community

Czech Republic:
>   Ms. Miroslava Kopicova, National Training Fund

Germany:
>   Mr. Georg Hanf, BIBB
>   Mr. Jochen Reuling, BIBB

Switzerland:
>   Mr. Peter Gentinetta, Formation Musique Recherche Zulauf
>   Ms. Madeleine Zulauf, Formation Musique Recherche Zulauf

Netherlands:
>   Mr. Ben Hövels, Knowledge Centre Vocational Training and Labour – KBA

United Kingdom:
>   Mr. Tim Oates, QCA

International organisations

EUROPEAN TRAINING FOUNDATION:
>   Ms. Evelyn Viertel

OECD:
>   Mr. Patrick Werquin, Head of project
>   Two additional countries acted as observers only: Italy and Poland.

ANNEX E

List of Acronyms

ACCS	Accumulation of Credits and Certification of Subjects (Ireland)
ACE	Adult and Community Education (New Zealand)
AFPA	*Agence pour la formation professionnelle des adultes* (Adult Training Organisation, France)
ALL	Adult Literacy and Life skills survey
ANPE	*Agence nationale pour l'emploi* (Public Employment Service, France)
ANTA	Australian National Training Authority
AQF	Australian Qualifications Framework
ANUIES	*Asociación Nacional de Universidades e Instituciones de Educación Superior* (National Association of Universities and Higher Education Institutions, Mexico)
BIBB	*Bundesinstitut für Berufsbildung* (Federal Institute for Vocational, Education and Training, Germany)
BTS	*Brevet de technicien supérieur* (Technical Degree at Tertiary Level, France)
CDIP/EDK	Conférence suisse des directeurs cantonaux de l'instruction publique (Swiss Conference of Cantonal Ministers of Education)
CEDEFOP	*Centre européen pour le développement de la formation professionnelle* (European Centre for the Development of Vocational Training)
CFC	*Certificat fédéral de capacité* (Federal Certificate of Capacity, Switzerland)
Céreq	*Centre d'études et de recherche sur les qualifications* (Research Centre on Employment and Qualifications, France)
CESS	*Certificat d'enseignement secondaire supérieur* (Upper Secondary Education Certificate, Belgium)
CINOP	*Centrum voor Innovatie van Opleidingen* (Centre for Innovation in Education)
CQP	*Certificat de qualification professionnelle* (Job-Related Training Certificate, France)
CVTS	Continuous Vocational Training Survey (European Union)
DfES	Department for Employment and Skills (United Kingdom)
DGEFP	*Direction générale de l'emploi et de la formation professionnelle* (Division for Employment and Vocational Training of the Ministry of Labour, France)
EC	European Commission
ECTS	European Credit Transfer System (European Union)
ECVET	European Credit Transfer in Vocational Education and Training
EDK/CDIP	Swiss Conference of Cantonal Ministers of Education
EDUQUA	*Éducation de qualité* (Quality Assurance System in Adult Learning, Switzerland)
EFA	Adult Education and Training Courses (Portugal)

EKEPIS	*Εθνικό Κέντρο Πιστοποίησης* (National Accreditation Centre for Continuing Vocational Training, Greece)
ETF	European Training Foundation
EULFS	European Union Labour Force Survey
Eurydice	European information network on education (not an acronym)
FD	Foundation Degrees (United Kingdom)
FDA	Foundation Degrees for Arts (United Kingdom)
FDS	Foundation Degrees for Science (United Kingdom)
FETAC	Further Education and Training Award Council (Ireland)
FOREM	*Office wallon de la formation professionnelle et de l'emploi* (Walloon Office for Vocational Training and Employment, Belgium)
GCE	General Certificate of Education (United Kingdom)
GCSE	General Certificate of Secondary Education (United Kingdom)
GNVQ	General National Vocational Qualifications (United Kingdom)
HEFCE	Higher Education Funding Council for England
HE	Higher Education
HERO	Higher Education Research Opportunities
HES	*Hautes écoles spécialisées* (Specialised Tertiary Education College, Switzerland)
IALS	International Adult Literacy Survey
ICT	Information and Communication Technology
IDBE	Lifelong Learning Institutes (Greece)
IKA	*Kompetenceafklaring* (Individual Competence Clarification, Denmark)
ILO	International Labour Organization
INCUAL	*Instituto Nacional de las Cualificaciones* (National Institute for Qualifications, Spain)
ISFOL	*Istituto per lo Sviluppo della Formazione Professionale dei Lavoratori* (Institute for the Development of Vocational Training for Workers, Italy)
IT	Information Technology
ITO	Industry Training Organisations (New Zealand)
LLL	Lifelong Learning
LM	Labour Market
MCEETYA	Ministerial Council on Education, Employment, Training and Youth Affairs (Australia)
NAfW	National Assembly for Wales
NCEA	National Certificate of Educational Achievement (New Zealand)
NCVA	National Council for Vocational Awards (Ireland)
NCVQ	National Catalogue of Vocational Qualifications (Spain)
NCVER	National Centre for Vocational Education Research (Australia)
NFER	National Foundation for Educational Research (United Kingdom)
NQAI	National Qualification Authority Ireland
NQF	National Qualifications Framework(s)
NQS	National Qualifications System(s)
NUD-IST	Numerical Unstructured Data – Indexing, Searching and Theorising
NVQ	National Vocational Qualification (United Kingdom)
NZQA	New Zealand Qualifications Authority
OECD	Organisation for Economic Co-operation and Development
OEVA	Observatory of Entries into the Working Life (Portugal)
OFFT	Federal Office for Professional Education and Technology, Switzerland

PISA	Programme for International Student Assessment
PMETyC	Project for the Modernisation of Technical Education and Training, Mexico
PSE	Open-choice study programmes in higher education (Greece)
PTE	Private Training Establishment (New Zealand)
QCA	Qualification and Curriculum Authority (United Kingdom)
QF	Qualifications Framework
RNCP	*Registre National des Certifications Professionnelles* (National Vocational Qualifications Directory, France)
ROME	*Répertoire opérationnel des métiers* (Job Directory, Belgium and France)
RPL	Recognition of Prior Learning
RTO	Registered Training Organisations (Australia)
RVCC	Recognition, Validation and Certification of Competences (Portugal)
SCQF	Scottish Qualifications Framework
SQA	Scottish Qualification Authority
SSC	Sector Skills Council (United Kingdom)
TAFE	Technical and Further Education
TEE	Technical Vocational Schools (Greece)
TIMSS	Trends in International Mathematics and Science Study
TSD	Technological Specialisation Diploma (Portugal)
UCAS	Universities and Colleges Admissions Service (United Kingdom)
VAE	*Validation des acquis de l'expérience* (Recognition of Prior Learning, France)
VAP	*Validation des acquis professionnels* (Recognition of Job-Related Prior Learning, France)
VET	Vocational Education and Training
VIZO	*Vlaams Instituut voor het Zelfstandig Ondernemen* (Flemish Institute for Independent Entrepreneurship)

ANNEX F

Three-letter Country Codes Used in the Tables and Figures

AUS	Australia
BEL	Belgium
BFL	Belgium (Flanders)
BFR	Belgium (French-speaking)
CAN	Canada
CHE	Switzerland
CHI	Chile
CZE	Czech Republic
DEU	Germany
DNK	Denmark
ESP	Spain
FIN	Finland
FRA	France
GRC	Greece
KOR	Korea
HUN	Hungary
IRL	Ireland
ITA	Italy
JPN	Japan
KOR	Korea
MEX	Mexico
NLD	Netherlands
NOR	Norway
NZL	New Zealand
POL	Poland
PRT	Portugal
SLV	Slovenia
SWE	Sweden
GBR	United Kingdom
USA	United States of America
AVG	Average

OECD PUBLICATIONS, 2, rue André-Pascal, 75775 PARIS CEDEX 16
PRINTED IN FRANCE
(91 2006 04 1 P) ISBN 978-92-64-01367-4 – No. 55299 2007